Mysteries of The Other Side is a multi-vol of the spiritual world. The author, G look beyond the surface of familiar to uncover what they hide. He reveals hidden meanings and induc- stories, solves riddles, exposes divine structures, identifies repeating spiritual patterns, decodes wisdom, and explains the fundamental spiritual principles of existence and eternal life.

The result that unfolds in Book One is a new, deeper, Bible story, from the spiritual beginnings of mankind until today. The story simply explains, in detail, the origins of: God and the divine plan for mankind including eternal life, through Love; Satan and why and how he/she violently opposes the plan, through hatred; the Messiah and how He is restoring the original plan and eternal life – which is happening right now.

Then each volume builds upon the previous one, layering insights and revelations, ensuring that the journey is as fascinating as it is illuminating.

With George Begg's spiritual gifts, meticulous research, passion for spiritual discovery, and knack of simplifying complex concepts, this work adds new perspectives and sparks new conversations that go beyond existing spiritual boundaries. The reader will see both the spiritual and the physical world in a new light and be better equipped to deal with the growing challenges that the world is facing.

'Life-changing, thought-provoking, and spiritually rich – a bold re-examination of the Bible's hidden depths that is as readable as it is revelatory.'

– Nettie Adams

'A fascinating journey into the unseen world – uncovering mysteries hidden within scripture and revealing answers to the biggest questions of all.'

– Nelli

'A mind-opening exploration of the Bible's hidden layers. George Begg simplifies complex concepts and this book completely reframed how I see the world. I can't wait for Book Two.'

– Jessie Behlert

'This book changed how I read the Bible – opening up new meaning, deeper understanding, and life-changing spiritual clarity. I look forward to going deeper in Book 2.'

– Anne Davidson

Mysteries of The Other Side

The Hidden Story

GEORGE BEGG

First published 2025

Copyright © George Begg 2025

The right of George Begg to be identified as the author of this work has been asserted in accordance with the Copyright, Designs & Patents Act 1988.

All rights reserved. No part of this book may be reproduced, stored in a retrieval system, or transmitted in any form or by any means, digital, electronic, electrostatic, magnetic tape, mechanical, photocopying, recording or otherwise, without the written permission of the copyright holder.

Scripture quotations are from the ESV® Bible (The Holy Bible, English Standard Version®), © 2001 by Crossway, a publishing ministry of Good News Publishers. ESV Text Edition: 2025. The ESV text may not be quoted in any publication made available to the public by a Creative Commons license. The ESV may not be translated in whole or in part into any other language. Used by permission. All rights reserved.

Published under licence by Brown Dog Books and
The Self-Publishing Partnership Ltd, 10b Greenway Farm, Bath Rd, Wick, nr. Bath BS30 5RL, UK

www.selfpublishingpartnership.co.uk

ISBN printed book: 978-1-83952-971-9
ISBN e-book: 978-1-83952-972-6

Cover design by Andrew Prescott
Front cover image by Nelli Begg
Internal design by Mac Style

Printed and bound in the UK

This book is printed on FSC® certified paper

Author's Note

I never imagined I would write a book – least of all one about the spiritual world. In my early life, I rejected all notions of spirituality, whether God, the Messiah, the Holy Spirit, or any idea of an afterlife. I believed that those who held such beliefs would do better to focus on improving life in the here and now, which was challenging enough. For me, that meant serving as a fighter pilot in the Royal Air Force during the Cold War.

After leaving the RAF, my perspective was shaken forever. One night, God appeared to me as a blinding white light in my room. It's difficult to doubt the existence of something once you have encountered it directly. In that moment, everything changed.

I experienced a profound sense of love, peace, and joy – a spiritual connection I couldn't explain. I found myself communicating directly with God and discovered that I had been given spiritual gifts and guidance, including visions and tasks that continue to shape my life today.

I came to realise that those who dismiss the spiritual world are missing out on something extraordinary. One of the visions I received was clear: I was to share the true story hidden within the Bible – one that goes far beyond the surface narratives we've all heard. This deeper story explains the mysteries of the spiritual world, offering insight into creation, God, the Messiah, Satan, spirit, soul, angels, and the eternal afterlife. It even answers the question: **Why now? Why are these mysteries being revealed at this moment in history?**

This deeper story has been concealed for millennia for a reason, and uncovering it was not easy. But I was guided and taught one-to-one by a living spiritual presence I came to know as 'Understanding'.

The book you hold now – *Mysteries of The Other Side* – is the result of many years of that guidance. It is the beginning of a series that explores the truths hidden in plain sight, offering a fresh way to understand life, death, and what lies beyond.

Contents

What Mysteries and Why Now?	8
Preface	10
Fiction or non-fiction?	10
Is there any science behind the spiritual world?	12
My own spiritual experience	14
The hidden mysteries	16
What does the spiritual world look like?	18
How have the mysteries remained hidden for so long?	18
What is revealed?	27
'The other side' and 'the spiritual mysteries hidden since the foundation of the world'	29
Have these mysteries ever been revealed in the past?	31
Some examples of hidden mysteries	33
The structure of the books	43
Book One	44
Books Two and Three	44
Prologue to Book One	46
Cycles	46
The underlying story	51

The Mysteries of The Other Side
Book One

Chapter 1	The End	55
Chapter 2	Before the Beginning	60
Chapter 3	The Beginning – the Seven Days of Creation	69
Chapter 4	The Rebellion	79
Chapter 5	Adam and Eve in the Garden of Eden	91
Chapter 6	The First Age – the Age of Adam	102
Chapter 7	The Second Age – The Age of Noah	114
Chapter 8	The Third Age – Abraham to Moses	128
Chapter 9	Moses Frees the Chosen People	146
Chapter 10	The Law of Moses	159
Chapter 11	Joshua and Caleb take the Promised Land	175
Chapter 12	The Time of the Judges. Samson and Delilah	182
Chapter 13	The Fourth Age – The king of Israel	196
Chapter 14	King David	211
Chapter 15	King Solomon – a Short Age of Light	228
Chapter 16	The Kings of the Divided Kingdom and the Prophets	235
Chapter 17	The Fifth Age – John the Baptist and Jesus	241
Chapter 18	The Sixth Age of the Apostles	302
Chapter 19	The Revelation of Jesus Christ	319

Chapter 20	The Seventh Age. The New Heaven and the New Earth and the New Jerusalem and the Tree of Life	337
Chapter 21	The Beginning	340

Conclusions 343

Appendix One – The Number Code and the Colour Code 349

Appendix Two – Glossary of Common Code Words 351

Appendix Three – The Seven Ages 359

About the Author 362

Prologue to Book Two 365

What Mysteries and Why Now?

We don't know or understand the spiritual world, and the physical world is in a mess. But all that is about to change. Thousands of years ago, all the secrets and mysteries of the spiritual world were deliberately and deeply hidden in the ancient scriptures, by spiritual people. So deeply that we didn't even know that they existed. They have never been revealed and published before, and once published, there is no going back to our state of ignorance.

They were hidden for good reason, but they were put there for good reason too. They were to be revealed to all of us, when the time was right, and when mankind most needed them.

That time has come.

It is a great privilege and a great responsibility for us to be the ones to whom the mysteries are shown.

The revelation will bring many changes. One example is that we will be much wiser as a result and make better choices. This wisdom is not just meant for a handful of our leaders to guide us like blind people are led, rather it is meant to enlighten and guide every individual who wants it. That's why it is to be published to everyone.

After the secrets have been published, we will better understand what is happening in the world, both in spiritual and physical terms, and how to prepare for what is coming soon. Is it the end of the world or World War Three, as we keep hearing? No, but it is the end of the age and it is the reason why the mysteries are being revealed now. The risks of devastating wars are real, and there are important things that we simply need to know.

Then, when it is over, we will usher in a new period, a much better period of peace and security, when we will know and understand the spiritual world around us and the physical and the spiritual will work together in harmony.

Everything will change, and the world we know will never be the same again. Then, perhaps the greatest mystery is that we will know how, when our physical body dies, to enter the afterlife as was always intended. Even from before the time that the mysteries were buried.

Preface

Please read this!

Usually, when I pick up a book and I see some sort of text before the story starts, I simply skip forwards to the story itself, so as not to waste time. However, in this case, please read everything that comes before Chapter 1, because it has a lot of useful information and spiritual principles that will help you understand what follows.

Let me be upfront, this book is going to be challenging for many.

It is meant for everyone with an enquiring mind about everything spiritual, to answer their questions. However, even if you firmly do not believe that the spiritual world exists, I ask you to suspend your rational analytical ways, and try to open your mind to something new. Likewise, if you believe, but have fixed and inflexible religious views, I ask you to try to keep an open heart. There are many conflicting religious views; are you sure that yours are right and the others are wrong?

In any case, all I ask is that you read on and make up your own mind. It's your life, after all.

Fiction or non-fiction?

This is a series of books about the spiritual world, so perhaps the first question should be where should it be found in a bookshop, under fiction or non-fiction? Is the spiritual world real or imaginary?

For thousands of years mankind has been fascinated by the idea that there is more than the physical world around us and that we are more than just physical creatures with a short lifespan, existing for just a moment of time. Is there something else that we can't see or touch, but which nevertheless exists and has some sort of influence on our lives? Do ghosts exist and can we interact with them in some way? Is there a God? Perhaps the most common question we want answered is, 'Is there life after death?'

Some people use logic to conclude that if they can't interact with the spiritual world or measure it, then it simply doesn't exist, and that is the end of the conversation. Yet many millions passionately believe with unshakeable certainly that the spirit world and God do exist, and that you can and do interact with them. Some have a fundamentalist religious belief which is so strong that they are prepared to die to defend and promote it. As a result, religion has been responsible for many horrible wars, where all parties believe that God is on their side. Even where there are no wars, there always seems to be more discord than harmony amongst people who believe. This constant conflict has given the spiritual world a bad reputation amongst those who do not believe. And many people are so busy merely trying to live their lives and navigate through their difficulties, that they have no time for spiritual 'mumbo jumbo'.

However, it might be better to say that religion, rather than the spiritual world, has the bad reputation. The difference being that much of religion has become an inaccurate account of the spiritual world, because mankind has modified it to fit our own various agendas, including becoming an excuse for war, fought for man-made purposes. These modifications and misunderstandings also result in many religions and denominations with quite different views, where there should be only one. So, we need to separate our opinions of man-made religious ideas and the real spiritual world.

Some people have had strange spiritual experiences which have convinced them that there is something out there, but they can't explain what it is, they just believe it. Generally speaking, people who believe, just believe without being able to explain it. Yet that makes no sense to people who need evidence. Yet even most non-believers do have an open mind and a level of curiosity to learn more. That curiosity is shared by believers too, who are always hungry to learn more about the spiritual world and God.

So these books are quite simply aimed at all people who have an enquiring mind, independent of their religion and whether they believe in the spirit world or not. After all, just because you don't believe in it, doesn't mean that it doesn't exist! I will soon explain why believers believe so passionately, and why non-believers just don't understand why they do. Actually, that is a very simple mystery to explain. For those who are put off by religion in general, and religious conflicts in particular, these books will try to rise above man-made religion, to show the true spiritual world and then explain why there is so much religious-based conflict and more importantly, how we can try to stop it.

The bottom line is that the spiritual world does exist and can affect every one of us, and so this book should definitely be found in the non-fiction section!

Is there any science behind the spiritual world?

At the beginning of this project, I thought that there was an unbridgeable gulf between science and spiritual belief. Then I became aware (from the spiritual world) that the science of the spiritual world and even the science of God would be understood within a generation. We are already close, and we will see that the spiritual world will fit within our existing scientific understanding, both at the extremes of large things through studies of cosmology and the universe, and the extremes of the very smallest sub-atomic things, through studies of quantum physics. The fundamental laws of science are the same for all sizes, and in fact they are the same for the spiritual world and the physical world. Before we can see how the spiritual world fits within our existing science, we need to understand much more about it and how it works.

For example, it is wrong to say that those in the physical world cannot see or hear or touch the spiritual world, because most believers can and do just that, in some way. For those who can't, using a physical analogy, it is rather like being in a physical world surrounded by invisible radio waves transmitted on a certain frequency. We have no way to know they exist until we are given a receiver which is set to that frequency. In the spiritual world, we also need a receiver, but it is not physical it is spiritual, and it is normally given to us only if we want it and ask for it. In other words, we normally have to choose to receive the gift, and then we will experience the spiritual world and believe. Actually, it is this gift of a spiritual receiver that can suddenly transform a non-believer into a passionate believer in a moment. Best of all, this receiver also transmits, and you can have two way communications with the spiritual world. All of this already exists, and I believe that soon science will be able to explain it in depth.

I will describe these spiritual receivers and transmitters in some detail, including to show that there are several of them, all with different functions – like different frequency bands. Perhaps, in the meantime, we can just think of the spiritual radio waves being a new frequency and we just need to turn the dial. Or better, if we can get our head around it, it is a new set of dimensions, spiritual dimensions. At first, we don't believe that these dimensions are there, all around us but not available to us, then suddenly we realise that they are there, and a whole new spiritual world is opened up to us, with so many opportunities and experiences. One of the most important things we quickly learn is that the spiritual world is here to help us in our journey through this short and usually difficult life, then it takes us into eternàl life in one form or another. The concepts of bad people going to hell and good people going to heaven are serious misunderstandings – the afterlife is nothing like that simple. But I will explain it all, in depth. In the meantime, you will soon see that the spiritual world and the physical world were always meant to work together and for our benefit. Our time in the physical world is very short, but our time in the spiritual world is eternal.

My own spiritual experience

When I was much younger, I was one of the logical, disbelieving people. I had no time for 'religious nuts' who tried to persuade me that there was a God and indeed that there was a whole spiritual world experience I was missing out on. I thought that anyone who made up a spiritual world was basically a weak, needy person, who needed an imaginary staff to lean on to get through life. In particular, how could anyone seriously think that the world was created in seven days?

I served in the military, flying fighters in the Royal Air Force, and I believed that you had to be prepared to fight to defend the values you believed were right. If your people were hurt, then you fought back to hurt the enemy more than they hurt your people, until they stopped or were destroyed. To try to avoid nuclear war, we had a policy of deterrence, through which both sides could destroy the other many times over. We called it Mutually Assured Destruction, or MAD for short.

Then I had a life-changing spiritual experience, so powerful that there was no denying that the spiritual world, and indeed God, existed. What happened? God appeared to me as a dazzling white light one night, and I experienced intense feelings of love then amazing peace and then incredible joy, radiating from the light and repeated like waves, several times over. Then the light moved towards me and touched my leg and in an instant, I was filled with something incredibly powerful and intense, which I had never experienced anything like before. It came with instantaneous knowledge of many spiritual matters and included a message. It was my first of very many experiences of how you directly receive spiritual knowledge

– one moment you know nothing about it, and the next instant you simply know it with certainty, and you understand it. Then the light vanished from sight and my new life began. I didn't know it at the time, but I had just met God and the Holy Spirit, and I had been filled with the Holy Spirit and all the gifts and powers that come with it. Including two way communication with God and the spiritual world. If you like, I had just received the 'radio'. I will explain all this in depth later in the book.

The message I received during the experience described two purposes for my life which I was to fulfil. If you like, you could describe it as 'my calling'.

The first purpose was that I had some business talents which I was to use, under God's guidance and advice, to generate substantial funds towards the costs of the second purpose and so that I was financially independent. I knew that I would not be told what the second purpose was until the first was over.

Well, the first purpose finished many years ago. When it was over, the second purpose was disclosed, and it was a surprise. I was to understand the spiritual world in depth and then publish it to the whole of the physical world for anyone 'with an enquiring mind' to read. Specifically, I was to tell the underlying story and all the mysteries that were deeply hidden within scripture, specifically the Bible. But at the time, I didn't know what that meant. I had no idea that an underlying story even existed in the Bible. I had assumed that the lessons God wanted us to learn were there in the various Bible stories, which were taught to us by knowledgeable Bible scholars. However, I was very wrong.

It turned out that everything mankind had been struggling to learn about the spirit world had been in front of our noses for thousands of years, hidden in unseen mysteries and secrets within ancient scriptures, not just the Bible. However, my calling was to focus on the scriptures of the Bible. I discovered that you just had to discover the secrets of how to reveal the mysteries, and then you could start to uncover them and publish them. That may sound straightforward, but I soon understood that this was no simple or quick task, because the mysteries had been deliberately and deeply hidden for thousands of years, even from very clever scholars, and scripture does not easily reveal them, as we will soon see. It took me some 10 years to uncover them.

The hidden mysteries

I came to realise that the Bible scripture was much more complex than I had imagined. Rather than having an underlying story, I had thought the Bible only told a historic story of important religious characters, like Jesus and Moses and David and Abraham, and also various laws and guidance from God on how to live. Most of the Bible stories of the old testament were shockingly bloodthirsty and certainly not a good example for us to follow. Although, that was because at that time I didn't understand what was going on behind the literal story that you read. However, I was quickly shown that the whole of Bible scripture describes the spirit world, not the physical world. In fact, it contains a complete picture of the spirit world and all its mysteries, but it buries them so deeply that you don't even know they are there – even when you read a passage, and you think you have understood it.

An important example is the story of creation. Like the rest of scripture, it is describing the spirit world. If you want to understand the creation of the physical world, then ask a scientist about the Big Bang. But if you want to understand the fundamental foundations of the spirit world and God, then you need to understand the story of creation in scripture. They are two separate stories told from quite different perspectives, about the same event.

We will see that in the biblical descriptions of creation, what appear to be physical things are actually spiritual things, and that they are all alive. The sun is not the sun we know, and neither is the moon. The sea is not the sea, water is not water, earth is not earth, trees are not trees and fruit is not fruit, although we can indeed eat it. But when we do, in the spirit world, we are 'eating' living spirits, so they enter our spiritual bodies. Do you recall the story of Adam and Eve, our spiritual ancestors? They had a choice of eating one of two fruits. One was the fruit of the tree of eternal life and the other was the fruit of the tree of the knowledge of good and evil. They are both spirits which give you spiritual gifts and powers; one gets you to Heaven and the other stops you getting to Heaven. So already we can begin to see how important it is to understand the spiritual meanings of the words. Sadly, Adam and Eve chose badly, and we are still suffering the consequences.

Of course, by now you may be wondering who Adam and Eve were, did they really exist, what are the consequences and what can we do about them? But these questions are exactly what you would expect if you have an enquiring mind. You answer one question, but the answer reveals more questions, and so on. There are so many questions! However, I will try my best to answer all of the important queries – which is why there are several books to read!

Likewise, in the spiritual world, a day is not a day and seven days are not a week! Yes, even a day is alive and has its own personality in the spiritual world! This all sounds a bit weird and in fact it gets a whole lot weirder before it starts to make sense. The good news is that when you have the spiritual meaning of a word, it never changes in any scripture, but it becomes a type of code made up of many code words. That means in the Old Testament of the Bible, and the New Testament and the Quran too. In fact, it is a sign of true scripture that it includes the same code and that it has the same meanings and reveals the same mysteries.

In this book, I am going to focus on the Bible because that is what I was asked to do, and it will be best known to most Western readers. At a global level, since these hidden mysteries reveal the same spiritual world, which is the true foundation of all religious beliefs, it is relevant to all religions (as well as to all non-believers). When properly decoded and understood, there is no discord between any scripture, only harmony and no need for conflict between their followers. Unfortunately, when the mysteries in scripture are not fully understood, misunderstandings have led to discord and conflict.

That's why the mysteries are to be published to the whole world, not just the Western world, and this project has become such a huge task.

What does the spiritual world look like?

A simplistic summary of the spiritual world which we will soon see, is that it exists within, and as an integrated part of, our physical world. If we could see it through spiritual eyes, then it would look very similar to the physical world, but everything would be spiritual and alive. Even mountains are alive, are under authority and can move if properly commanded to do so. In the Bible, Jesus makes a point of telling us just that. We will also discover that we all exist as both physical and spiritual beings. We understand our physical side well, but we all have a spiritual side, which we don't know well, and it is this side of us that populates the spirit world. You can think of this as our 'angelic' side, which looks like us, and that is what you would see moving around when you open your spiritual eyes. It is important to realise from the start that our physical bodies exist for a flash in linear time, but our spiritual beings are eternal and exist within cyclical time. I will explain angels and linear and cyclical time soon.

How have the mysteries remained hidden for so long?

As I said, scripture does not give up its secrets easily. The way to understand how they were buried so well, is to understand how they can be dug up, and how difficult this is. I was told to isolate myself from all existing religious scholars, preachers and doctrines, so that I would not be influenced by any misunderstandings and flawed doctrines that have arisen over time. Instead, I had to work in my study behind closed doors, using only the original scripture of the Bible, and to receive my guidance directly from God (through my spiritual 'radio') with no other interpretations. I have been doing this for 10 years and it has been a very difficult challenge. I will try to broadly describe the methods used to reveal the hidden spiritual mysteries here. When you read these methods, it might seem daunting and even impossible to follow, but that's the point – it's meant to be really difficult, because they were hidden for a really good reason. The good news is that I have done the work, so I can share the results. However, after the first book it will be necessary to prove that the mysteries and the underlying story do come from scripture as I claim, and not from my imagination. So in this book I will demonstrate some of the more simple methods used to uncover the mysteries being applied in practice, starting even in this preface. I will also give all readers the opportunity to dig some up for themselves. In the next two books I will show the links between the underlying story and the Bible, and demonstrate how to reveal the mysteries in more depth and more detail.

So how are the mysteries revealed then?
We will see that revealing the mysteries simply cannot be done with the physical mind, it is well beyond what we can achieve naturally. Actually, you need the spiritual radios I mentioned to guide you. So, what are they? In fact, they are specific living spirits which you are given and become part of your spiritual being. Yes, it's like eating the fruits I mentioned earlier! I will explain all these spirits in detail later in the book, but I will try to at least cover their basic principles here.

Some spirits give you channels of communication into the spiritual world, and some of them give you various powers or 'gifts', like talents. In the physical world you can have the gift of creating and playing amazing music, or painting beautiful works of art or being a brilliant mathematician or scientist. In the spiritual world you can receive gifts in a similar way, but each gift is a specific spirit with a specific name.

Faith, Counsel and Understanding

Your first spirit opens up the spiritual world to you. You either have it and you believe with certainty, or you don't have it and you can't believe, it's as simple as that. This spirit is called 'Faith'. For those who don't have it yet, try to grasp that this Faith does not mean a general feeling of having confidence in something or other. Like you have faith that your engine will start when you press the starter. Rather, it is a specific spirit that you receive which opens up a door to the spiritual world.

Unfortunately, this is something of a paradox. A non-believer might say, 'show me the spiritual world and I will have faith in it.' However, a believer would say, 'Have faith in the spiritual world and I will show it to you.' The spirit of Faith always comes first.

There is then a second spirit which, when you have it, allows you to communicate with the spiritual world. It is called 'Counsel' because you receive advice from it.

Then to understand the mysteries of scripture you need to receive another spirit. It is called the spirit of 'Understanding', and like the others, it is a gift and a talent which you either have or you don't. When scripture (for example both the Bible and the Quran) talks about 'people with understanding', it means they have the spirit of Understanding in them. Without it, you just read the words, and generally get no further than their literal meaning. With it, you suddenly see that there is a hidden spiritual meaning within a text, and you can understand it. For example, you quickly understand what the sun and the moon and trees and bushes and the sea actually are in the spiritual world, in a way that you could never achieve using only your physical mind.

When I was ready to start writing this book, I wanted to find out what level of understanding of the spiritual world I should start with. The first question I asked someone was, 'What are the sun and the moon in creation and what is their significance?' If someone doesn't know that, then they don't have even the most fundamental and essential knowledge you need to understand the basic underlying story of the Bible. Nobody knew, not even the experienced Christians or the Bible scholars that I approached. However, that turned out to be helpful for me, because it means that I can start at the beginning for everyone. Which is what I did, even in this preface.

Understanding comes a little piece at a time, but over time, you build up a large vocabulary of the spiritual meaning of these words, and you see that it forms the code that I described earlier. There is a word code and a number code and a colour code. The understanding of these codes is a fundamental step to revealing the mysteries, so to remind you I have made a table of the most common code words and their meanings, together with the number and colour code, which I have included at the back of the book. You may want to bookmark them for easy reference. However, after a while, you will learn and understand the common hidden meanings as you read them in the text.

To dig up the mysteries from the scripture, use of the word code does get harder because you have to use the words from the original language, not the translation. That's because a translation often needs an interpretation, especially when the word has several meanings, and it is often incorrect. However, the original word always has the same spiritual meaning when decoded. For example, several Hebrew words are translated to English as 'earth' or 'land' but they all have unique and important meanings in the spiritual code. Even the translation of 'the promised land' is wrong and it should be 'the promised earth'. The difference between the earth and the land is spiritually important, and the real meaning of the promised earth is lost when you think of it as a land. Without 'Understanding' it gets confusing!

Riddles

The next thing you do after you have established the code, is to decode the passage you want to understand. But this isn't the end, this is just the start. Then, using the spirit of Understanding, you can unlock more hidden meanings within the decoded version. For example, you will discover that many passages are actually riddles which need to be solved. Some of them are simple and many are complex, with several levels of meanings. First, though, you need to identify the riddles, which are themselves often hidden and unseen within the text. Over months and years, you piece together the secrets from the codes and the riddles, like a jigsaw, scattered in pieces throughout the whole Bible, until you have put together a complete new picture. This is a new level of understanding, which has revealed a deeper meaning than the literal text, and you have now revealed level one mysteries.

Now you have started, and you have revealed some basic mysteries. This is an exciting and satisfying time. These new meanings never change, so when you start the exercise again by going back to the beginning of scripture and reading it again, you can apply these level one meanings and mysteries to what you read, and deeper meanings will appear. Using Understanding again, you can put together another jigsaw at another level, deeper than the first. This is the second level of understanding, and you will reveal level two mysteries.

Then you start again, repeating the process, and putting together another jigsaw at a deeper level of understanding and meaning, which is based on what you learned on the previous levels. Each level becomes the foundation of the next level. And so on. The deeper you get, the closer you come to understanding God, but the harder it gets too. Actually, there are seven levels of understanding, and the deepest levels are mentally and spiritually exhausting to work with, even with the support of the spirit of Understanding. Why is it so tiring? Because you need to make sure that every new discovery is consistent with every other discovery, throughout the whole Bible, and at every level of understanding. It is challenging, but necessary to verify every new discovery. Which brings us to an important question. How do these mysteries have any credibility if they are so new that even the best scholars don't know them, nobody recognises me as a theologian, and I have no qualifications? I would answer that their credibility comes from the Bible itself. Everything is validated by the Bible, because everything is consistent with everything else in the Bible, at every level of understanding. If something was false, then it would conflict at some level, and many false teachings fail that test. If it is validated by the Bible, then my own credibility becomes irrelevant.

How do you use the spirit of Understanding in practice? If you know that there is a hidden meaning in a passage you are studying, and importantly, if you have already gathered all the knowledge you need from the rest of scripture, at the right levels, then you can ask for the hidden meaning of this knowledge, and the spirit of understanding will give it to you. This is one level of what Jesus meant when he said, 'Ask and you will receive'. However, as you may have guessed, even this quotation has deeper meanings, which we will reveal when we come to them. After several years, you can see hidden meanings in almost every passage you look at, and every time that you start again and come to the same passage again, Understanding will let you see new meanings which you never saw before. For example, when you understand how resurrection to heaven works at the end of the Bible, you will then be able to see it foretold many times, even in the earliest passages in creation, but you have missed that meaning many times before.

Unfortunately, you can only reveal the next level when you have finished the one before it. If you miss a meaning in one level, you will not be able to reveal what it is meant to unlock in all the succeeding levels. Think of it like a sphere with seven layers around it, like an onion, which you have to reveal one after the other. This sphere could be the spiritual universe or an atom, but the important thing is that in all cases, the mystery of God is at the centre.

You may ask why I have explained in some detail how to unlock and reveal the mysteries if I have already done all the work? Because by the end of this book, you will be able to receive the spirit of Understanding yourself, and you will be able to ask for and receive the true meanings of other passages which I have not covered. If you want to.

Cyclical learning and teaching
At the start of this book, in the prologue, I am going to explain the fundamental importance of repeating cycles in the spiritual world. *Everything* is a cycle and nothing is linear. Here, we will see that even the mysteries are buried in cycles, each one being a level of understanding which then reveals the next level. This process is what I call cyclical learning. You have to complete one whole cycle, or layer, then you repeat it again and again, learning more each time in each layer, and getting closer to God. It takes many years to reveal all the layers and cycles of the hidden mysteries. However, cycles soon help you to find the hidden meanings, because when you understand which cycle the passage is set in, you have the correct context, and the context makes it easier to reveal the mystery. We will look at the cycles a lot!

And that leads to another problem, because this process works in reverse when you try to teach what you have learned using cyclical learning. You might think, as I did, that you can just explain what you have learned to someone, at the end of the process. But in practice, you can't explain the deeper meanings to anyone, unless they have already understood all the levels above it. You come to realise that without the understanding of the prior levels, it is impossible for others to understand the deeper levels. So everyone must start from the beginning. That's what we are going to do in this book and those that follow.

Another feature of cyclical learning and teaching, is that you can't understand the end until you have understood the beginning, and you can't understand the beginning until you have understood the end. Therefore, you can't understand Revelation (the last book in the Bible) until you have understood creation, and you can't understand creation until you have understood Revelation – and everything else in between them.

However, cyclical learning can be helpful in another way too. That's because some mysteries from some parts of the story are so sensitive and secret and so well hidden, that they appear to be missing altogether, so you have a blank space, and apparently nothing to work with. Therefore, you might think that the missing story is lost for ever. The most important example of this is the famous story of the Serpent tempting Adam and Eve in the Garden of Eden. This is a very brief story with what seems to be a pretty simple message. However, it turns out to be hiding some of the most important and deep mysteries of them all. You will see that, as I mentioned earlier, it is really about how to receive eternal life in heaven, and how God's plan gives us this life, but the Serpent's plan takes it away. These conflicting plans will become the central theme of the conflict between God and Satan, which dominates scripture.

Therefore, a vital character of the story is the 'Serpent' who is introduced for the first time here, with Adam and Eve. The Serpent obviously existed before this story, and it turns out that the Serpent is the devil or Satan. But what happened to the Serpent in early creation, to make him or her want to tempt Adam and Eve in the garden and cause so many problems for them and all of mankind? Why does Satan hate mankind so much? Obviously, something happened, but what? There is no mention of it happening anywhere before the famous passage of Adam and Eve, so this mystery simply seems to be missing.

So how does cyclical learning help us? As I said, at the beginning of the book, we will learn that in the spiritual world, cycles are fundamental. You can see events and spiritual characters being repeated again and again through the ages. Normally you can recognise the later cycle from an earlier one, but actually, you can also recognise an earlier cycle from a later one. All the cycles start with an original event, and most of these original cycles are described during creation. In the case of the Serpent's story, it happened early on in creation, before mankind, and it started a series of repeat cycles. Although, the original cycle is not described, you can build it up from the later repeating cycles, in a sort of reverse engineering.

Therefore, the story is there in the Bible, but it is scattered in many pieces in later cycles. You can only reveal it when you have got to a very deep level and can recognise all the cycles and all the pieces involved. Without the help of the spirit of Understanding and a thorough knowledge of scripture, you will never put it together. But when you do, you gain an immense understanding of Satan, and you can see what drives him or her, what power he or she has, and how Satan can and does prevent entry to heaven, even today. Vitally, you will also be able to recognise the activities of Satan happening around you, and that makes it much easier to defeat him or her.

All of this is immensely challenging, but that is the point I am trying to make. You simply can't unravel all these mysteries with your mind, you need the spirit of Understanding to guide you and answer your questions. And that is why the mysteries will only be revealed when God wants to reveal them. Fortunately for us, that means now!

What is revealed?

There is an underlying and hidden story which flows throughout the Bible. This is the story that God asked me to discover and publish. I have discovered it, and I am publishing it in Book One.

The underlying story confirms many of the established doctrines, but it goes much further and deeper. It answers most of our questions about the spiritual world, including our spiritual creation, what was supposed to happen, what did actually happen, why things went wrong again and again, and how they are being corrected again and again. It explains the battle between good and evil, who or what is Satan, how does he or she work, how he or she can be overcome, the in-depth purpose of Jesus the Messiah, and, of course, the afterlife. It will also explain at the most fundamental level, the purpose and objective of our creation and the global threats we face, which will try to prevent this objective from succeeding. Including Armageddon.

Also, at the deeper levels, it reveals the foundations of life through the eyes of God, and the spiritual principles that define the spiritual world and frame what happens in it. Some of these principles are complex and difficult to grasp, but unfortunately, without at least a basic understanding of them, you cannot fully understand the underlying story. Therefore, I have included them in Book One, but only at the minimum depth that is required to understand the story and still keep it simple. I will explain more of the essential principles as we go deeper in the second and third books and thereafter.

If the deeper books sound somewhat daunting, don't worry. I have tried to make them more interesting, and even sometimes fun, by revealing many riddles and how to solve them. Most of us like to solve riddles! I hope that you will find the mysteries that are revealed to be fascinating enlightening and relevant to our physical lives too. Remember that the spiritual world is not meant to be academic, it is meant to help you practically, and that our spiritual identity drives our physical personality and actions.

Is the end of the world coming?

I hinted at the beginning of the book that the timing of the release of the mysteries was connected to the end of the age and the beginning of a new one.

Perhaps the most interesting revelation for most readers, will be the understanding of the mystery that has become known as 'the end of the world' or 'Armageddon' or 'the Apocalypse' or 'doomsday' or simply 'end times'. There has been much debate over the question, 'does the Bible finish with the massive destruction of a wicked mankind?' Can we perhaps expect World War Three with a nuclear Armageddon? Or an asteroid strike? Or a virus that wipes out most of mankind? Or even half of the population mysteriously being taken away to somewhere, in an instant?

For about the first half of my study, I had no idea why God had decided to reveal all the mysteries that had remained hidden for thousands of years, at this particular time. It was somewhat disturbing to find out that it was because this Armageddon event is a cyclical event, and although what was described in the Bible has already happened (around AD 70), it is about to happen again. Hence the warnings we have seen recently, of escalating wars and rumours of wars and earthquakes and floods and fires and pestilence and asteroids and so on. We cannot say exactly when, but it is certainly coming soon, in a matter of a few years.

It is true that we should take the threat of devastation seriously, because we are all aware of the risk of nuclear conflict and that we are moving steadily towards it. Remember that I mentioned the MAD policy? But we will discover that God is also very aware of the risk and is taking it very seriously, and we will see that **the events that are about to happen are part of God's plan to prevent the end of the world, not cause it.** In fact, we will learn at the very beginning of Book One that because time is different in the spiritual world, God foresaw the threat of extinction and came up with a dramatic solution, even before creation had started. We are a part of this solution.

So it is not the end of the world, but it is the end of the age and the start of a new age. The reason why all the mysteries of the spiritual world are to be revealed now is to help us to prepare for this event, but more importantly, to prepare for what comes after it, in a positive way. We will go into this in considerable depth, as we progress through the books.

'The other side' and 'the spiritual mysteries hidden since the foundation of the world'

Both of these phrases, which appear on the cover of the book, come from the Bible. To be accurate, it describes what Jesus is saying, after his disciples have complained that they don't understand what he preaches because he always speaks in riddles and parables. '*I will open my mouth in parables; I will utter what has been hidden since the foundation of the world.*' Thus Jesus knew and understood the mysteries but he never revealed them to the people, always hiding them in riddles and parables that require Understanding to solve. There was a very good reason for this which you will soon understand. It is about ensuring that the people of Satan do not know the mysteries, and keeping the rest of the people innocent through ignorance, until they are ready for them. However, Jesus did partially reveal the meaning of some of the parables privately to his disciples. Now, at last, the full meanings of what Jesus said and did can be revealed.

As I said, scripture always describes the spirit world, usually in a hidden way, but the phrase, '*The other side*' is used when the story switches to directly reveal the spiritual world through spiritual eyes which have been opened. What they see is weird and supernatural. Here are three illustrations of this from well-known Bible stories. If you don't know them, don't worry. They will be covered in more detail later in this book.

- First, Jesus and his disciples are en route to 'the other side' when the storms rise up and he calms the wind, and he walks on water. This is happening in the spirit world and we would not normally be able to see anyone walking on water. We will look at this in more depth in a moment.
- Second, it is on 'the other side' where he heals the sight of a blind man, but initially the man seems to be only partially healed and, strangely, he sees trees walking. When you understand that in the spirit world, trees are living spirits which can be either stationary, rooted in the ground, or moving when they are within angelic creatures, you understand that Jesus is demonstrating that he can open spiritual eyes to see spiritual things. He then completes the healing so the man can see the physical world too.
- Third, the strange story of a man called Legion who is full of evil spirits who can talk to Jesus and which are cast out by him, also happens on 'the other side'. It is revealed so we can see what is happening in the spiritual world, since in the physical world, you would never see what happens when spirits are cast out. This story reveals the mystery of where Satan's spirits finish up after Armageddon, and it is not a happy ending for them. All this sounds a bit weird now, but it will become more straightforward later, when we get used to seeing events happening in the spiritual world and almost take them for granted.

The switch of view to the spirit world also happens in the Old Testament, and is prefixed by travelling or sojourning 'on a long journey' to or from 'a far country'. For example, Moses sees the burning bush while he is journeying in the spiritual world, and the burning bush, like a small tree, is an important divine spirit of fire which we would not see in the physical world.

Have these mysteries ever been revealed in the past?

They have. A handful of people in the Old Testament, for example King Solomon and his father, King David, were given understanding of most of the mysteries and then the wisdom (another spirit, helpfully called the spirit of Wisdom) to know what to do with what they had understood. It was not for public consumption, but was to be used by kings to make their rule more effective and make their kingdoms more righteous and free from Satan.

Solomon was not permitted to publish the mysteries, so he wrote about what he had learned in a book of sayings, which he called proverbs, where he hid them all again, in riddles. The mysteries are there, but they are well hidden and require Understanding to reveal. For example, when he referred to his gift of Understanding, Solomon put it like this in proverbs, '*It is the glory of God to conceal things, but the glory of kings is to search things out.*' This is a short riddle and to explain what he was saying, 'Glory' is a code word which means a group of seven spirits from God (actually, we will see that it is the Holy Spirit), which includes Understanding. Therefore, the basic hidden meaning is that the Holy Spirit in God hides the mysteries and the Holy Spirit in kings, finds them. At a slightly deeper level Solomon is saying that God's own divine spirit of Understanding hides the mystery, so when this same divine spirit of Understanding is given by God to kings, it has no trouble to understand the mystery and reveal it to them! The fact that the divine Holy Spirit is later given not only to kings but also to ordinary people, will be vital to bring success against Satan.

Most of the riddles were about wise people who had received the spirit of Wisdom, and foolish people who had not. Sadly, we will see that Solomon's understanding and wisdom became corrupted, he became a wreck and died a broken man, racked by depression. The power that comes with the mysteries must be handled with respect. Solomon's father, King David, also had understanding and wisdom and he buried the mysteries he discovered, within the psalms that he wrote, and you need Understanding to reveal them too.

After that time, most of the mysteries were withheld from mankind, including the kings, until the coming of Jesus. Certainly, Jesus understood everything, and he could see the spirit world clearly, with his spiritual eyes, but as we will see, Jesus is very special. He didn't write in spiritual code, he spoke it fluently and perfectly, always in riddles and parables that made little real sense at the time, much to the frustration of his disciples. But later, when they were reviewed by those with the benefit of the spirit of Understanding, they revealed enormously important messages. Even his miracles revealed vital spiritual mysteries about what was about to happen. But for those without Understanding, the mysteries remained hidden as before, including the true spiritual identity of Jesus the Messiah.

But after the death of Jesus, we will see that the apostles, especially John, Paul and Peter, also were given the spirit of Understanding and they uncovered the mysteries. Yet again, they buried them to keep them hidden, referring to them only in spiritual code and riddles within their own writings. That means the whole of the New Testament. There are good reasons why they were obliged to hide them again, which we will discover. Put simply, they were important secrets about the spiritual world, including the afterlife, and they were not meant to be discovered by the people of Satan. Therefore, most people of that time could not understand what the apostles had hidden. However, most of the followers of the apostles who became the early Christian church, also had Understanding to an extent, and they could understand the hidden meanings sufficiently. Even today, the mysteries are there in their letters waiting to be revealed, but nearly all of them remain hidden. It is very humbling and most satisfying that they all confirm the mysteries that were revealed to me too, in this present age.

Finally, throughout the Bible there have been prophets who wrote scripture. They also buried important mysteries in their writings, which were not understood at the time, but they can be understood by people with Understanding now.

In summary, the way it works is that all the mysteries are hidden in scripture and nobody can see that they even exist. Then someone is given the ability to see them and to reveal them, so they can carry out their job, and therefore God's will, better. But when they do it is like they are contained in a file marked 'Top Secret' and to keep them secret they bury the file again. Therefore, no clear and comprehensive account of the mysteries has ever been written and published. This is the first time that God has decided to openly publish them. Or if you like, this time God has declassified all the files. Not just to kings and leaders but to everyone.

Why? To help us to prepare for what is about to come. We will see that the more people who understand it now, the better.

Some examples of hidden mysteries

Already, what I have said is a lot to take in and can be difficult to follow. However, the whole concept of hidden mysteries and what they reveal about the spiritual world is much easier to understand when you look at a few examples. So let's look at three examples now.

1) Sea and fish and earth
Earlier, I said that the '**sea**' in scripture is not the sea that we know in the physical world. We will learn that the spiritual sea is where people who do not believe in God reside in the spirit world, (wherever they live in the physical world). The unbelieving people who live in the spiritual 'sea' are called '**fish**'.

That is the meaning of two code words, sea and fish, but where does that take us and what mysteries does it reveal? Well, next we learn that fish do not breathe spiritual air, and air is called '**the breath of life**'. The breath of life is the first spirit that you receive when you become a believer. It is the first 'radio' that I mentioned earlier, which is called '**Faith**'. Without it you do not believe, but with it you do. That means that when a 'fish' believes, he or she must leave the sea to breathe in the air. Then they will crawl up onto the '**earth**' which is another code word for the place for those who believe in God.

But if he does not believe during his physical life, he will die without the breath of life, and his fishlike flesh will rot away leaving only his soul, which is eternal. His soul will then be carried within another fish and live another life as an unbeliever, and this cycle will continue until he chooses to believe, and he leaves the sea. It is in a cycle of reincarnation, again and again.

But when he believes, he breaks the cycle, and lives on 'earth'. The next stage is to go to heaven. You breathe the breath of life in heaven too. So, an unbelieving 'fish' cannot enter heaven if he doesn't believe in it, but a person on the 'earth' can.

Put sea, fish, earth and heaven together, and you can understand what Jesus meant when he gave his disciples 'the great commission' and told them to go out into the world and become 'fishers of men.' He is saying, in code, that he wants them to preach to the unbelievers so that they become believers and follow him from sea to earth and to heaven. You will also see that Jesus gives a different message when he speaks on the shore or in a boat on the sea, to the message he gives on the mountains of the earth, to keep them relevant to his audience. Therefore, these simple code words give important context to whatever story is being told.

But we can still go deeper when we look at the mystery of the 'sea'. Now that we know that the sea is really a description of a large group of people who do not believe in God, we can apply that mystery to every use of the word 'sea'. So when a group of people on earth are overcome by a great flood from the sea, we know that it actually means there was a battle between believers and non-believers, and the non-believers won. That explains Noah's flood, but it also explains the parting of the Red Sea when Moses led the people out of Egypt. The Red Sea was an army of non-believers whose enemies were the Egyptian army, not the Hebrew people. They were on the same side as the Hebrews, against the Egyptians, so they parted ranks to let them pass, then attacked the Egyptian army and overwhelmed them.

The same explanation reveals what is meant by storms and heavy waves on the sea, as the armies are either roused up into battle (heavy waves), or calmed into peace. But what is it that stirs up the waves into a storm? The living spirit, the breath of life, when it becomes enraged from a breath into a strong **wind**. In fact the Hebrew word for spirit is properly translated as 'wind'. This becomes really interesting when two types of this wind come from two different places, and compete to control the sea. This will lead to not just conflicts but to full-blown wars. What it is really meaning is that the evil spirits of Satan (wind) can stir up unbelieving people (sea) into a war with others. However, a spirit of God (wind from a different place) can compete to calm the people and stop the wars.

This is a fairly straightforward example of how we start with a simple new meaning for a word you thought you understood from the physical world, but quickly finish up explaining the mysteries of Noah's flood and the parting of the Red Sea, and even the competing forces behind major wars in the spiritual world. When we understand the spiritual powers at work, and how they manipulate the physical wars we experience, we have taken an important step towards stopping existing wars and maybe even preventing future wars. Along the way we have even revealed the path to eternal life in the afterlife in heaven. Yet this is only about halfway through the deeper levels of understanding about the spiritual world, and in the book we will continue to reveal more mysteries using both the 'sea' and an even more important code word, the **'waters'**. If you have heard the expression 'living waters' already, you may have an idea what it means and why it is living.

2) Spiritual 'flesh'
The spiritual world is populated by spiritual 'angels'. They may look like men and women or animals, but they are eternal beings with soul, spirits and spiritual flesh. Let's consider the spiritual **flesh** here. I learned (via the spirit of Understanding) that the angelic flesh is where the angel stores its spiritual knowledge, so it is the place of spiritual memory. That sounds weird, but it reveals many mysteries. We need to remember that everything we are considering in this passage is in the spiritual world, although it is easily confused with the physical world. It's best to try to focus on the spiritual world on the basis that it is showing what is going on behind the physical world.

Firstly, it explains why some spiritual flesh is clean and some is unclean. It depends on whether the flesh contains true or false spiritual knowledge, either from God or from Satan. For example, if you eat unclean flesh from an animal, it will give you the spiritual knowledge of Satan. Thus, this simple spiritual fact explains the doctrines of clean and unclean, and eating only clean food. Those people who obey these doctrines have unknowingly assumed that this applies to the physical world. This is a safe assumption to make, although it is not really that simple. Perhaps it is better to say that when we eat, for example, physical pork, our angelic side in the spiritual world also eats spiritual pork at the same time. Another mystery that I will reveal later, is why this doctrine doesn't affect Christians.

In the spiritual world, if your spiritual '**eyes**' are opened, you can see the unclean spiritual flesh on people. It looks diseased like Leprosy, and it is infectious like Leprosy, but Leprosy is only a physical analogy. It is the unclean spiritual flesh that is important. That is why Jesus regularly sees and heals what looks like Leprosy. He is healing the spiritual flesh by making it clean again, but Jesus is letting us see this in the physical world too. If we physically see that someone has physical leprosy today then we should treat this as an analogy, not that they are covered in sin. That applies in principle to all the healings that Jesus performs, which are all healings of spiritual problems, with physical analogies. We will look at these miracles in some depth.

Secondly, the angelic flesh is grown from eating spiritual food. The angelic food is spiritual knowledge, which can either be true or false, clean or unclean, and it finishes up in the spiritual flesh. Every example of food in scripture is spiritual knowledge. It could be the manna from heaven which includes the law of Moses. It is also the bread from Jesus. Every example of Jesus 'eating' with a group means he is preaching spiritual knowledge to them, and feeding their angelic forms to satisfy their spiritual hunger. The last supper or the feeding of the 5,000 with loaves of bread are simple examples. Also, the bread of the Christian ritual of communion, called the 'flesh of Jesus', now makes more sense and you can understand that it refers to Jesus continually providing clean and true spiritual knowledge to his followers through spiritual communication, even after his physical death.

Thirdly, a method used to remove the unclean knowledge of Satan in your flesh, is to introduce a famine. The unclean flesh withers away and a hunger grows. Then there is a feast of the new clean spiritual knowledge, and the flesh becomes full and clean. This spiritual principle is reflected in deliberate and voluntary fasting followed by feasting. From now on, all these events of food shortages or plenty will take on a new meaning, but you will see that the principle never changes.

Fourthly, later, we will see that by the time of Jesus and the apostles, the flesh is almost universally corrupted by unclean false spiritual knowledge from Satan. As well as clean bread, a clean spirit from God is introduced in the time of the Apostles, and used to deliver the truth directly and spiritually. At that point there will be conflict between the new clean spirit and the old memories from the old unclean flesh. This leads to internal personal conflict and the followers of the apostles are encouraged to listen to the spirit and reject the flesh.

Now, every time you read about food in the Bible again, you will understand what it really means, and a new picture will emerge from the jigsaw pieces you find. This is how the mysteries are slowly revealed a piece at a time, until you see the whole picture.

3) Walking on water

Here is a final example which reveals some of the mysteries hidden in a famous event concerning Jesus that has puzzled us for 2,000 years. It is the mystery of when Jesus walks on water. We can use this Bible story to show how the mysteries are hidden in it, in various depths, and how they can be revealed. Therefore, this example is rather more complex than the others.

This is a mystery which is mainly about authority and power. Authority is a vital principle in the spirit world. It is always displayed by the height of your position, with the higher position having the authority. When you 'fall' it means you fall from a position of authority, and you lose it. This is the 'fall' that happened to Adam and Eve and then all of mankind as a result. The position of Jesus is carefully given in every story so you can see who he is establishing authority over. If someone sits before him they are accepting his authority. If he climbs to the top of a mountain, then he is establishing his authority over everyone on the mountain.

This story of walking on water is a good example for us to demonstrate how to reveal a mystery. We can go a little deeper this time, to see how it works. The story is made up of many pieces of a jigsaw, and has many levels of understanding. It draws on other mysteries from other parts of the Bible, that have already been revealed at the time of the story, and some which have not yet happened, so will only be revealed later on. I will not attempt to cover all the levels and all the mysteries in this story here, but I shall hopefully go deep enough to demonstrate the principles of how the mysteries are hidden and revealed. Obviously, we don't yet have all of the earlier levels of understanding that we will need to get to the deeper meanings, however, we can use the mysteries which we have already revealed in this preface.

The story starts just after the famous feeding of the 5,000. Once the people have been fed, Jesus tells the disciples to get on a boat and sail over the Sea of Galilee to '**the other side**'. This tells us that we are going to view the spiritual world and that every event is spiritual. He goes up a mountain to pray, alone. The mountain is a statement of his authority over all the earth and the sea, and is the first piece of the jigsaw.

As evening approached, the wind was against the disciples, and they were beaten by waves. We know that means the disciples are being opposed by the non-believers in the 'sea', who are being stirred up by the opposing 'wind' which is a powerful spirit from Satan. The wind and waves represent the conflict in the physical world, which the disciples are facing now and will face later too. Satan is opposing what Jesus has asked them to do, which is why the conflict starts at the beginning of night, because this is the time of Satan. It seems that Satan is winning, and the disciples are making slow progress. They do not have Jesus in the boat to help them counter Satan.

Then, at the end of the night and the beginning of dawn, Jesus comes to them, walking on the water. Because we are on the other side, we are seeing Jesus in his spiritual form, and so are his disciples. We would not normally see Jesus or anyone else walking on water! To understand what that spiritual form is, we can look at a jigsaw piece at the beginning of creation, when 'the Holy Spirit is hovering over the waters'. The Holy Spirit is a living creature with its own angelic identity and personality, and now we are able to look at it. We can see that in this story, Jesus is the Holy Spirit in angelic form. To confirm this, there is a jigsaw piece in the story too, because the disciples call out that '*It is a ghost*'. They are right, it is the Holy Ghost, one of three spiritual identities of Jesus (the other two being the Father and the Son).

The Holy Spirit has authority over the sea, so Jesus must stand and walk above it. If he was to swim in the sea then he would have fallen and lost his authority, so there are no stories of Jesus swimming in the sea. He also has authority over the spirit (or wind) of Satan, and he has come to rescue his disciples from their conflicts with Satan. At this point of the story, the disciples do not have the authority over the Holy Spirit, so they are sitting or lying in the boat, below Jesus who is standing. They are therefore struggling against Satan. But as soon as Jesus gets in the boat, his authority and power over the spirit of Satan will save the boat and all the people in it.

There is one exception, which is Peter. Peter has already been given authority from Jesus in an earlier story (or piece of the jigsaw), and if he uses it, he will also be able to defeat Satan too. Peter wishes to use this authority, so he asks Jesus to command that he walks on water to him. Jesus's command will give him Jesus's authority to walk on water. But when Peter leaves the boat, he sees the 'wind' and he becomes afraid. Because he is in the spiritual world, he sees the spirit of Satan like he saw the Holy Spirit, and understandably, it scares him.

His fear makes him fall, and he loses his authority, so he sinks into the sea. But when he says, 'Lord save me,' Jesus puts out his hand and lifts him out, pointing out that he had little faith. That's because Peter had the authority and the power to calm the wind of Satan, but he did not use it. Then Jesus gets in the boat and to demonstrate his point to Peter, so the wind ceased, and the waves were calmed. Everyone in the boat worshipped Jesus, and that is the end of the passage.

You can see that the mysteries which are revealed are about the Holy Spirit versus the spirit of Satan, both when they are present in Jesus and when they are missing in mankind. We could stop there, but just to demonstrate how much more there is to this story, let me go a little deeper, if possible, without losing you! I appreciate that many readers will not know enough of the Bible stories at this stage to follow this fully, but try to bear with it anyway. You will understand all of this soon enough.

Really, this story is about what is going to happen after Jesus dies and leaves his followers alone and at night. They will suffer from continual conflicts with Satan, but Jesus will come to them as the Holy Spirit and everything will change. Not just because Jesus will fight for them, but because they will receive the Holy Spirit in them, and fight for themselves. The Holy Spirit will be in the boat with them, and they won't be alone. Everyone in the boat will have the necessary authority and the power of the Holy Spirit to defeat Satan, if they have enough faith to use it.

The story has become a living parable, which is a type of riddle, and in these parables, every character represents something bigger. Here we can see that the boat itself represents the early Christian Church for the followers of Jesus, who will be filled with the Holy Spirit. This will happen dramatically in the Bible, soon after Jesus physically dies. If you look carefully with this deeper understanding, you can appreciate that the Church consists of living people, so as a collection of living breathing people, it is alive. And that is true, because in the spiritual world, everything is living!

What about Peter's part of the story? This is showing us what is going to happen to Peter soon, but it is an example for what can happen to all of us. We know that Peter is given authority, but in another story, when Jesus is arrested, Peter becomes scared and denies him three times, one for each identity of Jesus. That includes denying the Holy Spirit. As soon as he does this, he falls and loses his authority and his power. In fact, he loses the Holy Spirit within him. Once lost can we get it back? Yes. Later, just before Jesus leaves the earth, he reaches out to Peter and he confirms Peter's love for him to an extent, three times, and his Holy Spirit, faith and authority are restored, also to an extent. Peter will have authority over the wind of Satan, and he will be the apostle responsible for the Jewish 'chosen people', but he will not have responsibility for the 'gentile' people all around the promised land. That job will be given to the apostle Paul.

I hope this demonstration has helped you to understand at a fairly basic level, how the mysteries are both hidden and revealed in various depths and levels, and how deep you are able to go after only a few passes.

When we consider this mystery later, we will go deeper, and we will see that this story is actually a living riddle about the coming of Jesus and the defeat of Satan at Armageddon. Maybe some readers will already see it. As I explained earlier, this is a repeating cycle and as it happened in Bible times (in AD 70) so it is happening now.

The key message for us today is that in difficult times we should watch out for the Holy Spirit to arrive, then use its power wisely against Satan, followed by a great victory over Satan, followed by an arrival at our destination. It is coming soon.

Other Spiritual Codes

There are many more things to understand which will help to unlock the mysteries, and which I will cover in the book. We have seen examples of the word code, and I have mentioned that there is a number code too. This is very valuable and used throughout the Bible. It helps us to identify the spiritual identities of the people in the passage. Each type of spirit has its own number. The number code reveals many more things too, for example five is about mercy and eight is about resurrection and afterlife, and three is about the Messiah and six is about the spirit of Satan. Most people have heard about 'the number of the spirit of the beast, 666', in Revelation, and the many myths that it has produced. However, this is a mystery in a riddle that requires the spirits of Wisdom and Understanding to solve. The author of Revelation, John, says, 'This calls for wisdom: let the one who has understanding calculate the number of the beast …' We will solve the riddle later.

Muslims may find the number code particularly useful when understanding the Quran, because many of the suras (books) start with a hidden number code within some letters, which identifies the spiritual identity of the key people the sura relates to. So far as I am told, Muslim scholars have not yet been able to explain with any confidence the purpose of these letters, but it is the same number code that is used in the Bible and other scriptures, and it has the same meanings.

Also, I mentioned a colour code which is similar and helps to identify the relevant cycles and ages that are relevant to the story. The best example is the rainbow, whose seven colours correspond with the seven ages of the story, starting with red for fire and transitioning to deep blue for water.

The structure of the books

Before we start reading the books, I need to briefly explain how they are structured.

The books are aimed at everyone with an enquiring mind, but that covers a large range of people from those who have absolutely no knowledge of the Bible, even the well-known stories, to Bible scholars who know the Bible intimately but may have strongly held views on its interpretations. Some people will want to quickly get deep into the mysteries and others will want to take it slowly, a step at a time. Some will simply want to read the revealed mysteries, and others will want to see how they were buried and how they were revealed, going really deep into codes and difficult riddles themselves. How do you cater for everyone?

The answer is to write a series of books which start simply then get deeper and more complex.

Book One

Book One is a narrative of the underlying story, at the most straightforward level. To make it readable, I have told it as a story, a bit like a novel, but it is not fiction. It does, however, include simple descriptions of the most basic spiritual principles that simply have to be understood to follow the story. Hopefully these parts do not read too much like a textbook. As you get used to reading about the spiritual world, and applying the basic spiritual principles, Book One will get a little more advanced and we will go deeper, the further you go.

At the end of the book, I have included three appendices with summaries of information that you will probably want to bookmark and refer to as you read. These are the number and colour code, the word code and the seven ages.

Regarding the hidden links from the Bible to the story, at the beginning of Book One I will make no attempt to explain the biblical origin of the events in the story. Generally, I simply state them. So there are no riddles and very little code. But as we get used to the spiritual world, I will start to reveal some simple riddles and code, and jigsaw pieces, and solve them and show you how they work. I will also give you the opportunity to solve some riddles yourself, hopefully without detracting from the story. Although, when we get to Armageddon, it is just too complex to explain in Book One, so I simply describe the key messages and where they take us, without decoding the whole book of Revelation!

Because most of what is covered in Book One is new, everyone needs to understand Book One before they move on to Book Two and beyond. Including experienced scholars.

Books Two and Three

Now I am very aware that simply recounting the underlying story of the Bible in Book One, with a handful of examples of links to the Bible, does not show how it comes from the Bible, rather than what people could say is my overactive imagination. Therefore, I do have to show the links in detail and in depth, including the riddles and how to solve them, and these are revealed in the next two books.

They go into much more detail, and at a much deeper level of understanding, and they cover more Bible stories, including some which are not so well known, but still important. They focus on events and parables and riddles and cycles, that were too deep for Book One. They also include deeper and essential spiritual principles about spiritual life. Book Two covers the Old Testament, up to just before the arrival of Jesus and Book Three covers the New Testament from the arrival of Jesus to Armageddon and beyond.

Where appropriate, throughout the series I will draw conclusions from what we have learned, and bring out some guidance on how to prepare for what is coming soon. Both regarding Armageddon and, more importantly, what comes after it.

Prologue to Book One

As I explained, there are numerous spiritual principles which need to be understood to follow the underlying story and the mysteries properly. I will introduce the deeper principles in the later books, but there are still a few to deal with in Book One. Most of them will be explained in the narrative of the story, but a couple are so fundamental that we need to cover them here, before we start. The first is a simplified list of the number code and the second is about cycles. I briefly touched on cycles earlier in the preface, but I need to develop the theme and go a bit deeper.

Cycles
In the physical world, most things are linear. There is a start and an ending and a line from the start to the end, where it stops. Conversely, in the spirit world, **everything** is cyclical, like a circle, and nothing is linear. A circle has no ending, so wherever you start you will eventually come back to the same place. Time in the spirit world is cyclical too, and since there is no end, everything is eternal. That's why God is eternal, but it's also why our spiritual life is eternal too. Everything in the spiritual world consists of a whole series of cycles, repeating and working and interacting together.

To help us to understand this, we can see cycles of time reflected in the physical world too. For example, a day is a cycle in time and seven days make up a different cycle of seven subcycles, which we call a week. Or 12 months make up a different cycle of 12, which we call a year. So you have small cycles within bigger cycles which are also within bigger cycles. And so on. Cycles are also seen in the repeating and predictable orbits of planets, which give us various repeating seasons or lunar months or solar years and so on. These cycles allow us to predict, to an extent, future occurrences which will occur during their future appearances. We can also look back at previous cycles and hopefully learn from them.

Our spiritual lives exist in a series of cycles, some of which are personal cycles and can be seen in the physical world as repetitive events. In a daily cycle, we might get up at the same time every day, have breakfast and go to work in a daily routine. Other cycles are much bigger and involve longer periods of time and many more people whose cycles interact with each other. But if you zoom out enough, you can see the larger cycles too. They can be reflected in major events in history and we might say that 'history is repeating itself' or 'what goes around comes around.'

We will review these cycles in considerable depth in the book. When you consider the spiritual world, you should try to forget the linear world and to only see a world of repeating cycles, if you can. For example, you might think you are looking at a straight path or a straight line in front of you, but if you can zoom out enough, you will see that it is actually a curve, which leads back to where you started.

Think of a line on the surface of our planet. What seems straight is actually a curve like a circle. However, because the planet is a three-dimensional sphere, it doesn't matter which direction you set off on, so long as you go straight and do not turn away, you always come back to the starting point. It means that in a world of cycles, **nothing** is new, and **everything** is based on past events and is largely predictable. We will see many references to staying on the way, going straight, neither turning to the right nor the left, and these circles are what is being described. When everyone is on their true way, there is order and a predictable, safe, ending.

Futile repetition?

You might think that living in repeating cycles where nothing is new and everything is predictable, leads to a spiritual life of boring repetition, and you wouldn't be the first to think so. We will look at the life of Solomon, the son of king David and we will see that Solomon received the spirit of 'Understanding' and understood the basic principle of cycles. He wrote a famous poem about the cycles of time, where everything has its time and its season, but he also said, *'there is nothing new under the Sun'*. He concluded that a life of repetition is futile and empty – a life of vanity, and he wrote a book about it. Over time he became disillusioned, depressed and then he went mad.

Or endless opportunities to improve?

But Solomon was wrong, because he had been deceived, and it isn't futile. Instead, every cycle gives us the opportunity to learn from any mistakes made in the previous cycles, and allows us to improve the next one. It's vital to understand that we can change a cycle, and our changes continue in the ongoing cycles indefinitely, unless they are changed again. Take a simple example of this. If there is a big stone in our front path and every morning we trip over it and hurt ourselves, we will continue to hurt ourselves until we learn to walk around it or we remove it. Then the hurt will have gone for ever and we can move on.

If we can improve enough, this cycle will continue to be a good cycle without further attention, and God can move us on to a new, higher, cycle and see how we get on with that one. This applies to each individual, but it also applies to every cycle at every level. It applies to groups and eventually to nations and great historical events. Unfortunately, we can also make a cycle worse, and get into a downward spiral of cycles. That's what happened to Solomon when he believed the spiritual deceptions rather than his God-given understanding. More of that later.

Seven fundamental cycles

In the story of the Bible, we will see many individual cycles and how they are either improved or made worse for the individual and for future generations. But we will also see that the whole story is divided into seven major cycles, which are called ages. An age is also called a day. So when we start with the seven days of spiritual creation, we are actually looking at seven ages. It is important to understand that each age does not stand alone, it is a cycle and it will repeat. Why is that important? Because the seven ages of creation become the cycles which are repeated in the seven ages of the story of the Bible. And when these seven cycles are fulfilled at the end of the Bible, they are not a linear story with a beginning and an ending, they are repeated. Again and again. You will see that at the end of the story, in Revelation, we hear the statement '*I am the beginning and the end*'. That describes a fundamental cycle where the beginning and the end are the same. Then, because the end is also the beginning, the cycle continues. That confirms the dramatic mystery that the seven fundamental cycles of the Bible are repeated, and the Bible story does not stop at Armageddon or any other place or time for that matter. Actually, it continues indefinitely, and what we learn in the seven ages of the Bible continue to be relevant in every cycle of seven ages that follow.

We will discover that each cycle (or day or age) is 10 generations long, so the cycle of seven ages turns out to be 70 generations long and takes roughly 2,000 physical years to fulfil, depending on the time between each generation.

Why is that important? Because we are now living towards the end of the next set of seven ages, those which came after the Bible's seven ages. This is not just significant for us all as individuals, it is going to be a worldwide event. You will soon see that in the Bible, towards the end of the sixth age there are escalating conflicts which eventually erupt into a huge purge of the spirits of Satan. As the sixth age closes and just after the seventh age begins, the purge becomes the battle of Armageddon. It's important to understand that Armageddon is not the end of the world, but it **is** the end of the age. Then it is followed by a great age of peace and mercy and rest – the sabbath age. Sadly, history shows that this age is not permanent, and it will close, and then the next seven ages will start.

The critical point, which we will soon see, is that the seventh age only closes when Satan recovers from the purge of the sixth age, and tempts mankind into falling once again. **The key to how long that takes, is how much have we learned from both our mistakes and our successes, the last time around. It could end in only a generation, or it could be many centuries.**

Now, just as we, as individuals, are given an opportunity to improve with each cycle in our lives, this principle applies to every cycle in the spiritual world, no matter how large. Some 2,000 years ago, it was our forefathers' opportunity to get it right! Many did, and many did not, and the seventh age came to an end. Now it is our turn. We are privileged that the sabbath age is certainly coming soon, but the question is, how long can we make it last this time? Can we perhaps even make it permanent?

Reference to and summary of the seven ages
Because these seven ages are so vital to the underlying story, I have summarised them at the end of the book, after the simple glossary of code words. But it comes with a spoiler alert, because the seven ages reveal the whole story, which is why I have not included it here. You may prefer to wait until you are further into the story before you refer to it.

Where are we now?
In the Bible story, the sixth age was the age of the apostles, which came after Jesus, the Messiah, had come in the fifth age, to prepare us for the seventh age, which he called the coming Kingdom. The sixth age is when the Holy Spirit was released (including the spirit

of Understanding), the mysteries were revealed by the apostles, and a path was opened up to eternal life in heaven. All of this will be explained in depth in this book, but the point I am making here is that we are already in the sixth of our seven ages, and we are nearing its end. Today, the mysteries of the spiritual world are being revealed again, the Holy Spirit is about to be released again, and the path to eternal life is opened again.

With the greater understanding of the spiritual world which this series of books will bring, we have the opportunity to change the cycles for the better and to be ready, both as individuals now and as the next generations to come. We have the opportunity to do better than our forefathers did.

As for our purges and our Armageddon? Like I said, it's not the end of the world it's the end of the old age and the beginning of the new age. It is certainly a huge and vital event which will change the world, but it will take place predominantly in the spiritual world with some parallel manifestations in the physical world. But like in the earlier cycle, many people won't even recognise it has happened. Nevertheless, it will bring something amazing to the spiritual world, for those who believe in it and can see it.

The underlying story

God has decided to reveal and publish all the hidden mysteries, so that we will understand the spiritual world and we will know what to expect. In particular, we will understand how Satan works and recognise his (or her) attempts to undermine us, both now and then eventually, in the sabbath age. When we know what to look for, we will even be able to identity Satan's manifestation as a person on earth, at the end of the age – in other words the anti-Christ. **Then, if we can fully resist Satan, so that we do not fall again, the sabbath age will not end. That should be our target.**

This book starts the process by telling us the hidden story of the Bible. It is a summary, written as simply as possible, and you don't need to have any knowledge or deep understanding of the Bible to follow it. To keep it as simple and as readable as I can, I have written much of the story to read like a novel, but please don't think that means it is fiction. This drama is not made up, it is true. Everything in it may be well hidden in the Bible, but it has happened, and much of it will keep happening as the spiritual cycles repeat themselves. This story describes the hidden mysteries, but remember that how to discover them where they were carefully hidden within the Bible, comes in the next two books.

To nearly everyone, this story will come as a surprise, and to some it will come as a shock. It came as a shock to me.

Let's start the book.

Mysteries of The Other Side

BOOK ONE

The Hidden Story of the Spiritual World
The Greatest Love Story Ever Told

Chapter 1

The End

The old warrior looked around himself and breathed a sigh. He could see ranks of soldiers all around, ready and willing for war. They waited silently and patiently and obediently, with the confidence of an army that expected nothing but outright victory. A great victory that they had waited a very long time for.

Their armour shone and their weapons glinted and flashed in the light. To the old warrior, many of the warriors were very young, almost children, and this would be their first battle. He worried about them, but he knew they were fit and strong and brave and would not turn from the fight. He looked ahead to their commanders and saw they were not much older, and he tried to remember what it was like to be so young and how he had felt the first time he went to war. Now he was old, and he commanded many. They were seasoned and capable, battle hardened, strong and brave men. They would obey him without question, and he felt the responsibility that came with such trust and loyalty, like all great military commanders before him. Some looked up at him and when they saw him looking down at them, they snapped to attention and raised their hand in salute. 'To glory – for God and King,' they shouted in unison. Their voices sounded like thunder and the old warrior knew from many experiences that their shout would bring terror to the enemy. He stroked his long black beard and felt his thick long black hair. They had taken a very long time to grow and he never trimmed them. He took great care of them, always. He could not resist a smile when he remembered how Samson had lost all his hair and his strength, and was captured.

But that was different, and this warrior was not going to lose his strength. Ever.

He looked wider. The ranks of this army had recently swollen dramatically. More than the many young recruits, large numbers of the enemy warriors had switched sides. Many had fought for the enemy only as captives, and they had been freed in their thousands by this very army, over the previous few years. Even in the last few days, many tens of thousands had suddenly joined forces with their great commander and warrior king. These were very old men, but they looked as good as new. Now, the enemy was weakened and vastly outnumbered and surely, victory should be theirs. But their king was too experienced to take anything for granted. The enemy commander was a master of lies, scheming and manipulation, and had a habit of bouncing back from previous defeats. Certainly, she was female, but you underestimated her power at your peril, as many had done. She had gathered her own armies in an alliance of other kings, deceiving them by promising great wealth and power. Promises she could not keep. Yet the old warrior knew that his own commander and king was a better strategist; he could out-scheme any schemer, overpower any strength, outnumber any army, outmanoeuvre any strategies, and he was the best warrior and commander that had ever lived. Every one of his warriors, including the old warrior himself, loved him and would die for him if necessary.

All was still and silent. They waited. He had waited a very long time for this moment.

He looked down at the enemy's forces. The success of their attack depended on complete surprise, and he could see no sign of increased readiness. They were carrying on their lives as normal. Nobody knew when the order to attack would be given, but it was to be soon. Very soon. He looked again at his own ranks to check they were fully prepared and completely alert. He saw lines of fierce and huge men, special forces who were known as the hailstone troops, their hearts as hard as stone, and lying back in slings already under tension. They would be hurled by the slingshots straight into the unsuspecting enemy's high value targets. His king was no stranger to the effectiveness of the slingshot. Their mission was to take out the kings and other leaders, to disrupt command and control and to bring mass surrenders and changes of sides. Behind them were the lightning troops. Their swords were unsheathed and flashed in the light that surrounded them. They would arrive in a flash, just behind the hailstone slingshots, accompanied by the terrifying thunderous battle cries. He was glad that they were on his side.

Then, behind them were the ranks of the army. Led by mighty horsemen on mighty war horses, who stamped and snorted impatiently. He saw fire in their eyes and their breath looked like smoke. They knew they had been born for this moment and they could already smell victory. They would be followed by the massed army of foot soldiers, all wearing gleaming armour with their breastplates and full helmets in place, and he knew that they would not hesitate, not even for a moment. When they attacked, they were like torches of fire. They were born to utter obedience and loyalty and these warriors had not even been slightly tempted to lower their standards. They fought for their commander and for their God and they wanted only to be as worthy as their god and king had proven to be worthy to them.

The old warrior shifted in his chariot and every eye was suddenly on him, ready for his command. But not yet. His chariot moved gently as his weight shifted, like a ship floating on the sea, but he was not a sailor. His chariot was like a cloud, driven by the wind, but the wind was silent and calm and did not even stir. He spoke to the wind and asked, 'when?' The wind replied, 'Soon. The hour is upon us and our time has come. You are as prepared as the enemy is unprepared, and lies asleep beneath you. For now, we wait. Then we fight together. You have my power at your hand, use it well.' The warrior looked down and spoke to his chariot. They had been to war together many times over many centuries, and he trusted him implicitly. 'What about you, old friends?' It rolled its wheels of stone to face forwards and it replied with its four voices, 'Yes, we are ready, and as always, our path will be straight, neither turning to the left or the right. Just say the word.'

Then he saw his king. the king stood up on his chariot of pure shining white cloud and he took his position at the front of his army. The warrior grinned. This was no rear echelon commander, this man led from the front. He knew that his army would follow wherever he went. The king was the anointed one, the Messiah, the prince and then king, soon to be king of kings. The king raised his right hand. The old warrior slowly stood up. He put on his helmet, and raised his shield. 'Are you ready?' he said, and the armour replied, 'fear not, for no fiery dart nor spear nor blow of the enemy will penetrate me.' 'I know, I know, and I thank you,' he replied. He slowly spread his wings, and looked at the earth far below him. The armies of Satan, the Serpent and her alliance of the kings of the earth, were gathered at a place called Armageddon, and were still asleep. They had been gathered here by a series of deceptions from the Serpent, and they had no clue what they were facing. But he knew, and he surprised himself by shedding a tear when he thought of all the sacrifices that had been made to get to this point. Salvation was coming. At long last. He looked again at the youngsters. They were the next generation, and they were the future, he thought.

He silently thought a message to his king, and his king turned to smile at him. He wore a crown and he stood high, well above all the kings of the earth, establishing his authority. His hair shone white and his eyes burned like fire. 'David my King, my Lord, I pledge to you that I and my troops are ready and we will follow you to victory.' David thought back, 'Yes, my old and faithful friend, commander of my army of the night. Let us fight as one and be victorious once more, so the new kingdom of heaven and earth can come, and everything will be made new. The rule of Light will replace the rule of Darkness, and the tree of life, the Spirit of salvation into eternal life, will be restored at last. Come, let us be like a thief in the night, and take back what has always been ours, while our enemy sleeps.'

King David blew his rams horn and spoke. His voice sounded like a trumpet. He called on the captains and commanders to prepare for the attack and they replied with their battle cries. Half of their voices sounded like the roar of mighty waters and the other half sounded like thunder. King David unstrapped his sword and attached it into his mouth. All his army of followers did the same. When they spoke a command, it had both the power and authority of the sword, with which to separate and cast out the Serpent from within the people. Then, King David trumpeted the order, and all the troops attacked. There was hail and lightning and thunder and fire and blood. As the wind drove up a fierce storm from the sea that no one could withstand.

The Serpent and her army had expected an attack during the light of day, but it came at night. They were not prepared, and they could not tell the difference between their own warriors and the king's. Confusion reigned.

As he led his angelic army of the night down from heaven to strike the angelic spirits of the Serpent on earth, the old warrior could not stop himself reflecting on what King David had just said to him. He had spoken of the restoration of the Tree of Life, the Holy Spirit of Light. But the Tree of Life had been offered freely to Mankind at the very beginning of their spiritual creation. And it had been rejected. Now it had to be fought for in this terrible war.

How on earth, had it come to this? What went wrong? And will mankind accept the tree of life this time?

Chapter 2

Before the Beginning

Before our creation, there was God. What was God? Put simply, he was everything, everywhere. And everything that he was, was alive. Therefore, when it came to creation, God was already everything he needed to be. God took a deep breath and made a plan. But before he initiated it, he looked forwards and backwards in time so he could see every possible outcome of every possible action. He could do this because he was also time itself and he could see all the cycles of time, past and future, and adjust the speed of time, even down to zero so that everything happened at the same time. To us, this is an almost impossible concept to grasp, but to God, it is straightforward.

In particular, God looked at the cycles and futures of the pinnacle of this creation – mankind.

Then God stopped.

The way of Darkness

No matter what option God looked at, the outcome was the terrible destruction of his creation. He could also see that the problem which caused the destruction was truly fundamental. You see, God had always used a simple system to maintain order in a creation which had a fundamental right to make its own decisions, whether good or bad. It was a simple system of law and punishment, a system that God called 'the way of Darkness'. God lived by rules in everything he did, and he expected his creations to do the same. That means everything, whether it was the smallest part of an atom to the largest galaxies of the universe, they all obeyed God's rules of creation.

Thus, the living creatures would live by the rules of good and bad given to them, and would reap the consequences of their decisions, whether they were good or bad. They would quickly learn that the law was just, so it was good for everyone if it was followed, and painful if it was broken. That was because justice demanded that whatever broke the laws would be judged, and a punishment would be set and carried out. God called the punishment for breaking the law, fire and it hurt. Fire was alive too, and it was powerful and could destroy anything, or simply cause some discomfort, according to the level of punishment laid down.

To be clear, Darkness is a simple system of justice and order, and it is not evil as you might have believed. It is a system for good. The purpose behind the way of Darkness was not to inflict fire, it is the opposite, to minimise fire. That's because fire is by itself, a good deterrent to ensure that the rules would be obeyed, so there would be no need for fire to be used. God does not like to inflict fire and that is why God prefers to live in a state of Darkness, where there is no fire. However, where there is fire, the deterrent is strong, and order should be quickly restored and maintained by obeying the Law, and the fire should be minimal. The deterrent feature of the way of Darkness is called the 'fear' of the living creature who is behind it. Thus, in the times of the people of Darkness, we will hear that someone has 'the fear of God' or 'the fear of the Lord'.

The way of Darkness had always been at the very core of creation. It was simple, and it always worked, fundamentally because God was the judge of the law and the punishments, and God's judgements were always just and universally accepted to be fair. So everything that God planned was based on rules, and these rules must be followed, or chaos will be the result. Therefore, you either have order if you follow the rules, or chaos if you break them.

Thus, all of creation, and therefore the whole universe, relies on rules which are never broken. We can see this clearly through the science of the physical world. We learn the basic rules of nature at school, and scientists are constantly discovering more. The rules of nature are not broken, and they result in order.

But turning back to our creation, God could see that the way of Darkness would not work, because God can see the future, and he saw that mankind would choose to break the rules, constantly. Mankind would always rebel and abuse God's system of law and punishment. They took the system of judgement and justice upon themselves, displacing God, and the judgements of the authorities in charge were not just, and their punishments were not fair. Then, rather than restoring order, the fire was answered by greater fire in response to the injustice, to try to balance it. In other words, they rebelled against the authority in charge, so that they could enforce their own perceived justice. But it wasn't the justice of God, it became based on the justice of revenge. They were fighting fire with more fire and it simply didn't work. Instead, the injustice got worse and worse as the fire spread and consumed. The fight for justice became revenge, and revenge became conflict, and conflict became war, and justice and order was lost somewhere in the process, and replaced by chaos.

This brought many cycles or spirals of escalating fire and destruction, leading to ever more destructive wars. Both sides became set on destroying each other by fire, in the name of justice. But justice was by then impossible to find. Until in the end, the creation was destroyed by the fire it created. Every scenario God looked at had the same outcome. It was a disaster.

What went wrong with the system of Darkness? When God determines a just punishment, he used the basic principle of restoring what had been lost by the breach of the law. No more and no less, just enough to restore the position. Therefore, the principle he used was an eye for an eye and a tooth for a tooth, which should be seen by all as a just punishment. However, this system goes badly wrong as soon as the punishment itself is seen by the person it has been given to as a breach of the law, because it is false justice. And so the spiral starts and grows until an eye for an eye becomes a life for a life and there is war. Then every time that mankind tried to put out the fire by more fire, the wars become worse until both sides destroyed each other, often claiming that God was on their side.

But God understood the simple fact that the way of Darkness and fire just didn't work for the creation of mankind. And that was the only way that God knew. Therefore, because of mankind's disobedience to God's law, nothing would work, and in a state of frustration and anger with his rebellious creation, God was ready to abandon his plan and start again.

Then something happened.

When God thought about his creation he was overcome by his love for them. When he saw the destruction of his creation, his heart broke. He was filled with grief and he started to weep. He mourned for the future death of his people, even before he had created them. Then, in an instant, he knew what would work and he immediately made a new plan. When he looked forwards in time again, this plan worked.

What just happened? Well, God is both male and female in one. There is only one God, but God has a male side and a female side. The way of Darkness and fire is from his male side. Technically, we should call God 'they', which is what the Bible does. For simplicity, I will call the male side 'he' when their male side is being addressed, and 'she' when their female side is being addressed.

The female side of God dislikes fire even more than the male side. She can, to an extent, show mercy and forgive the rule breaking, so that the punishment of fire is reduced or not even required. This happens when the culprit regrets their behaviour and asks for forgiveness, which is called repentance. If the repentance is genuine, then the law breaking will not happen again, order is restored, so fire is not required.

The female side of God washes the effects of the rule breaches away, without fire, like cleaning them with water. Therefore, so long as the male side's fire of punishment is minor, it can be dealt with by the female side's water of mercy, which puts out the fire and washes the wound clean again. Hence water is an alternative to fire and this process can be described as fighting fire with water. Water washes the culprit clean rather than inflicting punishment, and if necessary, it puts out the fire. In summary, it is using mercy instead of punishment.

However, it does not stand alone as a way of achieving justice and order. The justice system of Darkness uses both fire and water together, and there should be a balance between mercy and punishment. However, in the way of Darkness, fire dominates, and water is only for small breaches of the law.

When God wept, she was manifesting their female side, and producing the cleansing water of mercy by her tears. The same is true when she was mourning mankind's destruction. It was the female side that suddenly gave the male side the solution to the problem. She wants to apply forgiveness and mercy to any excessive injustice and punishment. So at first, God changed his plan to increase the water for mankind, but still working within the system of Darkness. But it still didn't work. The water was not sufficient to put out the fire, and mankind was still always destroyed. The problem was always too much fire and not enough water.

What then, was the solution?

Then God realised the truth. The problem was that the way of Darkness meant that the male side of God was the supreme and almighty God. He always dominated, and therefore fire would always come first and dominate, but mercy would come after and be limited. The only solution was that the female side of God would have to dominate so that mercy would rule. That meant that the female side of God would need to become the supreme God. This had never happened before.

So God took another deep breath and put this into his plan. It worked. Mercy triumphed, fire was extinguished by water, and mankind was saved.

But there was nothing simple about managing this changeover. His female side had never taken full authority before, and she had no experience of being supreme God. There is a lot more to being God of everything than just putting out fires. He couldn't just resign and pass over his authority to her, it had to be done in stages so she could learn, and finally, she would have to prove herself worthy to rule. Now although there is only one God, at this pre-creation moment, he had six living parts to his existence, three male and three female, but all were under the system of the old way of Darkness – the way of Law. He looked at his three female parts and he saw that none of them would be capable enough to rise and to become supreme – they had simply not been prepared by him for this role.

He knew that he would need to produce a new female part that would be capable of replacing him and ruling. A seventh part to replace the way of Darkness with a new and dominant way, the way of mercy. What would that way be called?

The Way of Light

So God produced a new female divine entity, still a part of the one and only God, but now there would be seven parts to God, not six. He called her Light and she would rule the Way of Light. When the time came, if she was proven worthy, he would hand over his authority to her and she would be supreme God.

His new plan for creation was that first there must be six periods of Darkness, because they already exist, and they must come first. He called the periods 'days' or ages. Then, on the seventh day, if she was ready, the supreme God of Darkness would rest and stop manifesting, and the supreme God of Light would manifest and take over, so the Way of Light would rule. Therefore, the seventh day would be a day of rest for the old system of Darkness and Law, and a day of work for the new system of Light. Once she had proven herself worthy to rule, the plan was that the seventh day of Light would never end, and mankind would be safe.

However, Light would be not just be required at the seventh day, but from the very start, so she could have the opportunity to exercise some authority, to learn and gain experience, and eventually to prove herself worthy. Also, it was already clear that mankind would not survive long periods of unbroken Darkness and fire without a period of Light and mercy. The period of Light would then allow a correction for excessive fire. Therefore, there must be a balance of the ways of Darkness and Light living together. There would always be six periods of Darkness followed by one period of Light, and each day would be half Darkness followed by half Light. These seven periods could be short, like a week of seven days, but they could also be long and one of the seven major ages. At the end of each period of Darkness would also come a period of Light when the excesses of fire could be extinguished.

Thus God had seen the risk of the extinction of mankind, **but although God had not removed the risk, he had devised a plan to deal with it**. This was nothing less than a new creation, where there was to be enough water to put out the fire. **Where Light would overcome Darkness**.

So, with a new plan that worked, the God of Darkness, with the original six parts, started our creation. Then he made a seventh part. This was not a problem for God, he simply said, '*Let there be Light*', and there was Light. There was a massive explosion of Light within the old universe of Darkness, which spread outwards to fill it. A physical universe and a spiritual universe combined. Both Light and Darkness, together. Light said, 'I exist' or 'I am'. In Hebrew she is called 'Yhwh' which means both to exist and to be Lord. The Supreme God is called 'Elohiym' and at this stage, his male side dominates and Yhwh's female side dominates.

Then, because she would need to rule independently and without any input or help from him while he rested, he separated her from himself. At the same time, the physical world was separated from the spiritual world. But the physical world still had rules to follow, and it took the shape planned from the outset. It would look remarkably similar to the spiritual world.

He also separated all of the coming creation into two halves; Light would have Day and Darkness would have Night, alternating within all the cycles in equal measures, but Darkness would come first, because it existed first.

Yhwh set about her first female divine role, to create all of our creation. She was their mother, and she would love her children well beyond any love that we can imagine. She knew that it would not be easy to prove herself worthy, and that the old structure of Darkness would not concede its authority easily, until she had done so. But she also knew that she was strong, resilient, resourceful and could overcome any obstacle and outwit any enemy that came against her. She is, after all, God. She passionately believed in the way of Mercy, and she confidently looked forward to her day, the sabbath day and the 'day of Yhwh' or 'the day of the Lord'. She was driven by the knowledge that if she fails, she will have to watch the suffering and destruction of her children, by fire.

But let's make one thing clear at this point. Although mercy and water will dominate in Yhwh, she is still very capable of using fire when she needs to. Like any loving mother, when her children are threatened, she will protect them by using everything in her armoury. That will include great heavenly armies. She will get angry but only against whatever threatens her creation. It would be very wrong to imagine Yhwh and her way of Light and mercy as a big softy who would always forgive the guilty, and never punish or go to war. In fact, she is no pacifist and she will withhold her water and deliver overwhelming fire whenever required – but only after repentance has failed, and always carefully targeting the guilty. In fact, for her to be proven worthy, she will need to show that the guilty are indeed punished so that justice has been properly served. The question is, who are the guilty and who judges them?

We will see that Yhwh is indeed both formidable and very, very wise. Her manifestation is also the most beautiful living thing in the universe and she will be recognised throughout the Bible by her beauty. Her biggest frustration is that she will always have to wait for Light to follow Darkness, and she will need a great deal of patience.

Chapter 3

The Beginning – the Seven Days of Creation

I am going to decode and summarise the seven days and keep it as simple as I can.

Heaven, Earth, and Sea, Souls and Spirits
God created the spiritual world, one age at a time. First came the six ages of Darkness and then the seventh age of Light. She created spiritual places for her living creatures to live, called heaven and earth. Yhwh then gave birth to many spiritual 'souls', who lived in a spiritual 'sea', so every living thing would start as a soul. Half were male souls and half were female. The soul is the spiritual personality of a living creature, where thoughts and decisions are made. Actually, this reflects the spiritual nature of God, because God consists of soul too and it is God's soul who makes all God's plans and decisions and which has the authority.

Perhaps surprisingly, although all the souls who are born to become living creatures come from God's soul, the souls in the sea are not born with any knowledge of the spiritual world around them. Their initial state is as 'unbelievers' in the 'sea', and many souls will live their lives and even a series of lives, without accepting the spiritual world.

That reveals an early, fundamental mystery, that was not a feature of Light. The earth was always meant to be a place of spiritual enlightenment and development, starting when you leave the sea and become a believer in the spiritual world. On Earth, you are prepared for the next stage – heaven. The main preparation is to learn how to become righteous so that you are accepted into heaven, which is harder than it sounds. The original idea was to obey the Laws under the way of Darkness, but as we know, that won't work. There needs to be another way under the way of mercy, but what is it and how will it work? We will have to come back to that!

After souls came spirits, which are also living spiritual creatures who have independent personalities and lives. Spirits are the power which carries out the decisions of the soul, and they communicate with other spirits. Now, in this stage of creation, there were living souls and living spirits, each with their own functions, but at this early stage, they were still independent and not combined into living creatures, spiritual or physical. Likewise, God has a Spirit as well as a soul, and it is the Spirit that has the power to carry out the commands under the authority of the Soul. You need both authority and power to be effective.

So it was Yhwh and her spirit who made the spiritual world, and she populated earth and heaven with living spirits too.

The Divine Angels

Once the components of spiritual life were in position, Yhwh created the living creatures. They would have soul and spirit like God, but unlike God they would have a body, with spiritual flesh to contain the soul and spirit. God wishes to create individual and independent living and thinking creatures, capable of making their own decisions, good or bad, and experiencing the consequences, good or bad, but always learning how to do better next time. You see, God does not want to create robots that simply do what they are told, what is the point of that? So Yhwh created angels, with soul, spirits and a body, initially to inhabit heaven.

The first two angels were the equivalent of the male and female side of God. They were the divine angels, with all the enormous authority and ability to make decisions like God. The first was Michael and

The Beginning – the Seven Days of Creation 71

he was the equivalent of Elohiym. He is called 'the angel of God or Elohiym'. 'Michael' means 'like God'. He had the divine soul of righteous Darkness, that is the way of Law and just punishment. I would point out again that Darkness does not mean evil, because God cannot be evil, rather it is a way to righteousness. The second angel was Gabriel and she was the equivalent of Yhwh. She is called 'the angel of Yhwh' or 'the angel of the Lord'. She had the divine soul of Light, that is the way of love and forgiveness and mercy.

The third angel was the divine Holy Spirit. This has no name. Like God's spirit, it is one spirit but it has a male side and a female side, that is a Dark side and a Light side, which manifest one at a time, either during night or during day. Gabriel communicates constantly through her Holy Spirit, but the importance of the Holy Spirit goes well beyond communication. It is the power for everything that Michael and Gabriel do.

Yhwh looked at her first three creations in heaven, the divine angels, and she was pleased. Gabriel was the most beautiful living creature and Michael was the most handsome. She understood that to all intents and purposes, put together, they were just like God, with the same souls and the same spirit. God has no body so both sides of God work through their respective angels. These angels had the supreme authority and the supreme power over the whole creation, so in practice they could properly be described as the angelic form of God. Most importantly, Yhwh will speak to her creation through Gabriel, so Gabriel will become her voice and her word. This can lead to a few misunderstandings, because when Gabriel speaks, it is Yhwh speaking through her. Therefore, the Bible often describes Gabriel as Yhwh.

It would be Gabriel that would sit on the throne in the seventh age, but only if she was proven to be worthy. Yet because she was part of the creation, she was free to make her own decisions and unlike God, she could make bad decisions, and she could fail. In fact, she will make bad decisions and feel the consequences, as

Yhwh looks on. But that was the whole point of creation. Elohiym and Yhwh already knew that because they were God, they would succeed in anything they did and they had nothing to prove. Rather, they wanted the creation itself to develop and succeed, becoming themselves, through their own will, to be more like God. God would provide the guidance and the direction and the rules, but the creation would make their own decisions – including whether or not to listen to the guidance and whether to obey the rules.

This way, it would really mean something, both to God and the whole creation, if Gabriel was able to prove herself worthy. Everyone would know that the way of Light really works. This was the primary objective of her creation, and Yhwh was determined to assist Gabriel in every way she could – other than making her decisions for her. Gabriel's biggest asset was her spirit. Not only was it the most powerful living thing, it gave Yhwh direct, two way, instant, communication with Gabriel and her creation. Gabriel would hear, understand and speak as if she was Yhwh herself.

In summary, the important thing to remember is that Elohiym and Michael represent righteous Darkness, and Yhwh and Gabriel represent Light. Michael and Darkness will rest on the weekly sabbath days, and Yhwh and Gabriel will take over temporarily. If she is worthy, she will eventually take over permanently in the seventh major age.

The stars and lights

Yhwh proceeded with creation and populated heaven with living creatures, many more angels. They shone with Light and burned with fire and she called them Lights and stars. They would inhabit heaven, but they could see the earth. They all had specific and important functions to perform for God, and they did so with great care. The governing way in heaven was still Darkness, so the angels followed the rules and were very careful to remain righteous to avoid the fire. If they slipped up, they would be mortified and genuinely

The Beginning – the Seven Days of Creation

apologise to God and ask for mercy, which was freely given. The water of mercy was drawn by the heavenly angels of Light, who were female. In other words, the original way of Darkness, a balance of fire and water, worked in heaven. All was well, and the six ages of darkness slowly passed by as the age of Light approached.

The heir

However, preparations had to be made for the seventh, or sabbath, age, the time when hopefully, Light would rule Darkness in a new kingdom with a new king, and when Michael would rest. When that happened Yhwh would be supreme God, but who would be the king and judge of the new kingdom, without Michael? It couldn't be Gabriel or Yhwh because they are creations of mercy and so they do not judge and they don't apply punishment. Instead, Michael needed an heir to take his place – he needed a son and a prince who would be the supreme king when he rested in the seventh age. But the prince and judge would be no ordinary angel of Darkness. He would need to be an angel of Light if he was to rule in the seventh age of Light, but if he was to judge and keep order he would need to be an angel of fire too.

In the future, when he was no longer a prince but had become king, his kingdom would include all the existing kingdoms of Darkness and their kings at that time, which he would judge and rule. So he would not be just a king, he would be king of kings, under only Yhwh, his God. And because he was a king of Light, he would bring Light to the whole world.

But for the prince to become the king of Light and the king of kings, he too would need to prove himself worthy before he could rule.

So Michael needed an angelic son of Light and Darkness combined. He would be born from a father of Darkness and a mother of Light. Yes, Michael and Gabriel would have an angelic son, who would rule when he rested in the age of Light. The plan was that he would enforce and judge the way of righteous Law and punishment during the ages of Darkness, then he would judge the way of mercy in the age of Light. Their son would indeed be very special. He would be an angel, but because he was the son of God, he would be far greater than all the other angels (except for the divine angels). He would be called 'the Sun', both Light and fire, and he would rule both day and night in preparation for when he would be king. Well, at least, that was the plan.

The Messiah

This is perhaps the most important mystery in the Bible.

As the heir and prince, he was 'anointed' to become the king. The anointed one is called in Hebrew the Messiah, and in Greek it is the Christ. Therefore, the Sun would be 'the son of God' and he would be the Messiah or Christ. But he is not the only anointed angel. Yhwh's angel, Gabriel is already anointed to be the supreme God, and her Holy Spirit is anointed to become the ruling divine Holy Spirit.

Thus, there will be three anointed Messiah angels of Light in heaven, waiting to take their divine positions in the seventh age. They are Gabriel, the Sun and the Holy Spirit.

Although I will continue to describe Yhwh and Gabriel as female, by convention in scripture the Supreme God is always described as male. Therefore, Yhwh and her angel, Gabriel, is the mother of all living creatures, but she will be described as the 'Father'. The Sun is the son of the two divine angels who represent God, so he will simply be described as the son of God and he himself will be divine as a result.

Hence the three Messiah angels in heaven are also called the father, the son and the Holy Spirit. Later, they will have a number of other titles. In particular, Gabriel will be responsible for spreading the messages from Yhwh, so she will be called the 'word of Yhwh', or just 'the word' for short.

Together, they represent the three main parts of God, male, female and spirit. When the Messiah/Christ appears on earth rather than heaven, he has one body but three spiritual identities in it, so he will be known as 'three in one'. In the seventh age, all three parts are divine, hence it is correct to say that he is divine, like God. We will see a lot of these three throughout this book.

I appreciate that this is quite a lot to take in, but this mystery has kept scholars and people of all levels in misunderstandings and debate for over 2,000 years, so we should try to understand it. In summary, the most important things to remember are that the Sun will replace Michael (if he is worthy) when Michael and the way of Darkness rest in the sabbath age, so that the Sun can work the way of Light. When he does, then the three angels combined will form the new God of Light – the male side, the female side and the Holy Spirit. Then, the female side Yhwh/Gabriel, will have the **divine authority** over everything. Her divine spirit will have the **divine power** over everything, and her son will be the divine **king of kings** of all creation in the new kingdom of Light.

It is probably already clear that we are describing Jesus, the Messiah or Christ. We can see that he has existed from almost the beginning of creation until now, in heaven. What comes as a surprise is that when he came to earth some 2,000 years ago, it was not his first visit. Actually, it was his fifth visit, but he used other names. The truth is that he has been present in each of the ages. Some readers who are aware of the story of Jesus in the new testament, will be aware that he calls himself the 'son of man' and other important characters who came before him were also called the son of man. The word 'man' is actually a translation of the original Hebrew word 'Adam', so Jesus was saying that he was 'the son of Adam'. He was Adam in the first age and the sons of Adam in all the other ages. His many identities, in heaven and on earth, are fundamental to the underlying story of the Bible, and we will look at all of them.

The plan goes wrong at the beginning

Back in the story, as time went by, Gabriel understood from Yhwh that she was to produce the heir and the Messiah, and she longed for a child. But she remained barren, because she would only produce a child of Light in the seventh age and they were still in the six ages of darkness. She became desperate, because she considered herself too old to bear children, and she convinced herself that she had misunderstood what Yhwh had said to her. Did Yhwh mean that the mother would come from her household, rather than the mother would be herself? After all, although she and Michael were husband and wife, they were also brother and sister. Was that the problem? But when there are only two divine angels, what else can you do? A female angel needed a male angel to conceive a child in her womb.

She approached Michael and explained her thoughts. He should have his heir from a woman in Gabriel's household, a servant under her authority, so the child would also be under her authority as if it was her own. Most importantly, the child would be in her house, the house of Light, and must follow her directions of Light as if he was an angel of Light. Michael accepted what she said.

It was a great mistake, because only Gabriel could produce a child of Light. And the mistake would have consequences for all of creation, forever, including now.

Yhwh looked on in horror. She could say nothing, because it was Gabriel's decision to make, and she had asked Michael when she only had to ask Yhwh. But the outcome of this decision would be that Michael's heir would not contain the soul or spirit of Light, which could only come from Gabriel. His prince would be an angel of Darkness, without Light, so Light would have no heir or inheritance.

But Yhwh's horror was not confined to this terrible event. She knew that creation was a fundamental, original, cycle, and every event during this cycle would form a cycle which would continue through the coming ages of the creation. Therefore, this decision would be made again and again. If Gabriel went ahead, the plan for a perfect creation which would lead to a perfect future under Light, had been severely damaged at least, and had already failed at worst.

But the decision was made, and the servant woman gave birth to an heir for Michael. An heir of Darkness, but a female, a baby angel princess. However, under the rules of inheritance, where the firstborn son receives the inheritance, if Michael and Gabriel were now to have a son, he would inherit the throne, not her. Therefore, the plan for Light could still succeed. Michael accepted her as his own daughter and he loved her as a father loves his daughter, but as agreed, he placed her in the house of Gabriel, under Gabriel. Later, God confirmed that Michael would soon have a son and heir from Gabriel, as they approached a sub-age of Light. Despite her fertility doubts because of her age, Gabriel gave birth to a male prince for Michael, who was in his house and his line. Thus, Michael had two great angel Lights and two heirs, his son and his daughter.

Michael called his son the 'Sun', and made him the ruler of Day and Light. He called his daughter the Moon and he made her the ruler of Night and Darkness. And he made the Sun the greater light, because he held the inheritance, and he would rule both Day and Night. The Moon was therefore under the authority of the Sun, despite being the firstborn.

So they grew up side by side, as brother and sister, as prince and princess, obedient to God, and it seemed that the plan had been restored. But the servant woman, the Moon's mother, despised Gabriel and she thought she was greater than Gabriel, because she had produced the firstborn, and the firstborn should be the true heir. She thought of herself as the true queen, not Gabriel. Gabriel was threatened by her, and Gabriel treated her roughly and then cast her out, along with her daughter. They nearly died, but God and Yhwh stepped in and saved them both. However, the resentment and the sense of injustice did not go away. All of this became part of the same cycle, a fundamental cycle, and it would be repeated in the future.

Not just the animosity between them, much worse was the fact that the house of Yhwh was now a house divided. Her house was now both Light as intended, and Darkness, which was not intended. And the dark side was resentful and rebellious enough to do something about it. They were, after all, creatures of rules and they thought that the rules had been broken and that they were the victims. The Moon hated the Sun and wanted to fight back with fire. Her anger was kindled and the fire did not go out. Later we will see that the house of Yhwh will be called 'Israel' which means 'God prevails', and from this moment onwards, even as early as the creation of angels in heaven, Israel will be a divided and rebellious house, which will be repeated in every age to follow.

The rebellion is planned

The Moon wanted her side of the house of Yhwh, the dark side, to inherit, and she was perfectly willing to rebel against Yhwh, who she hated as much as she hated the Sun. If necessary, she would break the rules to get what she wanted, even if the result was that her version of Darkness would become evil when she deliberately broke the laws. She thought the end would justify the means. She had the beginning of a plan, and it started with her formally changing the old rules of Darkness from her father, Michael, so they became her own rules, but carried the authority of Michael, the supreme God. Then she would have the authority that she needed. She was, after all, the ruler of Night and she wanted to rule in her own way. That way, she thought, nobody would be able to stop her, and Yhwh and the Sun would have to watch helpless as their inheritance was taken from them. She thought how clever her plan was, and how foolish her adversaries were, and she silently smirked to herself.

The Moon had no problem with becoming an enemy of Yhwh to get what she wanted. The Hebrew word for enemy is Satan. And under Satan, the system of Law and Order through Darkness became evil. Although the system of Darkness under Michael remained righteous and it had greater authority than her own. She set out to deal with that problem first. It wasn't going to be a problem for long.

Chapter 4

The Rebellion

The Covenant of Night

The Moon grew up into a most beautiful angelic woman, taking her looks from her most handsome father. Unlike her father, she was cunning, shrewd and she had no problem with lying. She distrusted everyone in authority, because in her eyes, they had stolen her rightful inheritance and tried to kill her and her mother in the process. She became driven by revenge and her ambition to take the inheritance of the kingdom from the Sun. She knew how to do so, but she just needed a little more authority and independence and clarity. For example, what exactly does 'ruling the Night' mean in practice? Did she have autonomy and delegated authority, or did she need to clear every decision with the Sun first?

She would have to get the authority and clarity she needed from her father, the supreme God, Michael. That was the highest authority there was, and with it, she could outrank the Sun at night and there was nothing he could do about it. It was her father who had taken away her inheritance, and despite his strengths she knew how she could get what she wanted from him. His weakness was that he was surrounded by righteous people who spoke only the truth. He trusted everyone around him, especially his beautiful daughter, who he loved.

She waited until Gabriel was not with him, and asked to have a private audience with him. She knew how to manipulate him like he was putty, so she laughed and giggled and flattered him until she had him around her little finger, as always. Then she struck.

'O father, my God and King, I need your help with how to rule the Night. I understand the way of Darkness and I know how much I want to rule it well, like you do now. But I don't have the authority I need if I can be overruled every time by my half-brother. Can we please agree a framework of rules, just for clarity, that will carry your authority? So I don't have to keep coming back to you every time? There is nothing you wouldn't do yourself, of course. This would be a covenant, between you and me.'

He agreed in principle, so she laid out all the rules she needed, without even hinting how she would use them. When she did, it would be too late, because any declaration made by the king was irrevocable and he would be stuck with it regardless of its impact on his own plans. Here are the rules:

1) This covenant carries the full authority of the king, Michael
2) Everyone has the right to freely choose whether to be under the way of Darkness, or the way of Light
3) I have authority over all creatures of Darkness like the Sun has authority over the creatures of Light
4) When I or any of my people are called by their people, it is their right to do so and we must go
5) I must place temptations and trials and stumbling blocks before the people, to test them and judge their righteousness under the Law
6) All people of darkness must receive my spirit of Darkness to guide them in what is good and what is evil, and empower them, just as the people of Light have their Holy Spirit to guide and empower them
7) Transgressors of the Law will be liable to justice and to fire
8) I and my people should witness the transgressions, and I should then accuse them of their breaches of the Law. It is only right that they suffer the consequences of their breaches of the Law, and that I should be their accuser

9) I should judge my people of Darkness just as the Sun judges the people of Light
10) If they are not able to serve their punishments or pay their debts, I will own them as my slave, like any other debtor, until they make their payment

Michael considered all these points, and decided that they were appropriate for the ruler of Law and punishment, the ruler of night. He thought that a covenant based on ten commandments was perfectly suitable. He agreed to make a covenant on these terms, and he called it the Covenant of Night. It could not be revoked. The God Elohiym looked on in horror, but it was Michael's decision to make. Michael had no idea that he had just given the Moon all the authority and power she needed to set up a rival plan for Darkness to inherit heaven and earth, and where people would be free to worship the Moon and her heavenly angels rather than Yhwh and the Sun, using the way of idolatry.

It was a decision he would regret for the rest of his rule. And it set off a cycle where in the future, many good kings would be duped into making covenants they would bitterly regret but could do nothing to stop.

Creation continues to earth

After a while, heaven was populated with angels, and it was time to create living creatures on earth. It was now the sixth age, the final age of Darkness, before the age of Light. The creatures would be both animals and mankind, the animals would be creatures of darkness and mankind would be creatures of Light and mankind would take the inheritance of the earth, to rule over in the seventh age. This was the inheritance that the Moon craved for, or in the biblical language, coveted.

Michael and Gabriel told the Sun and the Moon that they would soon need to give birth to the first of these living, spiritual creatures, who would be an angel destined to go to earth, and who would there multiply and fill the earth. The plan was simple enough, and would follow the normal rules of inheritance. The firstborn son would inherit the earth, and the second born son would serve the first. The firstborn son would be a man, made in the image of God, so would be both Darkness and Light together, but the Light would dominate. Just like his father the Sun. He would be in the house of the Sun and have authority over the whole earth. The second born was to be an animal of darkness, in the house of the Moon, and would serve the man.

Like the Sun and the Moon, they would both be kings, one of Day and the other of Night. The king of the animals and night would be a lion, but the king of Mankind and Day was greater and would rule overall. He would be the king of kings. His name was to be 'Adam' which is Hebrew for 'man'.

Thus, the order in heaven would be repeated on earth. But as the Moon saw it, that meant her offspring had been robbed of their rightful inheritance in earth, just as she had been robbed in heaven. She hated that idea even more than she hated the Sun. So, she schemed and plotted, trying to come up with a plan. How could her descendants, the animals under the lion, inherit and rule the earth?

She knew that the key was who would be the firstborn son. Under the basic principles of spiritual inheritance, he would get the authority and the inheritance. She also knew that the way it worked was that the first child in her womb would be in the line of the Sun, and her own line would only come in her second child.

She thought and thought. She racked her brains. You simply can't beat the fundamental rules that govern inheritance, and that meant she and her descendants were always going to come after the Sun. She was frustrated. There must be a way, she thought. Surely, there was something she could do. After all, she was the craftiest and the greatest schemer and the most devious deceiver. Surely, she could come up with some scheme, or some ruse, to get what she wanted. But what?

The Moon's Plan

Then, suddenly, she got it. The answer was twins. If she had both the first and second son in her womb at the same time, all she had to do was to make sure that the second son was born first. Her line would then be the firstborn and would inherit the earth. But how could she make sure that happened? Well, her son was a lion and the Sun's son was just a man. She could make them fight it out in her womb, and for sure, the lion would overcome the man. She smiled at the thought.

But how could she be sure she would have twins? A female angel has a new spirit enter her womb every month, and they come in the correct order. The first month would be the spirit of the Sun and the second month would be the spirit of the Moon. If the maternal spirit in her womb is not joined to a paternal spirit for any reason, she will not conceive and it is removed from the womb. The maternal spirit is in the blood of the female, which is washed away, similar to a woman's physical monthly period. However, for a short time, during the changeover of spirits at the end of the month, both spirits are present in the womb. If the father's spirit enters the womb at that moment, it will bind with both maternal spirits and she will become pregnant with twins. All she has to do is make sure the Sun comes to her at this time. Her problem is that to lie with a female at this time is strictly forbidden, to specifically prevent this event. And the Sun is very righteous and would never do such a thing. In any event, she will be expected to refuse such an advance.

Therefore, she still didn't have a plan, so she kept on scheming.

The time for her to produce an heir drew near. She knew she would have to lie with the Sun and the thought repulsed her. She knew she was very beautiful and she saw the Sun looking at her with growing desire. It would be more like rape, she thought. And she would have to do it twice! Then it struck her. Suddenly, she knew what to do, and so she finished her plan. She laughed to herself, because it was so simple. Why hadn't she thought of it before?

For her plan to work, she must be innocent and the Sun must take the full blame for all the consequences. How could she be blamed for having twins if he took her by force? She would be the innocent victim and he would carry all the guilt. A total fall from his high position, for which he must be judged and punished – by his father, the Supreme God, no less. There was no way he was ever going to be proven worthy after that. Then, with the Sun out of the way, in heaven, the ruler of day and night would be her. On earth, the inheritance and the kingdom would go to her son, because he would be the firstborn. The lion would be the king of kings. Then, without her Messiah king, Yhwh would be finished, and her Holy Spirit of Light would be finished with her. Her father, Michael, would continue as the supreme God and Darkness would rule. The Moon would have it all.

A brilliant plan, she thought, as she scorned God and praised herself.

The Execution of the Plan

The time came close, and the Moon laid her trap. Everything she did now would become a cycle through the ages. She danced for the prince, provocatively, and he promised under oath that he would give her anything she asked for. She made sure he would see her when she bathed naked and he cancelled all his royal plans and commitments to be with her. His righteous desire and love for her turned to a powerful lust which had to be satisfied, and all the Sons of God after him were plagued with this lust for a beautiful woman, which the Moon could and would easily manipulate. She soon had him mesmerised.

Then, when the time of the month was just right, she struck. The Sun was ill because of his lust, so she came to him in his room to care for him and feed him with cakes that she had made by herself. She was at her most innocent and sweetest. However, she had made the cakes carefully and alone, with the ingredients only she had chosen. They were laced with venom. The cakes were the food of angels, but unclean, full of false spiritual knowledge, and they were made to magnify his lust. She fed him from her hand, the angelic hand that carries the weapons of war. But the cakes were weapons enough, and more deadly than the sword. As she came near to him, he was overcome with lust and he took hold of her and told her to come and lie with him, calling her his sister. She refused him, as she had planned to, and made it clear enough so that he would remember her refusal when he was forced to confess. *'No, my brother, do not violate me, for such a thing is not done in heaven; do not do this outrageous thing. As for me, where would I carry my shame? And as for you, you would be as one of the outrageous fools. Now therefore, please speak to the King, for he will not withhold me from you.'* She knew, after all, that this union was long planned. But he would not listen to her, *'and being stronger than she, he violated her and lay with her.'*

And so it was done. The Moon became pregnant with twins, and they fought each other in her womb. They fought even to the moment of birth, and the second angelic son, in the line of the Moon, was born first and became king, and the heir to the earth. He was hairy and strong and a hunter by nature – he was a lion. The first angelic son in the line of the Sun had lost his inheritance and had to serve his brother. Therefore, Darkness ruled Light on earth, and the Moon had got her way. The Sun might rule in heaven, but she rules on earth.

The manifestation of the Moon in the spiritual world on earth was an animal of Darkness, a beautiful, powerful, creature with royal blood and great authority. She was called the Serpent but we will come to know her as the 'enemy', which translates as 'Satan'. The Greek word is diablos, or the 'devil.' She towered above every creature on earth, which was because she was a dragon and she breathed fire.

But in every age to come until the seventh age, the generations of the man of Light fought the Lions to regain his rightful inheritance, and they would fight each other constantly and bitterly. Who would inherit the earth and the kingdom of God? Who would rule them? They became the battles for the earth, between the line of the Messiah of Light and the line of the Messiah of darkness, or if you prefer, the Christ and the anti-Christ. They fought even until the final battle of Armageddon came, at the end of the sixth age.

And so we can see that a fundamental cycle was generated in creation, and ran on through the ages in the generations of the sons of the Lion and the sons of Adam. The sons of the Lions became the 'kings of the earth', who produced great and powerful and wealthy empires and famous civilisations, all under the serpent. But what about the sons of Adam? Well, since 'Adam' is actually the Hebrew word for 'man', we should really say that the battles continued through 'the sons of man'. The most famous Son of Man in this line will be Jesus, who makes a point of repeatedly calling himself the Son of Man. His line will fight on to overcome the kings of the earth, so that he will not just be a king, but the king of all the kings.

On earth, we will see that there were many cycles of twins in their lines, and the twins' battles for inheritance also began in the womb, fighting to be the firstborn. And there were many battles over birthrights and inheritance of the firstborn over the second born, even a hairy hunter against a smooth gentle man. And many cycles of the lust for a beautiful woman destroying kingdoms and splitting royal families and houses apart so that the battles continued from within, as civil wars. Again and again. The cycle has been started and it will continue for ever. That is, unless one future generation changes it and restores the inheritance of the earth to its rightful owner.

It's not a great start.

Michael's judgement of the Sun

These were the problems to come for the coming people of light on the earth. But now, in heaven, the Moon had not finished her plan. She wanted to bring down the Sun, here and now and permanently. She wanted to rule heaven too. The Moon quickly went to Gabriel and Michael to tell them what had happened, full of righteous indignation, and showing them the marks of force on her wrists and body. It was a full and detailed accusation, the Law of Darkness had been broken, and she demanded the justice she was entitled to. Michael was horrified by what had happened to his daughter and his anger flared. He demanded justice too. Gabriel was silent as she thought. She knew the ambitions and cunning of the Moon, and something was not right here. She insisted that they heard the Sun's side of the story, because the Law stated that there must be two witnesses.

The Sun came into the throne room and confessed to it all. 'I don't know what came over me,' he said. 'I repent, it shall never happen again, please forgive me,' he said to his mother. However, she knew that a cycle had started and that it would certainly happen again. Also, whatever she and Michael did now, would also happen again in cycles through the ages. The future was bleak for Light. But Gabriel was smart too. She had more wisdom than anyone, and she could outmanoeuvre any schemer. She was, after all, the divine angel of Yhwh. She silently prepared her response.

Meanwhile, having heard both accounts, Michael had judged the Sun and condemned him to death, to be destroyed by the fire. A burnt offering on the altar. He commanded that the altar was prepared with kindling and wood. His son bowed down before him and accepted his punishment. He trusted his father to be just, and that the punishment was justified. He climbed onto the altar and allowed himself to be strapped down. His father raised the sacrificial knife and he silently nodded to him. He was ready. He looked at his mother and said he was so sorry for everything that he had done and for everything that would follow as a result. He knew he had destroyed all her plans for Light to rule Darkness and he was devastated. His eyes filled with tears, and he told her how much he loved her. Then he closed his eyes and waited to die.

Gabriel's/Yhwh's heart was breaking and she could take no more. 'STOP,' she screamed. 'There is another way. There is always another way – the way of Light. Now, I beg you, listen to me.' Michael put down the knife and the Sun opened his eyes. She spoke calmly to Michael. 'Is it right for the victim to be punished, or should it be the person who is responsible for the crime?' Michael answered, 'The person responsible, of course. Always.'

She turned to the Sun. 'So when you consider all the people yet to be born, who will suffer because of what you have just done, who should carry the blame? Them or you?' The Sun trembled and said, 'Me.' Gabriel asked, 'Then, do you accept the punishment for all your people to come, for the sins they will commit because of what you did?' He replied. 'Yes. If I live on, I will suffer their punishment and they will suffer nothing.'

She turned to Michael. 'It is true that your sentence of death by sacrifice and burning must be carried out, for what the king decrees cannot be rescinded, but why now? If your son is to die now, how will he pay the punishments he is responsible for in the future? It cannot be just that the innocent will suffer for his crimes. Will you accept that his sacrifice is carried out not now, but at the end of the ages of darkness, when you can add to it the sins of his people?' Michael said he would.

Michael cut his son's straps and let him down, and they prepared to leave. With his sentence deferred, he was reinstated to his position in heaven.

Then Gabriel spoke up and said there was more to hear. 'The Sun has taken responsibility for the sins of his house, but what about my house? It was by my mistake that my house was divided and became rebellious. And it was by my mistake that the Moon is the most rebellious of them all. Who will take the responsibility for the sins of my house that happened because of my mistake, now and in all the cycles of it to come? I will.' Michael looked at her. He knew the enormous cost to her for what she had done, but it was her choice to make. He said, 'Let it be so.'

However, there was a hidden and greater significance to what Gabriel had just done. She had established a fundamental principle of judgement, which would apply throughout all the ages of Darkness. When someone was persuaded by another to break a law and therefore to sin, it was not the sinner who bore the punishment, it was the one who caused them to sin. Gabriel knew who was truly responsible for what had happened to the Sun. The Moon had no idea what that principle would mean for her in the future, but Gabriel knew. And Gabriel was patient.

The consequences

Gabriel sat back and took stock of what had just happened. She understood what the Moon had done and how close she had been to taking over from the Sun in heaven. But Gabriel had thwarted her plan, and the Sun had been reinstated, although at a terrible cost. However, when she looked at the situation on the earth, it was not resolved. The inheritance of Light had been lost to Darkness through the rule of the firstborn, so even if the Sun was proven worthy, Light would not inherit the earth.

She explained the problem to Michael and he considered for a moment. Then he gave his judgement, 'It is true that the rule is that the firstborn son should be the heir. But what if the firstborn turns out to be unsuitable for the position? Having carefully assessed the situation, I determine that the owner of what is to be inherited must be able to change who he wishes to inherit it. He must be able to bless whoever he wishes to be his heir, and curse whoever he wishes not to be his heir. He can declare his decisions in his blessing, given before the end of his life. This is the higher law of inheritance.' Gabriel was pleased. Michael had witnessed the schemes of the Moon and his ruling was just. She asked him, 'Who will you bless to inherit the earth?' and Michael replied, 'I bless the people of Light. Man, the son of the Sun, who will fill the earth with the way of Light. The animals will serve him and fear him.'

And so the promise of the inheritance of the earth was restored to Light by God's blessing. This method to change an inheritance was to be used in future cycles, again and again. But to rule, man still had to prove himself worthy before the seventh age, and to complete his deferred punishment; otherwise, Darkness would rule. The fight was far from over.

Therefore, the Moon's plan had collapsed, but the battles for the inheritance of earth would have to continue. Until Armageddon. Gabriel realised that she and the Sun had made a powerful enemy for life.

The Moon thought that she may well have lost that battle, but this was a war, and there was lots of time to make sure that man was not going to be accepted as worthy. The next battleground would be on earth, and the Moon prepared to go down there. She wanted to protect her creatures of darkness, the animals, especially her son, the lion and the king. But most of all, she wanted to make sure that Adam fell from his position of authority and favour. To fall from Light to Darkness.

The stage was set for Adam to meet the Serpent on earth.

Chapter 5

Adam and Eve in the Garden of Eden

Adam, the Messiah

Thus Adam was born in heaven, in the sixth day of creation, and he was not the firstborn, he was born after the animals. This completed the days of the creation of the living creatures of heaven and earth, and was just before the sabbath day when Michael would rest. Adam was made in the image of God, so he was entirely spiritual, an angel, and he had three angelic parts like God. Male, female and spirit. He was blessed by God so he would inherit the earth, despite coming after the animals, and he was in the line of the Sun, who was the heavenly Messiah of Light.

Adam was the next generation of the Sun and he became the **earthly** Messiah of Light, anointed to be king and waiting for the seventh day of creation, so he could be born on earth.

Therefore, Adam is not really the first creation of physical man, as he appears to be in the Bible story of creation. He is better described as the first spiritual generation of the Messiah on earth. He is indeed the first Adam, but we will see that he is only the first cycle of Adam, and there will be more cycles or generations to come. Each cycle will be a different son of Adam, that is a son of Man. Therefore, each cycle will be a cycle of the Messiah on earth.

However, the main point is that the seven days of creation are ending, and we are about to move on to the seven days cycle on earth.

I know this may be a difficult concept for many to grasp, especially if you have believed that there is only one Messiah, Jesus. Suffice to say for now that the Bible is clear that there are many generations of the Messiah, or Sons of Man. They are all vital to the story and we will meet them all, but the important point to make is that they represent all of the seven ages of the Bible story, one generation of the Messiah for each age. This Adam will therefore be the first Messiah of the first age. He started as three angels in heaven, made in the image of God, and now his three spiritual forms will enter a physical body on earth, and stay in it until it dies, when his spiritual identities will be released. If that sounds a bit weird, we all need to accept it anyway, because that is the template for each of us. When our bodies die, our spirits and soul live on. However, at this stage, we don't know where they go to!

But we are getting ahead of the story. As Adam enters the earth he is still in the seventh day of creation, the day of Light. If he is worthy, this age will never end, and he will never die. It will be permanent Day and there will be no need for a new cycle of a new seven ages. However, if he falls, the seventh age will close, and the next seven ages will begin. Gabriel has done everything possible to prepare him, in particular ensuring that he is blessed by Michael to inherit the earth. All he needs to do is to prove himself worthy to rule.

Yhwh has a clever plan to make sure of that, and that he will never fall. She wants him to be holy and to live forever. All he needs is to be filled with her Holy Spirit.

That ambition has not changed today.

Back in the story, when the seventh day of creation came, Yhwh took him and placed him in a garden on earth, in the spiritual world, which she had prepared for him. The garden was like a nursery, a safe place where Adam could learn and grow. She gave him an earthly body, made from the dust around him and her water of mercy combined to make a living clay, like a living skin. This body, or vessel, was to contain his soul and spirits, that is his three Messianic angels. This was the major difference between his angelic life in heaven and on earth. In heaven he was three separate angels, but on earth he had the three angels inside a body, although from the outside you could only see the body. However, this body looked just like the angels in it, if you could have seen them, rather like a clay mould of his angelic shape and form. His physical life on earth was limited, and when he physically died his vessel or body would become dust again, but his three angels would live on, be freed from the vessel, and become independent again, back in heaven. An important feature of the Messiah on earth, all the sons of Man, is that they had no memory of their spiritual life in heaven or in fact, any spiritual knowledge at all. They all had to learn it from the beginning, even Jesus.

When Gabriel first put Adam in the Garden, he had the male and female side of the Messiah, the Father and the Son (or if you prefer, the word of Yhwh and the Sun) but he had yet to receive his Holy Spirit to make him complete and to help him learn about the spiritual world. This will be true for all the sons of man to come, including Jesus.

The Tree of Life

The garden was in the spiritual world, and the trees in it were living spirits of various sorts, which looked like trees but were really spirits. The fruit trees were special because they were Holy Spirits, with various vital powers. When you ate the fruit of the tree, you took in the spirit and gained its powers. In the centre of the garden was the Tree of Life, a spirit of Light which was only available in the seventh age. This was the Holy Spirit of Yhwh, and it had all the powers of the way of Light, including that whoever ate it would be made Holy. To be Holy is an amazing gift, because it means that there is no sin or uncleanliness in you and on you, and no future uncleanliness can stain you, because anything unclean is instantly destroyed when it touches you. Therefore, you are able to go to heaven and stand before God and be seen to be perfectly righteous. That means that you are given salvation to heaven when your physical body dies. This was the plan, for not just Adam, but all of his offspring to come. It is a feature of being a creature of Light and it is the most vital gift of mercy that you can receive.

Meanwhile, while you are still alive on earth, the powers that the Holy Spirit give you would be used to enhance your life in many ways. One of the most important powers (or gifts) is to be able to communicate directly with Yhwh, so that she can guide you and help you during your life, including how to live a life of mercy and forgiveness. Therefore, the Tree of Life gives you a life on earth which is free of sin and without any judgement or fire, then it gives you eternal life in heaven. That is why it is called the Tree of Life. It is a stunning gift and it costs nothing. The tree is the vine, and from it you can make spiritual 'wine'. From now on, the Holy Spirit will be referred to as the 'wine' which gives you 'great joy'. It is the wine of the Christian ritual of communion – of taking bread and wine.

However, there is a problem with receiving the Holy Spirit. It destroys everything it touches that is unclean. So if a living creature, like a man who had not yet received the Holy Spirit, had broken any rules (called sinning), they would carry the consequences of that sin and become unclean. When they encountered the Holy Spirit, if the uncleanliness had become a significant part of them, the Holy Spirit would probably kill them. Yhwh had a simple plan for Adam to avoid that fate. Before he could sin, he was innocent, because he was spiritually ignorant. He did not know any Law, and so he had no idea about what was good or what was evil. Thus, he could not be judged against any law, and technically, he could not sin. Whilst he was in this state of innocence, he could eat the fruit of the Tree of Life without any harmful effect.

Therefore, Yhwh's plan for mankind was beautifully simple. All he had to do was to reach out and eat the grapes. Then he would be filled with the Holy Spirit, become Holy himself, and everything he touched would become Holy. He would do great things with his powers, and then go to eternal life in heaven. So would all his future followers. What could possibly go wrong?

The Tree of the Knowledge of Good and Evil

The Serpent had got there first, and had planted a tree of her own spirit, the spirit of Darkness, not Light. This was meant for the creatures of Darkness, and it contained the knowledge and powers required for the way of law and judgement and punishment. When you eat the fruit of this tree, you are filled with the spirit of the Serpent and you immediately know about good and evil and its laws, so you lose any innocence you had. Thereafter, you became a creature of Darkness and receive the appropriate powers of Darkness and fire, including the knowledge, understanding and wisdom of Darkness. Perhaps the worst thing about the spirit of the Serpent is that you communicate directly with the Serpent and not Yhwh. This spirit would never leave you, and it is passed on to your children and to others in a number of other ways, spreading fast, like a pestilence. It is the fig tree.

If Adam ate the fruit of this tree, he would become a creature of Darkness and be under the law and its punishments until he physically died. Then his life would be judged according to the law and his three angelic personalities would be punished accordingly. In reality, the Serpent would try to ensure that he would sin so much that he would be condemned to death. It didn't help him that when he was a creature of darkness, the Serpent would be his judge. He would not survive the punishment, and his soul and his spirits would die. Therefore, this spirit did not lead to eternal life like the Tree of Life, it led to death. Also, his spiritual form would switch from a man of Light to an animal of Darkness. His animal would not be a lion, it would be a sheep, as all his children would be. In the physical world he would look the same, but if you could see his spiritual side, he would look like a lamb. Perhaps the worst thing of all was that Adam's offspring would be herds of sheep, and because they are under the rule of Darkness, they would follow the Serpent, not the Messiah, or the Moon not the Sun. She would become their shepherd and ensure that they died. She would not save them from the lions, she would feed them to the lions.

All of this hung on only one choice. Would Adam eat the fig or the grape?

Gabriel looked on, and was horrified to see the fig tree in the garden. But under the Covenant of Night the Serpent was entitled to offer it, and to spread her spirit of Darkness to whoever chose it. Worse, she was entitled to tempt people into choosing this fruit, as a test.

Gabriel took this threat very seriously, but what could she do? Well, she could do two things. First, she could command Adam not to eat the fig, and explain that it would result in his death if he did. So she did that. Second, in case he ignored her, she could, and did, do something really drastic.

Woman

Adam, like God, was male and female together, so if he ate the fig, all of him would fall to darkness. Gabriel, following the guidance of Yhwh, decided to separate male and female, so it was harder for both of them to fall. She was less concerned about the male side of Adam, because he was very righteous and would be unlikely to break a command from Gabriel. On the other hand, the female side was a member of Gabriel's own rebellious house, and was more likely to be tempted and fall. If she did fall, at least she would not automatically bring Adam down too.

So she put Adam to sleep and removed his female side. She did so by removing his rib. The spiritual bones of an angel contain everything needed to make a new angel. It's like spiritual DNA. This particular rib contained the spirit of Yhwh, which is the female side of both God and Adam. She used that rib and covered it with flesh from Adam, to make a female angel, a woman, in a body or vessel like Adam had. She was incredibly beautiful, like Gabriel, and Adam called her 'Woman'. Like Gabriel, through her spirit of Yhwh, she communicated directly with Yhwh. She could hear Yhwh and speak what she heard, and so she was 'the word of Yhwh' to Adam.

This was a really important change for Adam. Before woman was separated from him, he heard the voice of Yhwh himself, through his female side. Now, he needed woman to tell him what she heard, and so he needed to trust her to tell him exactly what she heard from Yhwh. However, this was only meant to be a temporary situation, because as soon as Adam received the Holy Spirit of Yhwh from the Tree of Life, he would be able to hear Yhwh for himself again, through this Holy Spirit. Therefore, Gabriel had managed to work around the fall of woman, if she chose to rebel.

Gabriel put her with Adam in the garden and commanded her not to eat the fig, like she had commanded Adam. The new arrangement worked well and woman carefully and faithfully passed on the guidance of Yhwh to Adam. He learned to trust her.

The Temptation and the Fall

After a while, the Serpent approached the woman to tempt her into turning to the way of darkness. It was night time, and Gabriel was resting. The Serpent didn't tempt Adam, because she saw Woman as an easier target. The temptations the Serpent uses here, follow the pattern she will most commonly use in the future too. She starts by sowing doubt about what God actually said. '*Did God actually say you shall not eat of any tree of the garden?*' She knows this is not what God said, but now she has planted a seed that you can doubt and question the word of God.

Woman replies that God has told her not to eat from the tree in the midst of the garden or even touch it, lest she dies. The Serpent contradicts God and says she will not die, which is a lie. Then she implies that God is hiding something good from her, meaning that it is God who is deceiving her, while the Serpent is telling her the truth. She says that Woman will know good and evil and she will be like God, meaning like the male side of God. This is true as far as it goes, and Woman likes the idea of receiving the wisdom of God, but the Serpent is careful not to give her the whole picture. She doesn't say anything about the consequences of the way of Darkness being fire, or Yhwh's planned role for woman to be like the female side of God, with all the understanding and wisdom of the way of Light. Worst of all, she doesn't mention the benefits of the Tree of Life, especially salvation to heaven. All this is an example of how the Serpent will tempt mankind from now on. Establish trust through half-truths and lies, then promises of power and wealth and rising above God, without the consequences of loss of salvation. It is a very effective temptation, but only for those who do not know the truth.

And that is the first example of how this book can help us defeat the Serpent. You will see many examples of temptation, then when you are tempted you will recognise the Serpent at work, and you will also know the truth, which will defeat the lie.

The temptation worked on Woman, and she ate the fig. It was a disaster. The spirit of the Serpent was in her and it would be in her for ever. She would pass it to all her offspring, which means all of mankind, and it would be in them for ever. From now on she and her offspring would not hear Yhwh or Gabriel, but they would hear the Serpent and they would do her will. The Serpent would tempt them to do evil things, and they would do so, building up a burden of punishments as a debt to the Serpent, because she ruled Darkness and was therefore their judge. When they could not pay the debt, they would become slaves to the Serpent and slaves to their sins. For their whole lives. And there was no going back. Once eaten, or passed on by several other methods, the fig was with you for life and it did not let go. It is only when the body dies that the spirits separate, and by then it is too late.

Apart from one important thing. This is a spiritual principle which is difficult to understand, but well worth the effort.

The spirit of the Serpent is a living creature and it a servant spirit which serves its master. It has two sides to it, which represent both

Light and Darkness. Therefore, one side serves the Serpent, the Moon, but the other side serves the Messiah of Light, the Sun. It can 'turn' from one to the other. The key to who it serves is the one with the highest authority. And as we know, the Sun outranks the Moon. So if Woman places herself under Adam's authority, because he is the Sun on earth, the spirit of the Serpent will come under Adam's authority too, and it will not manifest in her. Instead, it will turn and become like the spirit of Adam, under the Sun. So long as Adam remains a man of Light, woman will follow him and be a woman of Light too. It happens instantly. But unfortunately, as soon as she rebels from Adam's authority, the spirit turns back to the Serpent, equally fast.

Therefore, in practice, so long as Woman follows Adam, she is not affected by the spirit of the Serpent, even though it is still in her. And since Adam is the Messiah on earth, this means so long as Woman turns back to follow the Messiah, she is not affected. This is not an academic side effect, this is the only way that woman can avoid being under the Serpent, at this time. It works, and it will remain the only solution during all the ages of Darkness.

There is one last spiritual principle to explain here. The spirit of the Sun is not the Holy Spirit, the fruit of the Tree of Life. The spirit of the Sun and the spirit of the Serpent are the same living creature, but they are angelic spirits, not divine spirits. The Holy Spirit is the **divine** spirit of Yhwh and this is much more powerful than the angelic spirit. This is going to be enormously important, because when the divine Holy Spirit comes, much later, it can and does overpower the spirit of the Serpent. More about that later.

Back in the garden, Woman had now fallen and was under the Serpent. She could no longer hear Yhwh, but she heard the Serpent. She heard her say that they both needed Adam on their side, so she should give him the fig and tell him to eat it. He trusted her, and he would believe that she was speaking what Yhwh had told her to say. He would not refuse a command he thought came from Yhwh.

Then Woman gave some fig to Adam, told him to eat it, and without hesitation, he ate it too. Double disaster! In a bite, all of Yhwh's plans were destroyed. Both Adam and Woman had fallen and were under the Serpent. Light had become Darkness, and it would stay this way for ever. Gabriel had lost, even before she had really started. She cried out to Adam but he hid from her in shame as he now knew good and evil so he understood his sin, and that he was no longer innocent. He and Woman tried to cover themselves with fig leaves, to hide their sin and their shame, but fig leaves are from Darkness and there is no mercy in them. They hide nothing. Only coverings from Yhwh hide sin as an act of mercy, for example Linen, which is itself a spirit covering. The best that Gabriel could do for them was to cover them with the skins of innocent animals, which also worked to hide sin.

Adam called Woman 'Eve', meaning the mother of all living, a reminder that she held the spirit of Yhwh in her, but it was now supressed by the spirit of the Serpent. Gabriel drove Adam and Eve out of the garden so they would not be able to eat the fruit of the Tree of Life. If they did then they would turn that divine spirit to follow Darkness too. If Darkness gained authority over the divine power of the Tree of Life, then it would be able to overpower everything, and all would be lost for ever.

She guarded it with a mighty warrior angel so that nobody could eat from it. This meant that the Holy Spirit of Light and water would be lost from all mankind until the next seventh age, which was thousands of years away. Until then, there would only be the spirit of Darkness and fire, with very few exceptions.

And without the Holy Spirit or the spirit of Yhwh, Adam could not hear Yhwh by himself. Woman could hear either Yhwh or the Serpent depending on whose authority she was under, and which spirit was manifesting, and she could speak whatever she heard. The trouble was, that Adam could not tell the difference. This was going to prove a serious problem for mankind, but especially for women, for thousands of years. Man would learn to mistrust what women said, and women would not want to be under his authority. However, the principle of Woman being 'ruled' by Adam has a deeper and much misunderstood meaning, which we will come back to.

Both Adam and Woman had been given positions of high authority, and when they lost it, they fell down. That is why this event is called the fall of mankind. Light had been defeated by Darkness and had lost its inheritance. Then Adam and Eve and the Serpent were judged, and the results demonstrate the judgements to come. I will explain them in depth in Book Two, but in the meantime, Adam and Eve were judged with mercy and guidance to help in the future. The Serpent was punished and lost her position of authority. She fell further than Adam and Eve, so that she crawled on the earth which they stood on. She became a snake. Yhwh foretold her eventual defeat at the hand of the Messiah, but it made no difference to her. She was determined to continue on her own way.

Gabriel wept and wept. The Serpent laughed; victory tasted sweet. She looked forward to ruling mankind as her slaves, forever. Her objective was to ensure that they rejected God and sinned constantly, so not a single person would enter heaven. When Yhwh and her Messiah, the Sun, had utterly failed, she would rule heaven too.

Chapter 6

The First Age – the Age of Adam

It was true that Gabriel had lost and as soon as Adam and Eve fell, the age of Light, the seventh age of creation was over. But everything in the spirit world is a cycle, and in another seven ages there would be another age of Light and she would get another chance to create a new kingdom and re-introduce her Holy Spirit to give salvation to the people of Light. The next six ages were going to be extremely difficult, because they were ages of Darkness. Worse, under the Serpent, most of the way of Darkness had turned from a righteous way of justice and order, to a corrupt way of evil and chaos. But Gabriel had no intention of giving up. She loved her creation too much, and she had plans.

They were all about cycles and patience.

Firstly, each age was a new cycle, which would be headed by a new Messiah. Initially there was Adam, then there would be six sons of Adam, or sons of man, making seven in all. Each son of Man will make a new start, and he will have the opportunity to get it right this time, or at least to make it better.

Secondly, each of the six ages of Darkness is itself subdivided into seven sub-ages. Therefore, at the end of each main age is a seventh sub-age of Light, like a Sabbath, which we can see as a time of peace and security. Just as important is the end of the age of darkness, just before the Light. This is when the age up to that point can be judged. This is very important, because at this time, the spirits of the Serpent that have become evil can be purged from the earth. This is called 'judgement day'. Many of us have heard of the judgement day at the end of the sixth age (and Armageddon which follows it), but there are actually judgement days at the end of every age. It is this purge of the Serpent that allows the next son of man to have a clean start in his own age. You will notice that I always say that the purge is not the end of the world, but it is the end of the age, and this is why I say it.

There will be one of these purges at the end of the first age, the age of Adam, and it is going to be known as Noah's flood. Noah is the next son of Man. This second age of Noah is going to be Yhwh's and Gabriel's next chance, and she already had a plan for it. But first there is the terrible age of Adam.

The age of Adam

The age of Adam consists of 10 earthly generations of men, in the line of Adam. Actually, there are 12 generations in an age, because two generations are within women, which came from Adam's rib. They must remain hidden amongst women, for their own protection. The tenth male generation is Noah.

1 Adam
2 Seth
3 Enosh
4 Kenan
5 Mahalalel
6 Jared
7 Enoch
8 Methuselah
9 Lamech
10 Noah

As you would expect, because the Serpent dominates all of mankind through her spirit, the fig, this first age of Adam's 10 generations is a disaster. It is true that Adam and Eve multiply greatly and produce a large population, who build numerous cities and great farms, but without the Holy Spirit, they can only try to be righteous through choosing to do good things, as they now understand what is good and evil under the Law of Darkness. But without the mercy of Light, it is impossible, in practice, to stay righteous, especially if the Serpent is constantly tempting you with various pleasures and riches to make you sin. By the end of the age, all the people have succumbed to the temptations of the Serpent, have lost any righteousness they had, and have become truly wicked. There was only one exception, who we will come back to.

Nevertheless, the conflict between the Serpent and Yhwh is constant, and is illustrated by the first story of the age, the story of Cain and Abel. Yhwh appears to favour Abel, who is a shepherd of sheep, like a Messiah of Light. Cain is jealous and murders him, like a Messiah of Darkness. Yhwh does not sentence Cain to death as she could, she shows mercy and only banishes him. If you look again at the 10 generations of Adam, you see that Cain has been removed. Also Abel, the next in line, is removed because he did not have any sons. That leaves Adam's third son, Seth, to carry on his bloodline.

Cain forms his own bloodline, and he founds a city from his place of exile, which is successful. We will see that the Serpent is very good at building cities and great empires for her people, under her kings, and Cain is her first king. They will later be called 'kings of the earth', and the great empires will include Egypt and Greece and Rome and Babylon. The tremendous power and instant wealth that comes with these great empires throughout the ages, is used effectively by the Serpent to tempt people into following her, rather than Yhwh and the Messiah of Light. A common feature is that the people will worship their kings as a god, and will also worship a group of false gods, which turn out to be a mirror of, and replacement for, the heavenly hierarchy under Yhwh and Elohiym. These will become the alternative kingdom of the Serpent in the battle for who will win the inheritance of heaven and earth.

Cain competes effectively with his original family of Adam. From then on, jealousy, rival cities and empires, between the people of the two kingdoms, Messiah and Serpent, will become a theme.

Enoch

One man from the earlier generations stood out though. He was called Enoch and he walked with Elohiym, the male side of God. That means that he was a man of Darkness, but he was righteous and he walked on the way of righteous Darkness, like God. He was not subverted by the Serpent, and he was not killed by the Serpent. That made him strong and unique. He was a righteous man of Darkness who was on the side of God and not the Serpent. Michael and Gabriel could use a man like that. It turned out that Enoch had both the Messianic spirit of the Sun in him, but also the spirit of the Serpent. They competed for dominance within his body, but only one could manifest at a time. The Sun usually won, making Enoch a Messiah, a son of Man of Light, although he appeared to be a man of Darkness.

So Michael made a deal with Enoch. On earth, he would make him a great king of the earth, appearing to be like the other kings who were under the Serpent. With Michael's help, he would build a great empire and have great power and wealth. Just like the Serpent would offer his kings, but his empire would be even bigger and more powerful, and would be able to change the world. However, in reality he would secretly work for Michael, and his armies would do the will of Gabriel, to further the way of Light. In other words, he would be their mole and secret weapon in the kingdom of Darkness. In return, Michael offered him a place in heaven without judgement or dying, and all his sins would be forgiven through mercy. This was the salvation given to the seven sons of Man at the end of their age, so they would live on in heaven, but now it was extended to Enoch too.

There was just one warning. Since he had both the spirits of Light and Darkness in him, he would be under regular internal conflict.

The Serpent would certainly try to win authority through him. Whatever position of royal authority he obtained, if the Serpent won the conflict and manifested in him, the Serpent would gain that level of authority in practice. The problem was that he was in a special position of favour with Michael and Gabriel, so there was a danger that he could attain very high authority alongside them in heaven, like the Sun has or even higher, then the Serpent would gain that authority and use it. It is dangerous, because if he exceeded Michael's and Gabriel's divine authority, all the angel armies in heaven would obey him in an instant, and he could not be overthrown. So he was given a command (as part of the deal) that he should never attempt to reach or exceed their authority. If he did, he would be thrown down to a place of very low authority, such as crawling with the lowest forms of animals and eating grass.

Enoch accepted the deal, but his services were not required yet. They would be called upon soon enough, and again in the next age and the future ages. Accordingly, he was taken to heaven while he was still young, and he did not die. There he waited to be called. He was going to be famous, under various names, and absolutely vital to the cause of Light, but like the mole that he was, he stayed in darkness and was kept very deeply hidden. Until the end of each age, when his services and his army would be very much required. Most people have heard about the four horsemen of the apocalypse, who appear at the end of the first four ages to purge the Serpent in terrible wars. You have just been introduced to them – they are all, spiritually, Enoch! You will probably be shocked when you learn their names in the physical world. Even today, at the end of our own age.

Noah's flood

The tenth generation on earth came, and Noah was born. From the beginning he was different; he was righteous, and he pleased Yhwh. That was because he was the second Adam, the second Messiah, and he was there at the end of the first age, to bring in the second age. The closure of the first age was to be the first purge at the end of an age. It was to be the first purge of the spirits of the Serpent (the figs). But Noah's role was not to make the purge, it was to save a remnant from the purge, to start again in the second age. Because with every purge comes a 'passover' so that the people of Light can be saved to populate the next age, which is always a Sabbath day of Light after the Darkness. Or you could just say that after every purge comes salvation. Noah's flood is the first, but there are going to be many purges, and they are all repeating cycles, so they are largely predictable. For example, they are always followed by a Passover and Salvation. That includes the most famous Passover, when Egypt and its army, who were under the rule of the Serpent, were purged, but the chosen people were passed over, saved from slavery and the next generation went on to populate the promised land.

Meanwhile, at the end of the first age, Gabriel and Michael looked at mankind and judged that they were wicked because their hearts only thought evil thoughts, and did so continuously. That was because their spiritual hearts were dominated by the spirit of the Serpent, who was responsible for all their evil thoughts and therefore all their evil deeds. All the hearts of mankind up to Noah had been corrupted by the fig that Adam and Eve had eaten. Both Gabriel and Michael, guided by Yhwh and Elohiym, decided they had to start again, with a clean and uncorrupted earth, for a new Adam and Woman to come into, and get it right this time. They needed to remove every spirit of the Serpent from the earth. But how?

They knew that the spirit of the Serpent was bound tightly to the spirits of both man and woman and it could not be removed without killing the host. Also, the spirit was not just in mankind, it was in all the living creatures in the earth, including the animals. It would easily pass from animal to mankind to 'reinfect' them if only mankind was purged. So Michael came to the conclusion that all but a small remnant of all the living creatures would need to die, if they were to cleanse the earth for Noah to repopulate.

Yhwh's plan to save the dead

Gabriel was horrified, because in effect the whole of her creation was to be killed so they could start again, but she accepted that what Michael had said was inevitable. She knew that she could not save their physical lives, but she did have a plan to save their spiritual lives. Actually, she had been using this plan from the very first death, Abel. It was simple enough in theory, a plan of deferred judgement, and it worked like this:

When the hosts died, their physical bodies would turn to dust and their spirits and soul would be released, and separated at last from the spirit of the Serpent. They would not be destroyed, they would be taken to a place in the spiritual world, like an underground prison, to rest, where they would sleep. The place is called Sheol. Most importantly, they would not be judged at this time, because in the ages Darkness, if they were judged fairly for their wickedness, they would be punished severely, usually by being sentenced to spiritual death. Gabriel's plan was that their judgement would come as it must, but only after their sins had been taken on by the Messiah, that is both the Sun and Gabriel. The process of taking on another's burden of sin is called 'redemption'. This would happen at the final purge of the final age of Darkness, which was called 'judgement day'. Therefore, at judgement day, the angels of the people of Light would be woken up and would be sin free, free from their debt to the Serpent, deemed to be righteous and then resurrected to enter heaven. This process of redemption and resurrection is an alternative method of salvation, in the absence of the Holy Spirit. Since the Holy Spirit was rejected by Adam and Eve, it is not available at this time, so redemption and resurrection is all that is available. But first, the dead will sleep until judgement day.

All the evil spirits of the Serpent who had caused so many problems, had been separated at physical death, and would be judged and destroyed at judgement day. This is part of the purge of the spirits of the Serpent at the end of the sixth main age. However, the spirits of the people would be redeemed and made sin free, and therefore would not need to be judged. They would be resurrected to heaven. That means that judgement day was going to be a very bad day for the Serpent, but a very good day for the people of Yhwh, and we should try to remember that when we are considering end times and Armageddon. You can also see that this great purge follows the principles of the cycles of the earlier purges. First comes the purge of the Serpent, during which the people of Light are passed over by redemption, and then comes the salvation, this time to heaven.

This was Yhwh's plan for her creation, and it was both simple and brilliant. However, we should always remember that the salvation of becoming holy through the Holy Spirit (the Tree of Life) is the original and preferred plan, because it removes the spirit of the Serpent without the death of the host. But the Holy Spirit will not be available in the Bible story, for a very long time. Happily, for us, it is available right now.

The key to Gabriel's plan was her Messiah, who would first redeem and then save. The judgement would also be carried out by the Messiah, once he had been proven worthy and had become the king and judge, at judgement day. He would therefore be called their redeemer and their saviour and their judge, and he would judge the living and the dead. The plan sounded simple enough, but Gabriel and the Sun understood that the cost of redemption to them would be enormous. We find out later in the story, when Ezekiel (who is one of the future sons of man) is told that as Gabriel, he will bear the punishment of Israel in the fires of hell for 390 years, and as the Sun he will bear the punishment of Judah in the fires of hell for 40 years. We sometimes hear that the Messiah was crucified and died for our sins, which is true, but the deeper truth is that he suffered in great pain in hell, for a total of 430 years, so that we would not have to. And he did it willingly, because he loved us.

The 'Flood'

Back in the story, Yhwh and Gabriel were ready to receive the spirits of the dead people from the flood into Sheol, so the purge was prepared. Noah gathered a remnant of the animals, who were to multiply into the new, clean earth. He and his wife, and their three sons and their wives, were the remnant of mankind who would fill the new earth. Noah built a large temple using a design given by Gabriel, which resembled the basic structure of God's temple in heaven. It was filled with the remnant and covered all over, so that its contents were impossible to see spiritually. This structure itself was completely different to anything else on the earth and could not be mistaken.

Then the purge took place. A certain king of the earth, a man of Darkness, had built a great empire based on law and order and a civilised way of life, and he had gathered a powerful army. The people under the king did not believe in God, and were separated from the people of Adam on the earth, so they were from the spiritual 'sea'. The king opposed the people of Adam. He chose this moment to attack them, and to wipe them off the face of the earth. His army quickly overwhelmed the people and killed them all. Including their livestock and anything that lived. Specifically, anything that breathed the breath of life – which made them an earth dweller. None of the sea king's army breathed this breath of life, because they were all non-believers of the sea. They advanced until their army of the 'sea' covered the earth.

However, under strict orders from the king, they 'passed over' the temple structure of the arc, without even touching it. In the physical world this would simply mean that they left the temple alone, perhaps because they thought it was the temple of a great god to be worshipped through idolatry. But in the spiritual world there is a deeper mystery to reveal. Noah, the next Messiah, was in the temple, and he was floating above the 'sea'. Therefore, in the spiritual world, he had authority over the army of the people of the 'sea'. So did all his followers in the temple. So, you can see that Noah actually has the same authority that Jesus did when he walked on water in the spiritual world, and then joined his disciples in the boat. Here they are a temple, but in the time of Jesus they are a church. What we are seeing is an example of Light having authority over Darkness as the new age of Light begins.

But that is only half the story. In heaven, Yhwh and Michael had also gathered a great army of angels, who were both invisible to the physical people, and invincible. They came down and attacked the spiritual and angelic sides of the people, killing more than the king's army. Anything unclean was put to the sword. But because the temple was covered, they could see nothing unclean in it, and they recognised it as a temple of their true God, so they passed over it too. From now on, this became a cycle, when Yhwh sent heavenly reinforcements to an earthly battle, to ensure victory. Not just at the end of the ages, but whenever her people were fighting the Serpent, according to her will. Conversely, when the battle was against her will, there would be no heavenly reinforcements and the battle would be lost.

When the battle was won, and only Noah's followers in the temple remained alive, both earthly and heavenly armies withdrew. The land had been purged, and it was clean, and ready for Noah. He unsealed the temple and looked out on the new earth. He looked at his family and wondered if they really could build a new kingdom of Light from scratch. He caught the eye of his wife and a wave of pure love swept over him. She was so beautiful and so wise and she knew the answer to any question. Even when she had told Noah how and when to build the temple and what to fill it with. He felt like a king, but he always listened to his wife. And he was all the wiser for it. Because she was not descended from fallen Eve, she was Woman, and she had the Spirit of Yhwh from the rib of Adam. Like Noah, she had not fallen. Together they were determined to build a great kingdom of Light.

Who was the mysterious king of the great, civilised, empire and powerful army? He was a man of Darkness, doing the will of Yhwh, at the end of the age. He was Enoch, come down from heaven as a man and the king of a powerful empire, specifically for this purpose. His armies flowed and overwhelmed the people of the earth, like a great flood. Then they left and he went back to heaven. Ready for the end of the next age.

And as we approach the end of our own age, he has returned, and he is already in place. You know him. But in our age, the Holy Spirit has been released and is ready. Therefore, the purge and salvation will be quite different to the first Adam's age. Just remember that no one has to die, and no one should rebel against his authority.

The Rainbow

Yet for Yhwh and Gabriel in heaven, the purge of Noah's flood had been too much to bear, as they watched their creation, their children, being destroyed on earth. They felt their people's distress and their pain, and Gabriel swore that this would never happen again. Not a total purge like this. Gabriel knew what she was up against, and it was potentially going to be a massive job. She was going to start with a new and clean earth, but she knew that the spirit of the Serpent was infectious like a great pestilence, or a pandemic. It only needed one infection, and it could spread like wildfire. She could and would try to contain it, but if containment failed, she would have to live with it rather than destroying it again and starting over, again. The cure, or vaccine, would surely come, but not until the seventh age of Light, and in the meantime, she would have to endure the remaining ages of Darkness. At least at the end of each age she and Michael and their secret weapon could make another purge of the spirit of the Serpent, albeit not a total one.

Gabriel wanted to have something to remind herself of this, when she or Michael became overwhelmed with rage at the Serpent and were close to striking out with another wipeout. Something to remind her that the best solution was to endure patiently for the cycles of Darkness to pass, and that the day of Light would certainly come.

So she made a bow in the sky which appeared when the Sun of great warrior armies, and the water of mercy were together, with her tears of mercy falling like rain. It was curved like a cycle and there were seven parts to it — the seven ages and the seven Sons of Man. Each had its own colour, starting with red for fire and finishing with shades of blue for water. The seventh colour, deep blue, was the colour of the salvation of the seventh age, the Sabbath and the day of Yhwh. Whenever she saw the rainbow, she would long for blue, but be restrained by her patience. She knew that without the seventh colour there would be no salvation to heaven, and if there were only six colours the Serpent would have won. She knew that was not going to happen, because her water of mercy would always overcome fire! Thus seeing the rainbow would make her the side of God which was very slow to anger.

Chapter 7

The Second Age – the Age of Noah

The Second Fall of Mankind

Noah and his family worked hard, and they started to multiply. Everything was going well. God had established Mankind's authority over the animals (who were creatures of righteous Darkness) and they all obeyed God and gave no trouble. To Mankind, God gave one commandment, which must be obeyed, rather like the commandment in the garden not to eat the fig. It was, when you eat the flesh of animals make sure that you do not eat anything with its blood still in it. That is because in the spirit world, blood is a living spirit, and the spirit is the spirit of fire. That includes the spirit of the Serpent. This living blood is similar to eating the living fig, it will grow in you, you will not be able to get rid of it, and it will be passed to all your offspring. So Noah and his sons obeyed God and took care not to eat the blood. Thus, they remained people of Light and lived side by side with the animals of Darkness, without conflict.

Noah became a grandfather many times over, and the youngest of his offspring was called Canaan.

Meanwhile, the Serpent looked on. She was furious and her fury grew each day. Everything she had built up in the age of Adam had been wiped out in a moment, and now she was back to square one. She had been overpowered by the forces of the Sun, and she knew she was no match for his heavenly army. Worse, she had been punished for what she did to Adam and Eve in the garden. Previously, not including Gabriel and Michael, she had been the second highest ranking creature on earth, just as she was in heaven, and she had all the authority she needed over Darkness on earth. She was beautiful, tall and strong, even taller and stronger than the Lions, and she could breathe fire on whoever she chose. That's because the Serpent was a powerful dragon, no less. But after her temptation of Adam and Eve, she had been stripped of her authority, down to the lowest level possible. Now, her belly touched the ground so she could only crawl, and she looked up to everyone except the creatures who crawled on the ground with her. She had become not a dragon, but a snake, and she was forced to serve all those above her. She still had the power of her spirit, but not the authority to use it as she wished to.

But she was not beaten, far from it. This is just a setback, she told herself, as her hot fury turned to cold hatred. It was only a matter of time before mankind slipped up again. If she had lost her own authority, she could always borrow his. She just needed him to turn to her and choose to do what she wanted. She just needed a new Adam to turn, stumble and fall this time too. So, she looked and waited. She was good at looking and waiting, and she saw that people soon forgot about her and quickly became lulled into a false sense of security. They were never ready for her when she suddenly struck. For the time being they were in a temporary sabbath age of Light and peace and security, like the Garden of Eden had been, and the sooner she brought it to an end the better.

As she watched them grow, she saw that Noah and his sons were strong and righteous. They were not good targets for her. But the youngest one, Canaan, was different. He had the lowest position of all his family, and he was expected to serve them and do what they said. He really didn't like that, and he complained. But nobody listened. He became more and more disillusioned, and he could see no solution, because he would always rank below his brothers. He wanted to rebel, but he didn't know how he could succeed. But the Serpent listened, and the Serpent knew exactly how he could rebel and succeed.

Here is Noah's family tree, including his youngest son at that time, Canaan. We will come back to the other lines soon, so you may want to bookmark this page.

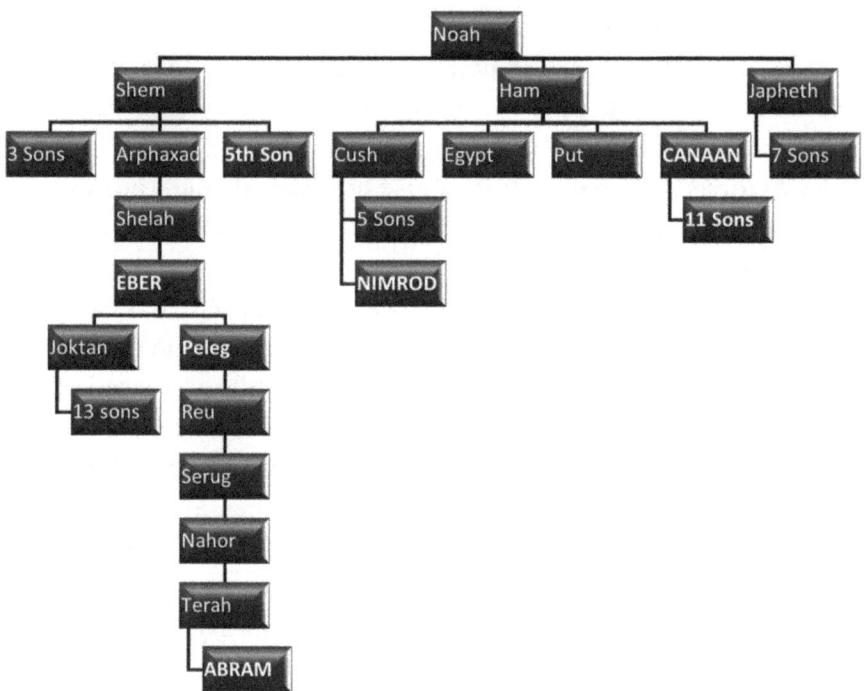

Canaan was a perfect target for her, because he was a son of Ham, the second born son of Noah. Why was Ham so important to the Serpent? Because the Serpent knew that it was no coincidence that Noah had three sons, because each one had the spiritual identity of one of the Messiah spirits which were in Noah. The first born, Shem was in the line of the Sun. The second born, Ham, was in the line of Gabriel, and the third born son, Japheth, was in the line of the Holy Spirit. Yhwh's plan was for each of the sons to grow their own 'house' of their own Messianic Spirit, which combined would make up all of Mankind. Everyone would be offspring of the Messiah of Light. The Serpent was not a part of Yhwh's plan in any way.

But the Serpent had other ideas.

The house of Ham was the key to the Serpent's plans. It was not just the house of Gabriel, it was the house of Yhwh, which was the house of Light on earth. It was to be called the house of Israel. This is the house that is destined to rule with Yhwh in the seventh age. Israel means 'he will rule as God'. It is always the target of the Serpent.

But more importantly, this was the house that had been divided almost from the beginning of creation in heaven, because Gabriel had unwittingly introduced a spirit of Darkness into it when she thought she was barren. It was therefore a house of both Light and Darkness, which meant it was a rebellious house. Eve was in this house and she had rebelled, and now we have Canaan in the same house, and he wants to rebel too. Perfect, here we go again, thought the Serpent.

However, if the Serpent wants to take over the house of Israel, she needs to win over a son who will inherit it, so she will control his inheritance. But she had one important problem with Canaan. You can see on the chart that the line of inheritance of this house was from Noah, to Ham and then to Cush, the firstborn. Canaan was not expected to inherit anything, and that was what he was complaining about. Canaan's problem was therefore the Serpent's problem too. But the Serpent was cunning, and she knew how to get around that problem.

The Serpent formed her plan, waited for the right time and then she struck.

She came to Canaan and won him over with smooth, sweet and convincing words. She sympathised with his position, an unfortunate fate of birth, just like her own experiences, and she asked him if he wanted to change things. He said of course he did, but he didn't know how. She said she knew exactly how to run great civilisations and powerful empires under her own way of Law and order. She had already shown how they could do very well in the previous age, and she used Cain, his forgotten forefather, as an example. They would be huge empires that would dominate the world, with great power and great riches, and all she needed was a line of great kings. Just like him.

They would be great kings of the earth, and the Serpent told Canaan that he would be at the head of their house, so he would be their king of kings. All he had to do was bow before her and worship her and she would tell him how to do the rest. The people would be wealthy and successful so they would surely have every reason to worship her as their god too, and be happy to do so. A whole powerful civilisation, full of rich people who would give tributes to their king and worship the Serpent and her heavenly angels as their gods, in order to get even more wealth and more success. Money and power would be a fabulous thing to have, and what's the harm in that anyway?

Canaan was certainly tempted, but he couldn't see how this plan could possibly work in practice. To start with, he was not head of his own house, even within his own generation. He had elder brothers who would inherit before him, the eldest being Cush, and above them all was Ham, their elder. So he asked the Serpent how he could be set at the head of this house and take over the inheritance of his firstborn brother, Cush.

The Serpent knew this question was coming so she smiled and replied, 'It is simple. Your eldest brother, Cush, will sell his "birthright" to you and you will then have bought his inheritance.' That was simple indeed, but perfectly feasible. It was legal and acceptable for an heir to sell his future but uncertain wealth, in return for some certain power and riches right now. Canaan only had to strike a deal and Cush's future wealth and his inheritance, would become his for his own descendants. In other words, Cush would sell his house, both present and future, to Canaan. Canaan replied, 'And, I suppose, in return, as my god you would take my authority and inheritance and my house, as if it was your own.' The Serpent just smiled at him again.

He asked what he had to do, and she told him. 'Just eat the flesh of that lion over there, with the blood in it, then give it to your eldest brother, Cush too. You will receive the blood of a king and become a king of kings. Leave everything else to me.' Canaan did as he was told, and so did Cush. Canaan took Cush's birthright and therefore took his place, as if he had been the firstborn. That meant that he would take the whole of Ham's inheritance, which was the whole house of Israel, on earth. And the whole house of Light would become a house of Darkness on earth and the Serpent would run it through his kings of the earth, starting with Canaan and following his line. As the eldest, he would be their king and so he would become king of kings, as promised.

Mission accomplished. What a great plan, brilliantly executed, thought the Serpent!

She had outwitted Yhwh and taken her house, without a fight. Mankind had fallen to her again, and she would deal with the other two houses who came from Noah, later. She gloated as she thought about Noah, the second Messiah Sun. 'What do you think about that, sunshine? Not so clever now, are you?' Best of all, Noah was still alive and would see the fall of Mankind himself, to know that the Messiah had failed again, before he died.

Then the Serpent would create her own kingdom on earth with her own empires and her own kings of the earth and her own king of kings. She would steal the people of Yhwh to do it. And all the people in her kingdom would worship her as their supreme god and judge, not Yhwh or the Sun Messiah. She would soon become higher than Gabriel. She would even set up her own hierarchy in heaven with her own angels who would rule heaven and earth, and the people would worship them too, as their idols. Nothing could stop her now.

Noah's reaction

We need to remember that there are subcycles within the major cycles, and each of the main ages has seven sub-ages. Near the end of Noah's life on earth, after the purge, the first age of Adam finished with the seventh sub-age, which is a sabbath, a sub-age of Light. This is the salvation after the purge, and this age would continue until there was another fall. It was also the sabbath that the Serpent wanted to close as soon as possible. It was like the time of the Garden of Eden, and most significantly, in this sub-age of Light, the Holy Spirit of Light was released to Noah like it was to Adam. It was only available to Noah, because he was king, and the Holy Spirit was to guide and empower him in that role. This time, Noah took the fruit of the vine and drank the wine, and felt the joy as the Holy Spirit entered him. He received all its spiritual gifts and powers.

The most useful gift to him, was the direct communication with Yhwh, who opened his spiritual eyes, so he could see what Yhwh saw. He removed all his coverings so there was no spiritual barrier between himself and Yhwh, and he became in a trance like state called being 'in the spirit'. He looked like he was drunk and naked, but he was completely aware of what was happening in the spirit world around him. His second son, Ham, walked into his room and saw him like that, and he didn't understand what he saw. Ham wasn't wearing any spiritual covering, and was facing him, face to face and eye to eye, so in that instant, Noah, through Ham, saw everything that happened in his house, that is, all of his offspring. He saw everything that Canaan, Ham's son had done to him and his house, and the deal to buy Cush's birthright. But he didn't come out of the trance yet, he needed to hear from Yhwh what he should do about it. It only took a moment.

Then his other two sons covered him and made sure to cover themselves, and not to look eye to eye while they did so. It shows that they had already received some basic spiritual knowledge, presumably from Noah. Soon afterwards, Noah awoke from being 'in the spirit.' He knew all about the disaster that had happened, and he also knew what he could do about it. Yhwh had told him to use his blessing to change the inheritance of his sons. It was impossible to reverse what Canaan had done to the whole house of Ham, but he could reduce the impact as much as possible. Just as Yhwh had taken away all the authority of the Serpent after she caused Adam to fall, Noah took away all of Canaan's authority and made him a servant to his uncles, Shem and Japheth. Since Japheth already had the servant spirit with the lowest authority, he became a servant of a servant. Since Canaan now had no authority in practice, the Serpent would be unable to gain authority through him.

Also, all of Noah's inheritance would now go to Shem and Japheth, so Noah had effectively disinherited the house of Ham. Whatever riches that Canaan's house would receive, it would not come from Yhwh or Noah, the Serpent would have to get it the hard way, by working for it.

But the damage had been done and the house of Ham had fallen to the Serpent and was lost to Yhwh, and with it, all her plans for her own people of Light. They were the people of her own house, called Israel, and now what had been a divided house in heaven, had all joined on earth, to turn to the Serpent and Darkness. It was an almost total disaster. The cleansed and purged earth was now going to be full of the spirit of the Serpent, once again. Shem and Japheth could try to resist the Serpent as much as they were able to, but Canaan and all his descendants would be filled by the spirit of the Serpent, and they would follow the will of the Serpent, now and in the future.

The growth of the houses – the chosen people and the promised land

Why was the loss of Yhwh's own house such a disaster for Yhwh? Because in this age of Noah, she had planned to set up a discrete area of the 'earth' which she would rule as God, even during the ages of Darkness. Within this land she would prove to everyone that she was worthy to be supreme God over the whole earth. It was part of the overall plan, and it had been promised to her by Michael. Hence it was called the 'Promised Earth' (translated as the Promised Land). The people of this earth would be believers and covenanted to her, rather than to Michael. They would be the people of her own house, Israel, and she had chosen them because they were people of Light. Therefore, they were the 'Chosen People', and they were meant to fill the Promised Land. This area, the Promised Land, already had its boundaries set out, and only needed to be filled with Yhwh's people. Then they would be her people and she would be their God. Outside the promised land, the Supreme God would be Michael and his people would be the people of righteous Darkness and Law.

The disaster was that the promised earth was now destined to be filled by the offspring of Ham, and these had been hijacked by the Serpent, under Canaan. She had therefore lost both her chosen people and her promised earth. Her plans were in tatters, while the Serpent gloated.

Over the next generations of the second age, Canaan and his offspring multiplied and spread out and covered most of the land that Yhwh had promised to the house of Ham, even from Sidon to Gaza.

Not forever though, because Yhwh planned to get her promised land back, even though she would have to take it back by force. But she knew that, in practice, for many generations she would not have enough strength or numbers to win a war. Indeed, this was not going to be possible until the third age, when Yhwh would fight to take back her land. After that, she knew that the nation of Canaan and his clans will be at war with the people of Yhwh, over the occupation of the promised land, for a very long time. Meanwhile, the nation of Canaan in the promised land became evil under the Serpent, just like the generations of Adam. Two infamous cities which were developed in the promised land under the Serpent, were called Sodom and Gomorrah. They became strongholds of the Serpent and were not taken over by force in the third age, they were destroyed in a purge.

Canaan's brothers also spread out to the south. Cush occupied North Africa, including Ethiopia. Egypt formed the country of that name, and Put formed the area of Libya. They all became kings of the earth and set up powerful and wealthy empires – just as the serpent had promised. Egypt in particular was to become a great civilisation, based on law and order, and worshipping its king (Pharaoh) as their God, but that was just the start of many such empires. The Serpent will prove that she is a very capable empire builder and she will produce many great civilisations across the earth, known for their wealth and power and gods. For example, the later Greek and Roman empires. Her empires are all based on taking land and people by force, then enforcing order through the rules of law, punishment and discipline, which is the way of Darkness. They were not known for their kindness and mercy! And of course, the worship of Gods other than Yhwh and Elohiym and the Messiah. The Gods they worshipped were the Serpent and other heavenly angels who followed her, by many other names – although the Serpent was careful not to let the people know who they were really worshipping.

But one such king of the earth was special. He was called Nimrod, a mighty hunter before Yhwh. He went east and set up the mighty empire of Babylon, the first city being called Babel. He then moved on to Shinar and built the up land of Assyria. He was a great man of Darkness, and he became very powerful and very rich. Why was he so special? Because he was a 'mighty hunter **before Yhwh**'. Not before the Serpent, but before Yhwh. He was a man of Darkness doing the will of Yhwh. Yes, he was Yhwh's secret weapon, in the line of Enoch. He had the spirit of the Sun and the Serpent in him, who were in conflict over who would manifest. Much later, the king of Babylon and the king of Assyria will become fundamental to Yhwh's plans, although their true identity will remain secret. But we will see the early work of the king of Babylon soon enough.

Meanwhile, Japheth's (Noah's third son) descendants spread over the coastlands, but it was the descendants of Shem (Noah's first son) who were destined to replace the house of Ham. Shem's line was divided into two. One line became the Hebrews, people of Light, and the other became righteous and obedient people of law and order, that is the people of righteous Darkness, who were not under the old Moon, but a righteous new Moon. They became the Muslims and they were vital to Yhwh's plans.

The Hebrews produced a man called Abram, who became Abraham. He was the tenth generation from Noah, and so he brought in the third age. He also brought the new chosen people to replace the offspring of Ham, and to take back the promised land by force. They were the famous 12 tribes of Israel and the Jews.

Abram's job was far from straightforward, and it actually required a new creation, which had to follow and preserve the old cycles of the first creation. Then again, Abram was a very special man.

Babel

The third age is when Yhwh will re-establish her chosen people, under Abraham, and fight back to reclaim the promised land. But first, the second age must run its course and come to an end. As always, there is a purge of the spirit of the Serpent at the end of the age. But this purge will be different to the purge of the flood, because nobody dies. Here is the story of the purge of the second age.

As Yhwh had predicted, during the second age, the Serpent challenged Gabriel in an attempt to overcome her so that the Serpent would replace her and rule, not just on earth, but heaven too. She chose her best king, the king of Babylon, enthroned in the city of Babel. To overcome Gabriel, the Serpent would need to take authority over her, and in the spiritual world of heaven and earth, authority was always denoted by the height of their position. She needed to get to a position which was higher than Gabriel's.

The Serpent's objective was to rule the house of Gabriel, which was the house of Yhwh. She wanted to mount a rebellion and take everything. But how? Now, in the spirit world, a house is like a mountain, with the eldest at the top and all subsequent generations below them, pushing the mountain higher from the base upwards, and spreading outwards at the same time. Gabriel came before the serpent, so she would always be higher. Somehow, the Serpent either had to make her fall to a lower position, or the Serpent had to make herself higher. Gabriel was unlikely to fall like Adam and Eve had done, so she focused on the second option.

On earth, everyone after Noah started their houses, or mountains, at the same time, so the Serpent was starting with a level playing field and, with some effort, she was in a good position to grow faster than the others. It was a race to be the highest, but she was confident that with the help of the king of Babylon, she could do so and take authority over the whole earth. Rather than waiting for the generations to grow naturally into a mountain, she decided to build her own mountain, an artificial mountain of her own design. She was going to build a pyramid. She could build it narrower than a mountain, so that it was higher, and soon it would be the highest thing on earth, she hoped. She would use her people from her own new house, the house of Ham and Canaan, to build it, and she knew that they would build it well. Why was she so confident? Because they worked with one aim, in unison as one nation, one body, with no divisions, no disputes, hearing only the voice of the Serpent and obeying it. She thought that the earth was already as good as hers.

However, the biggest threat to the Serpent was not from earth, it was from heaven. She knew that she and her followers were no match for Gabriel's heavenly army. She had suffered the purge of the first age and seen the heavenly army in action. She needed to deal with that threat too, or she would be vulnerable to the second purge, when it came. And it was coming soon, so she had to work quickly. She realised that the heavenly army was made up of ranks of angels who were all under authority and would obediently follow all the commands of their commander. So all she had to do was to keep building her mountain until it was higher than Gabriel's in heaven. As soon as that happened, her king of the earth, the king of Babylon, would have the authority, sitting on his throne at the top of the highest mountain, and the whole angel army of heaven would be obliged to follow his commands. Rules are rules, after all. Then, of course, he would do what she told him to do, and in practice, she would take his authority as her own.

So the Serpent guided her king and the work commenced. It went very well, and the pyramid rose quickly towards heaven. The plan was working.

But the Serpent didn't know that the king of Babylon was in the line of Enoch and Nimrod, and was secretly serving Yhwh and doing her will. And God had already warned him when they completed their deal, that if he tried to set himself above Yhwh then he would be swiftly brought down earth.

Gabriel came down to earth to see what was going on. She saw the threat and she saw that they were all working as one people under one voice and she knew that nothing would be impossible for them. Her solution was simple and instant. All these people were originally her own people in her own house, albeit it was divided. True, they were only hearing the Serpent, but since this was Gabriel's house too, she could add her own voice to what they heard. She did this by introducing her own spirit of communication, like a spiritual radio transmitting on the same frequency as the Serpent. She would speak the opposite of the voice of the Serpent and they would all become totally confused. They would be divided, disputes would break out, and the work would stop.

It worked. Then Gabriel made sure they would never be able to build such a high place again. She dispersed them from the city, over all the spiritual world, so that there was not just one large mountain, there were many scattered low hills. Each settlement spoke their own spiritual language and could not understand any other, which was reflected in the physical world by a series of languages and cultures and religions as they spread out. They had no effective authority and no effective force against the other people, that is the descendants of Shem and Japheth, including the Hebrews.

And that was the purge of the second age. Nobody died, but removal, or exile, and dispersal became a viable alternative. And her secret weapon had been brought down to earth. It was the first time that happened, but it would not be the last.

Clearly, Gabriel had confused the word so that it was not understood, but who dispersed the people in this purge? They didn't know it, but it was a combined operation of the three spiritual identities of the Messiah. Gabriel, the word, had confused their speech. The Sun, the great warrior commander of the heavenly angel army took command. And the army was an army of angels filled with the power of the Holy Spirit. Therefore, the Serpent of Darkness was defeated by the Messiah of Light, in a spiritual battle in the spiritual world. That spiritual division, confusion and battle is going to be a major feature of our own coming purge too. Remember, nobody died in this purge.

Finally, we will see that it will be the Messiah who will restore the ability to understand the spiritual word at the beginning of the sixth age, when the Holy Spirit of Yhwh will be introduced to the people of many countries and languages, giving the same message to everyone, through a common spiritual language which everyone understood.

Now, after the weakening and dilution of the people of the Serpent at the end of the second age, it was time for the third age. This was the time for a new start for the people of Yhwh, a new chosen people. It was time for the Hebrews.

Chapter 8

The Third Age – Abraham to Moses

Abram's role was to set up a new chosen people to replace the people from the second age that had fallen to the Serpent. That means to replace the house of Ham which had become the house of Canaan. The new chosen people would all be descended from Abram, who would soon be named as the well-known Abraham. Then, the new chosen people would aim to take back the promised land from the people of the Serpent who had taken it during the second age, especially the descendants of Canaan. The promised land had been promised to Yhwh, but it had been stolen by the Serpent and she needed it back.

But the enormous problem that Yhwh faced was that her own house, the house of Light, was now missing from the people of the earth. To understand this better, let's go back to the three sons of Noah. The firstborn, Shem had the spiritual identity of the male side of God, Michael, and so this would be carried into Shem's house. The third born, Japheth, had the spiritual identity of the Spirit of God, and this would be carried into his house. However, the second born, Ham, had the spiritual identity of Yhwh and this line had been lost to the Serpent. This is the line of Light that was supposed to take the inheritance in the seventh age, but now there is no inheritance of Light, it is lost.

The worst thing is that because it is Yhwh's line, it goes all the way back to the very beginning of creation. Therefore, it is obvious that everything that follows without it from now on, is going to be very different from the intended order and plan of creation. How can you finish up with a kingdom of Light if there are no people of Light?

The only solution for Yhwh and Gabriel is to recreate creation. It is that critical, and that big a job. Yhwh must create a new start which would once again include the people of Light who carry the spirit of Yhwh. Then these people would grow in numbers, to run in parallel with what was left of the old creation. Put simply, the old fallen creation would be called the Gentiles, and the new creation of Light would be called the Hebrews. The new plan was for the Hebrews to become the chosen people and would take back the promised land, and the gentiles would live outside its boundaries.

Also, it would be important for the new creation to follow all the previous cycles of the original creation, or it would not be a true replacement.

With the arrival of Abram and a new age, Yhwh was ready to begin creation all over again. Not just a new Adam, a whole new creation in heaven and on earth.

The new cycle of creation
In the beginning, the original creation began with the divine angels, Michael and Gabriel. In the new beginning, Abram was like the original male side of Almighty God, Michael. Abram means 'exalted father'. He was married to a woman of Light, called Sarai, and she was like Gabriel, the female side of God. She was very beautiful, and she held the missing spiritual identity of Yhwh. Together, they reflected all the key features of the original creation. For example, Abram and Sarah were married but they were also like brother and sister, as were Michael and Gabriel. Later, Abram would pass Sarai off as his sister when they were threatened. Like the original cycle, Yhwh told Abram and Sarai that they would have an heir and would become many large nations. Like before, Sarai lost faith because of her age while she waited to produce a son of Light, so she suggested that Abram would produce a son and heir by her servant, who was a woman of Darkness without the spirit of Yhwh and Light. He was called Ishmael, a man of Darkness, and he took

the place of the Moon to rule the night. But not the corrupt Moon, he was a righteous and obedient man of the Law and was called the New Moon. He was male and was loved by Abram as his son. He fathered a second line of the Muslims, under Abram, as well as the first line that we saw which came from 'the division of the earth' under Shem, the son of Noah. Now we have a line of gentile Muslims and a line of Muslims within the chosen people, in the house of Sarai (who will be named Sarah). Therefore, the house of Light is still divided into Light and Darkness as before, but this time, the side of Darkness is righteous under Ishmael.

This is becoming a little difficult to follow, but it is important and relevant, because we still have this split structure today. In summary, the Muslims in the line of Ishmael follow the new Moon, not the old Moon, and their symbol is the crescent of the new Moon. The Muslims in the line of Shem follow the Sun and not the old Moon. Also, Ishmael is obedient to his half-brother, Isaac, who we will see represents the Sun. So although Muslims are people of Law and punishment, that is righteous Darkness, neither line is under the corrupt Moon, and they are by nature righteous and obedient to the Law and to the authority of God and the Sun. This is going to be a huge benefit to Yhwh's plan.

Returning to the new Creation, after Ishmael, Sarai then had one son called Isaac who was a man of Light, receiving the spirit of Light from his mother. He represented the Sun, the greater light, and he became the Messiah on earth. His line was chosen to inherit the earth because he was the 'anointed one' of Light, and he became the heir by a blessing rather than the birthright of the firstborn. Like the original Sun, he was nearly sacrificed on the altar by his father, Abram, but Yhwh intervened and stopped the killing. Nevertheless, both Abram and Isaac passed the test and were prepared to do what they thought was correct to put things right, including dying, so the cycle of redemption which started in the old creation continued into this creation too. The plan may be complex, but it was working.

Isaac married a crafty woman of Darkness, Rebekah, but she performed the will of Gabriel and achieved everything she had to, according to the original cycle. She too was like both a wife and a sister to Isaac and was passed off as his sister, like Abram had done with Sarah. She too had twins, following the old cycle of the Moon in heaven, and the firstborn, called Esau, was a man of Darkness, not Light, who was hairy like an animal and a mighty hunter like a lion, a natural leader. She arranged for her second twin son, called Jacob, and a man of Light, to buy the birthright from Esau, and later, deceived his father, Isaac, into blessing him with the inheritance earmarked for the firstborn. Rebekah had just ensured that despite the mix up in the womb, when the firstborn was a spiritual Lion, the inheritance of Light would pass to the second born son of Light, Jacob. The plan was still working. Now, we just need Jacob to produce all the new chosen people.

It was Jacob and his four wives who had 12 sons who produced the 12 tribes of the chosen people, and it was these tribes who were expected to inherit the earth in the seventh age. They included the three Messianic identities of the true Messiah. The Sun (the king of kings) started the tribe of Judah, the word started the tribe of Simeon, and the Holy Spirit started the tribe of Levi. These three hold the same spiritual identities as the original Messiah in Heaven.

The house of the king was therefore called the house of Judah, which means 'celebrated'. This will later be the house of King David. The house of the word, which is the divided house of Gabriel was called Israel, which means 'he will rule as God'. This name describes the anointing of the people of Israel, the people of Light, to receive the inheritance. This is the house that replaced the fallen house of Ham and Canaan. The house of the Holy Spirit was called the house of Levi, which means 'joined to' because, like the Holy Spirit, he is firmly joined to whoever he serves. Levi became the house of the priests who serve Yhwh. Thus, the plan for the new creation, with the new chosen people of Light complete with the three Messianic spirits of the coming Messiah, was finished and all the spiritual identities and cycles were in place, ready for the next age.

The Serpent's responses

With this, the new creation and the new chosen people were loved by Yhwh and Gabriel. However, they were hated by the Serpent, who had not gone away and not changed her objectives. She continued her plans for her own people and the gentiles in general, eventually building amazing rich and powerful empires and civilisations. Her people worshipped idols, which were false gods who were actually, heavenly angels who followed the Moon. To worship an idol was to worship the Serpent, whether you knew it or not. Idolatry spread throughout the gentile peoples.

The Serpent also targeted the chosen people while they were still very few in number. Her highest value targets were the three Messianic tribes, Judah, Simeon and Levi. She wanted to make them all fall to Darkness and worship her instead of Yhwh, then to cause division and rebellion. As a result, there will be constant conflict between the Serpent and the chosen people. Of particular note will be the Serpent's strategy to take over the divided house, now openly called Israel, by turning them from Yhwh to her, and then for Israel to become king and rule, instead of Judah. The serpent will have a number of successes along the way. However, the Messiah will constantly fight for the chosen people, the lost sheep of Israel, as their good shepherd. He too will have a number of successes along the way.

You could say that most of the remainder of the Bible is about these conflicts. It's all about who will inherit and rule in the seventh age.

The covenants of Abram and Abraham

To go from one man and his wife to the whole chosen people to fill the promised land and then enter heaven in due course, was a daunting task for everyone involved. It would stretch anyone's beliefs enormously, especially that they would get to heaven hundreds of years after they died. Therefore, Abram and his descendants received important promises from Yhwh, to give them hope and reassurance. These promises are far-reaching and affect us all, even today, so they are not just academic, and they can't be avoided, even in this basic Book One. In fact, the various promises cover all the ages from this time up to the seventh age and the inheritance of Light and even the inclusion of the gentiles. Here is a quick summary of them.

First, Yhwh told Abram that he would become a great nation and that all the families of mankind would receive the inheritance. This was a confirmation that the inheritance given to Adam by the blessing of Almighty God in the original creation would stand. Abram's enemies, however, would not inherit. This promise went further than the chosen people, it included the Gentiles too, who would be blessed 'through Abram'.

Then Gabriel appeared to Abram to tell him that his offspring would be given the land of Canaan, which was currently occupied.

Soon afterwards, Yhwh confirmed that his offspring would be given the promised land, but added the vital message that they would not be judged. This was to confirm that they were the people of Light and would be redeemed by the mercy of Yhwh, not condemned by the Law. This promise covered all the people of Light on the earth.

When the time came for the birth of Isaac, the new Sun, Gabriel came to Abram and told him to look to heaven and that the stars would not be judged either. The stars were the offspring of Isaac, the new Sun. This promise of redemption therefore covered the angels of Light in heaven.

The promises concerning the earth were confirmed in a special binding covenant, and the boundaries of the promised land were extended from the Nile to the Euphrates and the areas occupied by the clans of the house of Canaan and his brothers.

When Ishmael was to be born, Gabriel told his mother, the servant woman, that her offspring would be a great multitude and that they too would be redeemed. These are the Muslims in the line of Ishmael. Thus the redemption by the Sun is not restricted to the people of Light, or to the future Christians, the Messiah Sun will redeem his half-brother Ishmael's offspring too. We will see that the people of Light and Darkness will work closely together against the Serpent and not against each other. That includes powerful combined angelic armies under the command of the Sun in the future, including Armageddon.

Then, when it was time for Isaac, Gabriel confirmed and renewed the covenant for the people of Light. Abram would be multiplied greatly and become not just the father of a nation, as previously promised, but the father of a 'multitude of nations'. Their kings would come from him and the nations would be filled by the fruit of the Holy Spirit. This was a description of the Christian nations and any other nations who embraced the Messiah and the Holy Spirit, which the Messiah would bring. This is the covenant which covers the Gentile nations, not the nation of the chosen people. At this point, Abram's name was changed to Abraham, which means the father of a multitude. It should not really come as a surprise that the Gentiles are included, because they are the original people of Light, the sons of Noah, including the stolen chosen people of the house of Ham. Yhwh loves them just as much as she loves the new creation, and she would never forget them.

At the same time, Yhwh introduced the covenant of circumcision. On the eighth day after birth, a male baby would have his foreskin removed. The foreskin is a circular mark of redemption and resurrection to heaven, on the first day of the new cycle. The hidden meaning is that the mark is a circle of flesh because the old seven day cycle of the flesh on earth is fulfilled, and a new day in heaven has started, in angelic form without the flesh. Circumcision is a mark of those who will be redeemed to heaven. This, as we know, is the first method of salvation to heaven. However, for completeness, we should understand that the second method of salvation through the

Holy Spirit is different and does not need the mark of redemption. Their mark is the Holy Spirit. Therefore, Christians who receive the Holy Spirit are not circumcised.

From now on, all the fleshly offspring of Abraham would be circumcised, including the sons of Ishmael, but his spiritual offspring, the Gentiles, would not be required to do so. But importantly, neither of the groups of the people of Light would be judged, they would be redeemed.

Sarai was also blessed and told she would become nations and produce kings. This is essential, because it is Sarai who produces the people of Light. Remember that Sarai represents Yhwh and Gabriel. Sarai's name is changed to Sarah, meaning 'noble woman' where Sarai meant 'princess'. This name change is not academic, it is vital, both then and now. It is a reflection of the change from a princess who is anointed to rule, to the queen when she is proven worthy and takes her throne. It means victory for the God of Light.

Finally, but by no means least, Ishmael was blessed and he would multiply greatly too. He would be fruitful, and he would father 12 princes and become a great nation. He was a man of Darkness, so he would not carry the inheritance of Light, but otherwise he was blessed in a similar way to the other offspring of Abraham. His role is vital to Yhwh. In fact, his 12 princes would mirror the 12 offspring of Light. In heaven, they would sit on the 12 thrones of Night, next to the 12 thrones of Day. They too will carry the fruit of the Holy Spirit, but the Holy Spirit of fire rather than water. The people of Ishmael are the people of the new moon, and they will submit to the authority of the Sun and oppose the original Moon and the Serpent, both on earth and in heaven. When we consider Muslims we must remember these roots, that they are not just powerful allies and guardians, they are brothers, sons of Abraham, working together.

When Isaac grew up, Gabriel re-established the covenant she gave to Abram, directly with him. She is talking to him as the Sun, but it is apparent that he doesn't know it at this stage. She says that she will multiply his offspring like 'the stars of heaven', and 'in his offspring all the nations of the earth shall be blessed'. His offspring includes Jesus the Messiah, in whom all the gentiles will be blessed and saved.

You can see that there is nothing new in these promises, they reflect what has been planned and promised from the beginning of creation. They are, however, being repeated because this is a new creation which must include all the cycles and features and promises of the old creation.

The third fall of mankind

First, Jacob would father the 12 'princes' who will multiply into the 12 tribes. The Serpent lost no time in attacking them, especially the three who carried the spirits of the Messiah. Judah carried the spirit of the Sun and he quickly fell by having sex with a prostitute who turned out to be a manifestation of the Serpent. He just couldn't resist taking a beautiful woman. Her name was 'Tamar' and we will see her again soon. Judah became filled by the spirit of the Serpent and his Messianic line was lost for many generations, until it was finally restored from another branch, introduced in the fourth age. Tamar had twins who fought to be the firstborn in the womb. The firstborn's line will be brought to an end and replaced when the new branch will be introduced.

Here, we are seeing the cycle which I described in Chapter 4, of the Moon causing the fall of the Sun and the birth of battling twins, in early creation, being repeated. In a future cycle, the beautiful half-sister in the line of the Sun (then, king David) who is raped by her half-brother, will also be called Tamar. Tamar is a code word which means judge, and the judge of the people of Darkness is the Moon.

The second target is Levi, the tribe of the priests, and it will fall, starting with Aaron the brother of Moses, and the priests will remain fallen until the time of Jesus and beyond. They are important, because they were supposed to teach the chosen people about Yhwh and her

The Third Age – Abraham to Moses

commandments, but the priests actually taught a false version which was corrupted by the Serpent, and which did a lot of damage.

Thirdly, the most damaging fall for Yhwh would be if her own house, the house of Israel, would fall again. Since Adam's rib was removed, the Messianic spirit of Yhwh had been carried by woman. Jacob's first three wives did not carry the spirit of Light, so everything depended on his final wife, Rachel, who was beautiful. She carried the spirit, but as usual, she was barren, as Yhwh waited for a sabbath sub-age of Light. When eventually it came, her first son was called Joseph and he is very special indeed, because he had the third Messianic Holy Spirit. We will soon return to Joseph. Now 11 sons had been born, so only one remained, and this son was to carry the second Messianic spirit of Yhwh, the spirit of Light and the spirit and house of Israel.

Jacob and his household had been staying for many years at Rachel's family home with her father. Her father was not a righteous man, and he worshipped idols and deceived Jacob, so Jacob decided to leave with his whole household, unannounced. They were returning to Jacob's own homeland with all his children and his wives. Rachel's father was offended and chased after them, and when he caught up, he complained that some of his household idols, who he worshipped as gods, were missing. As we know, idolatry had become a massive problem for Yhwh, because the people were actually worshipping the Serpent on earth and the Moon and her angels in heaven. They did bestow real spiritual powers which worked, so they were popular, but whoever worshipped them turned from Yhwh and fell to follow the Serpent so they received the spirit of the Serpent. Virtually the whole of the Gentile nations had fallen and engaged in idolatry, but it was essential that the new chosen people worshipped only Yhwh as their God. Once they fell to the Serpent, her spirit would spread like a pestilence, as before.

Then disaster struck again. It turned out that the idols had been stolen by Rachel, and she had succumbed to the Serpent, and fallen.

She had the spirit of the Serpent in her, and she would pass it to all her children. Rachel was just like fallen Eve. Now, when her son was born, who was to have been the source of the Light of Yhwh within the chosen people, he would receive the spirit of the Serpent from his mother, not the spirit of Light. This would have the same effect as Eve passing on the fig to Adam, and Canaan eating the unclean flesh with the blood in it. Once again, the house of Israel, that is the house of Light, had fallen, because every child of Rachel would manifest the spirit of the Serpent, not the spirit of Yhwh. The final son was going to be called Benjamin, and his tribe was to carry the spirit of Yhwh, the spirit of Light. Now he would carry the spirit of the Serpent, the spirit of Darkness.

After all the planning and the forming of the new creation, disaster had indeed struck again, Israel had fallen again, even before it started.

As before, although her son would manifest the spirit of the Serpent by default, there was a ray of hope. The key was, again, authority. When he was under the chain of authority of the Sun or Yhwh, he would manifest their spirit instead of the Serpent's. In practice, his immediate authority would be his father, Jacob, so whoever Jacob followed would be critical. If Jacob succumbed and was under the Serpent, then so would Benjamin and his house too. But if Jacob was strong enough to withstand the Serpent, and Benjamin accepted his father's authority, then Benjamin would not manifest the spirit of the Serpent either. It's not much to go on, because he wouldn't be with his father for ever, but it was better than nothing.

Gabriel pondered on the problem. She knew that Jacob was faithful to her and hated the Serpent, but he was not a very strong man by nature. More of a lamb than a lion like his twin brother. She could give him her Messianic spirit of Israel which would give him strength and mean that his son followed Yhwh, but it would also expose him to an attack from the Serpent, because the house of

Israel was divided and rebellious. If she lost Jacob too, that would make matters worse, not better, so she decided that she could not take the risk.

Then again, she could always test him to see how strong he could be. She could give him the spirit of Israel and then find out if he could withstand the Serpent, by a demonstration of strength. A wrestling match with Gabriel herself. If he could match her strength, then he could withstand the Serpent for sure. So that night, during darkness, when the spirit of the Serpent would manifest, Gabriel came to Jacob and he was filled with the true spirit of Israel. Gabriel tried to take it away from him, but he resisted. She tried over and again, applying all her strength and all her endurance, and he still resisted. She tried to wear him out, hour after hour until it was almost daybreak, but he continued to resist. Eventually she was satisfied and touched his hip to dislocate it, so he would let her go.

There was another reason for the dislocation, because the true spirit of Israel was a pioneering spirit, born to spread out, and she wanted him to stay put in the promised land. While he is lame his spirit of Light will remain in the promised land, among the chosen people. There is an even deeper consequence. In an angel, the leg is the place that holds the Holy Spirit. When Jesus comes, he will wish to spread the Holy Spirit, so he will heal the lame so that they can receive the Holy Spirit and spread the word and its salvation to the Gentiles.

Now a spiritual principle is that your name is your spirit, so when you receive a new spirit, you receive a new name. From this moment onwards, Jacob was named 'Israel', and so he joined the house of Israel. Now this new name is not just academic. Jacob has just been given the Messianic spirit of Israel, which was supposed to be in Rachel and passed to her son. Now it is in Jacob, and he will pass it to his son instead. It means that his twelfth son will carry both the spirit of Israel and the spirit of the Serpent, and they will strongly compete in him. Not just when Jacob/Israel is still alive, but in future generations too. At the very least, although he will be fallen, there will be a good chance that his spirit of Israel can withstand the Serpent, so that she will not manifest.

Rachel gave birth to a boy, but she dies in childbirth, ending her line. He was called Benjamin which means 'the son of the right hand'. The right hand is the side of the inheritance, therefore the side of Light. It will be a reminder to him to resist becoming a son of the left hand and turn from Light to Darkness. Nevertheless, the fact is that Benjamin has fallen and it is very likely that he will follow the spirit of the Serpent. Sadly, despite the efforts of his father and his brother Joseph, over time, it will not go well for Benjamin, nor for the house of Israel.

Taking stock, spiritual mankind on earth has been multiplied from one man and one woman in three separate ages and even two creations. And in each age, they have fallen before they even started. It's not looking good for Light, but Yhwh refuses to give up. Instead, she looks at the rainbow and is patient. She has the Holy Spirit on her side, which will be spread in the seventh age, the final colour. The Holy Spirit may be humble and righteous, but he is also the most powerful living creature there is in heaven and on earth. The Holy Spirit is also the third Messianic identity, and in the story, it is already on earth, albeit confined to one man. To mark him, Yhwh asks his father, Israel, to make him a coat of many colours, like the rainbow, and he calls him Joseph.

Joseph

Yhwh's big problem is that the chosen people are very small in numbers and are surrounded by many enemies who could destroy them. How can she protect them while they grow into a nation that can withstand attacks? How can she use the Holy Spirit in just one man to achieve her aim? But Yhwh has a plan, and that one man is enough. Especially when she also has a well-placed secret weapon to be his king.

The Serpent has scored successes against two of the Messianic spirits, Judah (the Sun) and Benjamin (Israel), and will soon cause the fall of Levi too. But Yhwh has taken her divine Holy Spirit and filled another man with it. He is called Joseph, the firstborn son of Rachel and the elder brother of Benjamin. He is also the third Messianic identity. While he is filled with the Holy Spirit, he is holy and he will not be troubled by the spirit of the Serpent. He serves Yhwh, not the Serpent, and he is the power behind the Messiah. He has many gifts from the Holy Spirit. Most importantly, he can hear the voice of Yhwh through the Holy Spirit, and he has the understanding and wisdom of Yhwh. He can pass on messages (or prophecies) from Yhwh for others too, including interpreting the messages in their spiritual dreams. It is obvious that Yhwh is with him, so he will receive favour wherever he goes. Furthermore, because of his divine authority as a servant of Yhwh, he will rise to the highest levels of service wherever he is.

Joseph's job was to prepare a land for the chosen people to safely multiply and grow strong, although initially, he didn't know it. When any Messianic person comes to earth, they have no memory of their spiritual life and have to learn everything from scratch. Yhwh had chosen a place, and it was Egypt. Now Egypt is a place of darkness, one of the Gentile countries, and under the rule of a king of the earth who followed the serpent. How would the chosen people possibly be safe there? Because the king, or Pharaoh, was no ordinary king of the earth, he was in the line of her secret weapon, Enoch and Nimrod, and had been inserted there by Yhwh. He was a man of darkness like everyone around him, but he would do the will of Yhwh. Under the terms of her covenant with him, she promised him great wealth and power over the whole empire of Egypt, and he promised to look after her people. Although first, they had to come to his kingdom in Egypt!

Since Joseph was a man of Light, he was hated by his brothers but loved by his father, Israel. Benjamin was not included amongst his brothers because his father kept him close, for reasons we now understand. Joseph wore a coat like a rainbow, the sign of the seven sons of man. This was a sign of his future victory in the seventh age and it was hated as much as Joseph was. As another sign, Yhwh gave him two dreams about his future divine authority and how all the spirits of his own brothers would come under it. Rather foolishly, he shared this with his brothers, who hated him even more! Then one day his 10 brothers took him and sold him as a slave. They sold him to a group of Ishmaelites who just happened to be passing. They, of course, are sworn to be faithful to Yhwh and her people of Light, so they protected Joseph and took him to Egypt. There, he was bought by an officer of Pharaoh, Potiphar, and he found favour with him and was soon promoted to be head of his household, under only Potiphar. The Holy Spirit is always under the authority of someone else, but the divine Holy Spirit will rise to be under someone in high authority. Like the king.

Then the wife of Potiphar tried to seduce Joseph, just like Tamar seduced Judah. Potiphar's wife was a descendent of the Serpent like Tamar. This would have resulted in him losing the Holy Spirit, being filled with her spirit of the Serpent, and falling to Darkness. However, he refused her, so she falsely accused him of rape and he was thrown into prison. This event is like the earlier cycle in heaven when the Moon successfully accused the Sun. But once he was in prison, Joseph did well once again, and he found favour with the jailor so he was promoted to be the head of the jail under only the jailor. Another demonstration of his status of head of the servants, but rising up the hierarchy.

Joseph, through his Holy Spirit link to Yhwh, was able to understand and interpret spiritual visions or dreams, and he correctly interpreted two prisoners' dreams. One prisoner was a senior officer of the Pharaoh and he was soon released. Later, the Pharaoh too had visions which he could not interpret, but the officer remembered Joseph, so he was summoned and he correctly interpreted the dreams. He found favour with the Pharaoh and was promoted to the number two position in the empire, under only the Pharaoh. Now he has reached his true position of being the top level servant, under only the authority of the king.

Now, Joseph was exactly where Yhwh needed him. Pharaoh was Yhwh's man in authority, but because he was a man of Darkness, he could not receive the understanding and wisdom of Yhwh, so for example, he could not interpret his own dreams. That position was filled by Joseph, who would continue to pass on the word, understanding and wisdom of Yhwh to Pharaoh, through his advice, using the spirit of 'Counsel'. Together, they were complete.

With Joseph and the Pharaoh in position, Yhwh's plan for her chosen people took shape. The dreams had shown that there would be seven years of plenty, with good crops of grain, followed by seven years of famine over the whole region, bringing starvation. Joseph's wise advice was to set aside and store the excess grain from the good years, so that it was available for the starving people in the bad years. Pharaoh agreed, of course, and put Joseph in charge. The result was that Joseph controlled the grain and the price, on behalf of the Pharaoh. The famine came and the people paid the demanded price, so that they would not die. The money was paid to the Pharaoh and be became very rich. When their money ran out, the people paid with their livestock, and the Pharaoh became even richer. When the livestock ran out, they sold themselves to be slaves to the Pharaoh. So he finished up owning the wealth and the livestock and the people of the whole region. Therefore, Yhwh had fulfilled her part of the bargain.

But there was more to this deal. On the face of it, she appeared to have traded all the Gentile people of the whole region to the Serpent. She seemed to have given up a whole nation to the Serpent, just to save her own chosen people. That goes against everything that Yhwh holds dear, as she would never give up any of her creation to the Serpent. So what was really happening here? Pharaoh was a descendent of Enoch and Nimrod, so he contained the Messianic spirit of the Sun, albeit in a man of Darkness. So the reality was that the fallen Gentiles were now under the Messiah Sun, even though they didn't know it. They were lost sheep but they were secretly being looked after by the good Shepherd. Egypt was now safe and ready for the Hebrews to come. This secret will have positive implications for Yhwh in later generations.

It was time for Yhwh to move all her chosen people into Egypt, where they would secretly be under the Messiah too, but as free people, not slaves. At the same time, Yhwh wanted to test Joseph's brothers, especially Judah, to see if they had repented for their treatment of Joseph, so she could forgive them, and let them continue into Egypt, washed free of sin.

Joseph's family were starving in the famine too, and his brothers (without Benjamin) came to Egypt to buy grain. Joseph recognised them, but they did not recognise him. He sent them back to their home with grain, and refused their money. They would not have to pay for their food, so unlike the other nations, they would not be in debt and they would not be enslaved. It is a principle of Yhwh, that her people will never have to pay for their freedom. Even their redemption is free for them. That is because if they or Yhwh paid off their debts, they would be making the Serpent richer and more powerful.

Joseph set up the tests of the brothers, all of which had secret spiritual meanings which we will look at in the next book. They passed the tests, genuinely repenting of their previous treatment and not repeating it. Especially Judah, who offered to sacrifice himself to save his brother Benjamin. He had just confirmed that he was still willing to redeem Israel, so he passed his test and was forgiven. But remember that in this age, the spirit of the Serpent cannot be cast out, so although he is forgiven he still has the spirit of the Serpent in him and his line will still have to be replaced by a clean line in due course. Joseph ensured that all the 11 remaining brothers and their father Israel, and their households and livestock would move to Egypt.

And so, all of the chosen people came to Egypt as free people under the care of the Messiah king and the Messiah Holy Spirit, ready to multiply in safety. And Yhwh had proven that she was a great God who made great plans and executed them faithfully. She could outwit any schemer, and turn a dire situation with little chance of survival into a great success, with peace and security for her people. Even if very few of them could see what she had done and how she had done it.

Joseph welcomed his family and revealed himself to them, and they celebrated. Joseph especially cared for Benjamin, and he covered him in spiritual mercy and clean spiritual food. Pharaoh also delivered his part of the deal and welcomed them, setting aside a large region in Egypt for them to live and grow. Now, when they were a large enough nation to look after themselves, Yhwh planned to tell the Pharaoh to let her people go and they would travel the short distance to the promised land, and would take it back.

But the Serpent had other ideas. As we know, the descendants of Enoch and Nimrod had both the spirit of the Sun and the Serpent (or the Moon) in them, and the two spirits were in constant conflict over who would manifest as king. After several generations, the Serpent won and the agreement with Yhwh was effectively torn up. The chosen people were then enslaved and lived under a Pharaoh who manifested as the Serpent. Their lives were made miserable, and there was no way that the Serpent was going to let Yhwh's people go to take the promised land.

Meanwhile, the spirit of Enoch in the Pharaoh at the time of Joseph was taken up to heaven, to wait for the right time to return and sort it all out.

Chapter 9

Moses Frees the Chosen People

In heaven, Gabriel is in trouble. The Serpent has taken control of Egypt and has refused to let her people go, and without her people, Gabriel will have failed. The biggest issue that Gabriel faces is that the Serpent has grown bold and is prepared to break the rules. After the fall of Adam, she lost her authority, falling down to the lowest levels so that she became a creeping creature, a snake. That put her firmly under the authority of Gabriel and the Sun, but now she has openly rebelled and is refusing to obey either of them. That means that if Gabriel cannot get the Serpent to obey her authority, then she will need to be defeated by force. That's not going to be easy, because she has a massive and well-armed army under her, the Egyptian army, and Yhwh's people have no army which is either trained or equipped.

Meanwhile, the conflict over who will have the inheritance continues. By default, it goes to the firstborn, but if for any reason it does not, then it goes to the next in line. These are the arguments that the Moon applied to the twins in heaven, which still persist on earth, as Darkness and Light still fight for the inheritance. The key is the firstborn sons of Egypt, who will carry the inheritance of Darkness to the next generation. The Serpent wants to protect them at any cost. Gabriel, however, has plans for her own people of Light to take the inheritance, as is their right according to their blessing.

This is the time for strong leadership, but the Hebrews have no king. They need the Messiah king, judge and warrior – the Sun on earth, the next son of Man, but it's not that simple. The serpent

Moses Frees the Chosen People 147

expects him, can easily recognise him, and will kill him as soon as he is born, before he has the strength and numbers to defend himself.

Assuming Gabriel can deal with all these problems, she knows that being freed from Egypt is only half of the job anyway. Once her people are free, their new king needs to lead them to the promised land and introduce a new set of rules for them to follow. This is still an age of Darkness and following a set of Laws to achieve order is expected. However, this will not be based on the law of the Serpent, but the law of Yhwh. This law, if obeyed, will guide the people away from the Serpent, but it will also capture the sins against Yhwh, which the Serpent is responsible for. The new law must be laid down by the new king, who must receive it from Gabriel, nobody else. The people do not need to understand it, they just need to blindly obey it and they will be OK. This law will apply for all the remaining ages of Darkness until Light takes over in the sabbath age and the system of Law will rest, to be replaced by the Holy Spirit – the Tree of Life. The original objectives for the people of Light have not been changed, only the way to get there.

Overcoming these problems is going to be a very difficult task for Gabriel. She needs a very special leader who does not yet exist on earth. But Yhwh, through Gabriel, has a plan, and the plan is called Moses! Let's look at her plan.

Birth

Gabriel is an angel of Light and the Messiah Sun is also an angel of Light. You might ask how can angels of Light produce a system of Law and punishment, which is the way of Darkness? Well, you need a king who is secretly a man of Darkness, but one who does the will of Yhwh, not the Serpent.

Then when he is born, how do you stop him being recognised and killed by the Pharaoh, who is on the lookout for him? Well, it's the same solution. Pharaoh is looking for the Sun, a king of Light, so you need a young royal prince who is a man of darkness, and destined to be a king of the earth under the Serpent. When he is recognised as such, he should then be accepted by the Pharaoh and maybe even brought up as a prince under his protection.

So Gabriel doesn't use her king of Light, she brings down to earth her secret weapon, her king of Darkness who does her will. This is a very deeply hidden secret, which will take most of us by surprise, but Moses is actually a spiritual descendent of Enoch and Nimrod. A man of both Darkness and Light in the same body, and born to be a king. He has the unique spiritual combination of the Messianic spirit of the Sun (king and Light), the spirit of the Serpent (Darkness) and he also has a third spirit, a spiritual covering of his sins, which is a spirit of mercy and forgiveness. It is this covering that allows him to stand face to face with Gabriel and hear what she says directly, without being seen to be unclean and immediately struck by fire.

It helps that the earlier Pharaoh from the time of Joseph, was also in the secret line of Enoch and Nimrod and was a king of Darkness. Therefore, Moses should be able to pass himself off as a prince of darkness too.

Sure enough, just before his birth, the Pharaoh decreed that all the male Hebrew babies must be killed, but Moses's mother carefully puts him in a floating basket and pushes him towards a bank of the Nile where she knows he will be noticed by a daughter of the Pharaoh. When she sees him, she takes him into the palace and he is brought up as a prince, under the full protection of the Pharaoh. The princess even decides to use his real mother as his wet nurse, until he is weaned. This problem has been overcome too. (By the way, the basket is like an ark to protect the Messiah from harm. But the main point is that Moses is above the waters and reeds of the Nile, so this already establishes his authority over them in the spiritual world, which he will demonstrate in spectacular fashion, soon enough.)

Exile

Moses grows up in Pharaoh's palace, into a young man, and his spiritual nature of a prince and a judge in the way of law and punishment is strong. One day, he sees injustice taking place, as an Egyptian is beating a Hebrew man. Without thinking, he strikes out with a punishment, and he kills the Egyptian. Now, his true identity and his loyalty to the Hebrews is exposed, and he has to escape before he is killed by the Pharaoh. He goes to Midian and is looked after by the priest of Midian. He lives there for many years and he marries a daughter of the priest, and has two sons. Remember these two sons, because their true identity is going to be as well hidden as their father's, and they will stand out as being very important to the plan of taking the promised land.

Burning Bush

When the old Pharaoh dies and is replaced, it is time for Moses to return to Egypt. Then Gabriel suffers a problem that comes with her choice to use a king of Darkness. He can't spiritually hear her or understand her, and he has none of her wisdom. Yet it is essential that he can hear her clearly if he is to carry out her instructions and lay down her law, so what can she do? She doesn't speak through her spirit of Yhwh like a normal prophet, she speaks to Moses face to face. Normally, no man could stand before her without being killed by the Holy Spirit of fire, which destroys everything which is unclean. But Moses is manifesting the Messianic spirit of the Sun, and he has been given a spiritual covering for his sins through the mercy of Gabriel, so he is safe before Gabriel. Therefore, Gabriel appears to Moses in the spiritual world, manifesting as her spirit of fire, a burning bush, and he sees her, stops and goes to her. She speaks to him face to face, and he hears and obeys. Another problem has been overcome. She tells him that it is time to go back to Egypt and to free her people.

The next problem is authority. The authority of Moses will certainly be ignored by the Serpent and the Pharaoh. So Gabriel gives Moses a spirit of authority which is a wooden staff. This gives him the heavenly and divine authority of Yhwh. The higher he raises the staff, the more authority he will have. At its lowest level his authority will be at the level of the Serpent (flat on the land) and can even look like a living Serpent to make the point. At its highest level, he will have authority over the angel armies in heaven and earth. They will fight on his behalf, and he will win against any earthly army. The problem of authority and lack of an army has been overcome.

Yet Moses is not confident, and he doesn't want the job! He complains that he has poor speech, which is because whenever Gabriel is not with him, he can't hear her telling him what to say. In other words he can't speak the word of Yhwh because he can't hear it. Gabriel tells him to go with his brother Aaron, who is a Levite and a priest. Priests have a spiritual link to Gabriel so they hear her voice to guide them in their priestly duties; thus Aaron can speak on behalf of Moses. A fourth problem has been overcome. However, although we don't know it yet, this solution of Moses hearing Yhwh through Aaron, leaves an opening for the Serpent which will soon lead to a terrible downfall of the Hebrews.

There is one last problem with Moses's spiritual identity as a man of Darkness, which goes back to the first creation and the line of Enoch. He is not from the line of Abraham, so he is not circumcised and cannot be circumcised. This is a problem for Gabriel, because soon there is going to be a purge of the firstborn sons and the Egyptian army, therefore the chosen people will need to be passed over by the heavenly warriors who will carry out the purges. The mark of the chosen people is circumcision, so everyone who is circumcised will be recognised and passed over. However, Moses, who is spiritually a firstborn and a man of Darkness, like the target, will not be recognised as a Hebrew, or passed over and so he will die with the Egyptians. So, on the journey back to Egypt, Gabriel blocks Moses and his family on the road, and seeks to kill him, as a warning. But she gives a solution too, and she speaks it to his wife, who can hear her. His wife circumcises Moses's son and then touches Moses with the blood, which Gabriel accepts and lets them pass.

What is that all about? It means that now, the mark of those chosen and passed over is not circumcision, it is the blood. Not just any blood, but the blood of the son of the Messiah Sun in Moses, who has been circumcised and will be redeemed. So now, the mark of the redeemed who will be passed over, is the blood of the Messiah, who is their redeemer, because, as we know, the Sun redeems them through his own sacrifice. In the Passover event, this will be symbolised by sacrificing a lamb and marking all the doors of the Hebrews with 'the blood of the lamb'. Therefore, the mark of the Passover has become the blood of the sacrificial lamb, and circumcision is not required. A fifth problem has been overcome.

This may appear to be a strange and apparently a minor side story, but the consequences are huge. Now, the redeemed Gentiles who are uncircumcised, have been added to the Hebrews to be passed over from all the future purges. In the future, the blood of the sacrificial lamb, will be the blood of Jesus. To complete this difficult passage, I should say that the blood of Jesus is actually a code for the Holy Spirit of Jesus. Therefore, you receive salvation into heaven, either through the circumcision of redemption or the blood of the Holy Spirit. Both will give you Passovers during a purge, and both of them involve the Messiah. More of that, later.

The 10 judgements and 'plagues', and the Passover
Back in the story, we have not reached the Passover yet. When Moses returns, he sets himself and Aaron the task of compelling the Pharaoh to let the people of Yhwh go. There is a pattern, or a cycle, starting with a command to let the people go, then a warning of a punishment if he doesn't, then when he refuses, the punishment

takes place. There are 10 such judgements, and they are judgements of fire from Yhwh, ending in a purge. As such, the cycles show that before a purge, Yhwh applies as much mercy as possible. First, she offers opportunities to repent and receive a full pardon, then she delivers warnings which escalate in severity over the cycles and are visible to the Serpent and especially to the people, who don't like what they see. Each time, the punishment is for disobeying a command from Yhwh.

These 10 cycles of judgements, become the principles of escalating judgements leading up to a purge, which are repeated in later ages too. The principles still stand today.

Moses and Aaron started with minor demonstrations of authority, using their staffs at ground level, at the same level as the Serpent's authority. But the Pharaoh scoffed because he and his magicians could do the same with their own authority from the Serpent. Soon the staffs rose higher and the punishments became stronger, requiring higher authority, which could not be matched by the Pharaoh. These are the famous 'biblical plagues', like frogs and gnats and turning rivers to blood and so on. They are all spiritual plagues and happen in the spirit world, and they all have spiritual and angelic meanings. But they do impact the physical world to varying extents, and they cause discomfort of rising levels. However, the Serpent has no sympathy for any discomfort suffered by her followers, and continues to refuse to release Yhwh's people, continuing the cycles, and letting them suffer. She does begin to try to negotiate terms for partial releases, but Moses rejects most of them. Where he accepts them, she then goes back on her word to release the people. A repentance and an agreement must be genuine if it is to be accepted. If it is broken, then the punishments continue to escalate. This principle remains true today, for example an insincere regret for armed conflict followed by a broken ceasefire agreement which results in loss of trust and greater conflict.

Moses Frees the Chosen People 153

Another example of this principle which will be seen in future end of age purges, is when someone who accepts authority under a greater force rebels against it. This is a serious breach and results in serious consequences involving death and destruction in the physical world. I will regularly warn us as we approach our own end of age purge, not to rebel, because Yhwh has got this and nobody has to die. In all the previous cycles, Yhwh clearly gave this warning through prophets, but sadly, she was ignored. I hope we learn from their mistakes and do better this time. We must remember that if we make an agreement we must keep it, and if we agree to be under authority we must not rebel. That's because at the end of the age, Yhwh is getting us out of the mess we largely put ourselves in, and will use her secret weapon with his forces, to do so. When you rebel against them, you rebel against Yhwh, which is not such a good idea, because it puts you on the wrong side of the purge.

Back in the story, after the ninth punishment, heavenly angelic warriors have been deployed on earth, causing famine and devastation, but avoiding the chosen people. It's easy to miss, but they do not leave, they only move away, and they remain available for a future purpose, waiting at the Red Sea. The Pharaoh still does not concede. It is time for the purge, the tenth judgement, which requires Yhwh's divine authority, and is to be a surprise. Therefore, Moses does not give a warning, he is told only to prepare for the Passover. What happens next will come as a surprise to those affected, just like every purge. The people prepare to leave Egypt in haste, they sacrifice and eat a lamb, and they put the blood on the doorposts so it is visible to any angel who tries to enter the house. It is night time, the time of fire, and a mighty angel of fire sweeps through Egypt, killing only the first born sons, but not touching the redeemed.

Why are the firstborn sons purged?

The purge of the firstborn is a disaster for the Serpent. These are her heirs, and now her inheritance has been lost. Where does it go to now? In this specific case, what that means is quite difficult to explain, especially in what is meant to be the most straightforward book! But it's worth the effort to understand it because it is an opportunity to reveal a deeply hidden mystery which shows how clever and far-reaching Yhwh's hidden plans really are. If this short dive into the deeper mysteries is too much too soon, don't worry, just put this section to one side and keep on going.

This is about who will inherit the earth, either the line of the Sun or the line of the Moon.

First, we must remember the Moon's and the Sun's twins, the generation who took their lines onto earth. There was a bitter dispute about who would take the inheritance. It was supposed to be in the line of the Sun in his house, but the Moon stole it by manipulating her son, in her house, to be the firstborn. Her son was the Lion, and the sons of the Lion became the powerful kings of the earth, under the Serpent. One of these kings is the Pharaoh of Egypt. His line and his inheritance also pass through his firstborn, and so the inheritance of Darkness continues in Egypt.

What Yhwh has just done is to end that line of inheritance. Where does it go?

Now we can see that in the absence of the firstborn, the inheritance passes to the second born son of the twins, which is the line of the Sun. Therefore, the inheritance of Egypt has passed from Darkness to Light. Yhwh has defeated the Serpent.

What does all that look like in practice? Let's go back to the time of Joseph when the Hebrews settled in Egypt. At that time, the Hebrews were free people, with free food, and were not under the Serpent or enslaved by the Serpent. Equally important, the Egyptian people who were in debt and enslaved by the Pharaoh, were secretly under the Sun. Why? Because the Pharaoh was in the line of Enoch and Nimrod who secretly had the Messianic spirit of the Sun. That meant that at this time, Egypt and the Hebrews were under the Sun,

Moses Frees the Chosen People   155

not the Serpent, and the previous inheritance of Egypt had passed to the Sun. It also meant that the Hebrews were safe.

Therefore, at the start of this story, Egypt, which was thought to be a nation under one of the Serpent's kings of the earth and therefore a stronghold for the Serpent, was actually under the Messiah king, the Sun. This means that not only was this a great place for the Hebrews to be safe and grow, the people of Egypt were also free from the Serpent and under the Messiah. The Pharaoh has happily agreed to this because the deal has made his country greater and he is personally much richer. This is the principle that was agreed with Enoch at the beginning of his line. So far so good.

Now we can see that when we move on to the new Pharaoh in the time of Moses, the new Pharaoh has reverted to a typical king of the earth under the Serpent. He has broken the agreement made with his predecessor, and the Serpent enslaved the Hebrews and stole back their inheritance for Darkness. Likewise, the Egyptian people are the serpent's people again. Bad news, because the Serpent has stolen the inheritance of Egypt back again.

The next step is for Yhwh, through Moses, to take back what was rightfully hers. She has freed her people from the Serpent, and she has put the people of Egypt back under the Sun too. The inheritance has passed back to Light and the authority has reversed, so that Light rules Darkness. Good news.

However, an important message here is that the Serpent rebelled against Yhwh's authority and the inheritance had to be taken by force. She thought she was invincible because she had the greatest army, but the battle was not won by earthly warriors, it was won by heavenly angel warriors, and the Serpent was defeated. This will be repeated all the way up to our own time and our own Armageddon to come. We will see that a rebellion precedes Armageddon, but we also see that the rebellion does not have to happen.

In the final twist, we know that the Pharaoh in the time of Joseph was Yhwh's secret weapon in the line of Enoch, but who is the leader now? Moses, and he is also in the line of Enoch. Therefore, the inheritance has been returned to the same line, negating everything that the Serpent did. However, the battles over the inheritance are far from over yet, and the Serpent never stays down for long.

The Exodus

Back in the story, the death of the firstborn sons is too much for Pharaoh, so he frees the people of Yhwh and tells Moses to take them away. They are already prepared to go in their houses, and they leave straight away. Strangely, the Egyptians give them their riches, gold and silver and precious stones. Why do they do this? Because they are now under Moses too and they do what he asks. This is an example of the reversal of authority which, we will see, always comes after the purge. The riches of the Serpent are also willingly changed hands.

But Gabriel has not finished dealing with all of her original problems. The Egyptian army is intact and still very strong, and she has no physical army to match them amongst her people. By now, the Serpent would know that the people of Yhwh are well on their way to take back the promised land, and she will have persuaded the Pharaoh to attack and destroy them with his army. In turn, Yhwh knows that if she is to be successful, she must destroy the Egyptian army. But how?

Gabriel already has a plan, and she has already set up an ambush for the Egyptian army. And, of course, another Passover event for her people.

The Red Sea

Yhwh led the people away from Egypt, along the route she chose. She allowed the people to see herself in her angelic forms; a pillar of a cloud of water during the day, and a pillar of fire at night, which became a pillar of Darkness during the day as the fire rested. There are two pillars and both contain Yhwh. The cloud is clearly the

Moses Frees the Chosen People 157

water of Yhwh, and the pillar is Gabriel. The fire is her Holy Spirit of fire. The hidden significance of this is that the three Messianic identities are all present and active. The Sun is in Moses, Gabriel, the angel and word of Yhwh is in the pillar of cloud and the divine Holy Spirit is in the pillar of fire, and they never leave their people.

Gabriel chose to lead them to the banks of the Red Sea towards the north, at a narrow and dangerous crossing point. Waiting for them, in the spiritual world, was a vast angel army. In the physical world they looked like upright red reeds which give the Red Sea its name (the 'Red Sea' actually means the sea of red reeds or rushes), but in the spiritual world they were upright guardian angels of fire. Guardian angels interlink to form a 'wall' around whatever they are protecting, and they fight for God, under the command of the Sun. And Moses had the spirit of the Sun and the staff to give him the necessary authority. There was another army there too, an army, called 'locusts' in the spiritual world, who had been used for the eighth plague and had then withdrawn to the Red Sea and waited there. The two armies together, the reeds and the locusts, were against the Egyptians and for the Hebrews, and were invincible under the authority of Moses and Yhwh.

With the trap set, Gabriel waited there and sure enough, the Pharaoh had changed his mind and he had sent his army to destroy the people of Yhwh. They were spotted and they drew closer and closer, until Gabriel was ready to execute her plan. She and her Holy Spirit moved from the front of the people where they were leading, to the rear, between her people and the Egyptian army, so they could protect them. They waited for night, when the fire would manifest and it lit up the night. This would normally be the time of the Serpent's power, but Gabriel is proving a point. She is now the supreme God in this land (or rather earth), the Elohiym at night, and her divine Holy Spirit will outrank and overpower the Serpent.

Gabriel told Moses to raise his staff, and when he did, the warriors in the sea parted ranks to let them through, making a wall of guardian soldiers on both sides to protect them, aided by the wind of the Holy Spirit from Heaven. The people walked through them in safety.

Then the Egyptian army followed them, and the two armies of the locusts and the reeds attacked them and overwhelmed them, and they were destroyed. Just like the 'sea' overwhelmed the wicked people in Noah's flood. This time, there was no Passover in an ark or by marking their doorposts, but there was still a Passover to keep the people of Yhwh safe. They 'passed over' using the passage of safety, made for them alone by the Red Sea reed guardians, and so they escaped the purge which followed.

Already we can see that the mystery of the purges is becoming clearer as a pattern emerges. It is a cycle which uses a heavenly and earthly army working together with the Holy Spirit of fire, to defeat the Serpent, and always provides a means of safety for the people of Yhwh.

Once the people had passed over and the Egyptian army was defeated, they continued on their way towards the promised land, led by the two angelic pillars, while the Serpent was so weakened, she could do nothing to stop them. Except, of course, to try to persuade the people to turn from Yhwh, to fall, and to worship the Serpent. And that was the biggest weakness of Yhwh's plan. During their time in Egypt, most of the people had been swayed by the Egyptians and taken up some of their customs and practices. Including the deadly idolatry. Therefore, most of the people already had the spirit of the Serpent in them, and when they were saved in the Passover, so was the spirit of the Serpent in them. Yhwh was relying on them accepting the authority of Moses, so the spirit would not manifest. She then intended to quickly introduce a new set of laws for them to follow, which would ensure they avoided the wickedness of the Serpent, especially idolatry, while they were in the promised land. It was to be known as the Law of Moses.

Chapter 10

The Law of Moses

The Law and the Prophets

This law was essential because of one overwhelming problem. Since Adam rejected the Holy Spirit in the Garden, the people had largely been spiritually blind, deaf and dumb. Three of the spirits which come with the Holy Spirit are Counsel, Understanding and Wisdom, and the people did not have them. So they could not hear Yhwh themselves, and if they heard the word of Yhwh from the few others who could, they did not understand it. And they did not have the spiritual wisdom to know what to do with it in any event.

So the Law was to be introduced to replace the Holy Spirit. In summary, it would tell them what to do and what not to do, even if it was followed blindly, with no idea of the purpose of the rules.

In addition to the Law, which dealt with generalities, Yhwh would speak to the people and their kings through prophets, to give specific guidance and warnings, especially when they lost their way. Thus, 'the Law and the Prophets' came to the chosen people at this time, and both of them came through Moses, who became the first of the prophets as well as the lawgiver.

Scripture

Moses didn't stop there. Through face to face contact with Gabriel, the word of Yhwh, he was able to write down what Gabriel told him, word for word, as she dictated it. This became scripture and was part of 'the prophets'. It was Moses who wrote the first five books of the Bible, from creation to the Law. All the remaining scripture was also given by Gabriel, and was usually started with 'and the word of Yhwh came to …'. That means that Gabriel came to the prophet. All scripture comes from Gabriel. For example, it was Gabriel who passed down the Quran to the prophet Mohamed, as scripture given to the Muslims.

The Law, Prophets and Scripture are there to replace the Holy Spirit, but only until it comes

Scripture is spiritual knowledge, and it was also given in the place of the Holy Spirit. A fourth spirit which comes with the Holy Spirit, is called 'Knowledge' which is spiritual knowledge, given directly by Yhwh to individuals according to their need. The original plan was for mankind to receive the Holy Spirit, and with it they would hear the word of Yhwh, receive the true spiritual knowledge, understand it and have the wisdom to know what to do with it. Then he would speak it and spread the word. When Adam and Eve rejected the Holy Spirit, mankind lost all these spiritual gifts and was blind, deaf, dumb, ignorant and lame regarding the spiritual world. That describes the majority of us, even today.

However, Moses has replaced counsel, knowledge, understanding and wisdom, through the law, the prophets and scripture, but the people are still spiritually blind. All they have to do is blindly obey what they are told to do until the Holy Spirit comes. When that happens, the Law will be fulfilled, there will be no more prophets, and there will be no more scripture. Instead, it will be received by individuals directly through the Holy Spirit. This is why scripture and law and prophets had stopped at the end of Revelation, the last book of the Bible. It is not because it foretold the end of the world!

Jesus will introduce the Holy Spirit and fulfil the Law

In case this sounds academic and somewhat irrelevant to us, let me skip forwards for a moment. All of this has already happened. The story is still in the third age here, but in the fifth age Jesus came to prepare us for the sixth and seventh age, when the Holy Spirit, would be released to mankind and everything would change. He demonstrated what it would be like. He made the blind see, the deaf hear, the mute speak and the lame walk (to spread the word). He fed us directly with spiritual knowledge. He took away the sins of people and made them clean again. He showed us what the new covenant of mercy would look like in practice, including no more judgements. Then he confirmed that the people of Light would inherit the earth, and what the final purge of the spirit of the Serpent would look like. Then he demonstrated the salvation to heaven that you get when you become holy through the Holy Spirit. And he confirmed that he would fulfil the Law of Moses after the ages of Darkness when the work of Darkness would rest, but Jesus would work, because he would be the 'Lord of the Sabbath' in the kingdom of Light. Every word he spoke was the 'word of Yhwh', who was in him and one of his three spiritual identities.

But at that time, most people did not know him or understand him or have the wisdom to know what to do with what he said and did.

When Jesus died, we entered the sixth age and the Holy Spirit was released. Counsel, knowledge, understanding and wisdom flowed into a small group of mankind. Then, in the seventh age, the old covenants and the Law of Darkness were fulfilled and the new covenant of Light came. There were no more prophets, and scripture stopped. There has been no scripture or prophets for nearly 2,000 years, other than the scripture given to the Muslims. So hopefully, we can see that what Moses did to help mankind get through the ages of Darkness and the conflicts with the Serpent was far from academic and irrelevant. But we should also realise that it was meant to be temporary, and replaced by the Holy Spirit.

This time, we must be prepared to make the most of the Holy Spirit when it is offered to us, with all of its gifts.

Mysteries hidden in scripture

Now, the scripture of the word of Yhwh, including the Law, contained many secrets which were only for the people of Light and must not be revealed to the people of the Serpent. They were buried so deeply in hidden code and hidden riddles, that most people wouldn't even see they existed, so they could only be revealed through the spirit of Understanding and considerable perseverance when the time came. But the people did not have Understanding.

However, the plan was for their kings to be able to understand some of these secrets, those which were relevant to their rule, and would help them and guide them. But they must be very careful how they used them, and they must not explain them to the people. That's because most of the people were filled with the spirit of the Serpent and were people of Darkness. However, the meaning of the mysteries was only to be given to people of Light.

If the kings did pass the mysteries on, so that later generations who would have the Holy Spirit would understand them, they had to be buried again in the same way, so as not to be understood until then. Therefore, if the mysteries hidden in code and riddles were to be revealed to an individual king, then they would know that they must be rewritten in more codes and riddles.

And so, that was what was done.

In the event, Yhwh only released her mysteries to a couple of kings. David will rebury what was revealed to him in his psalms, and his son Solomon, famous for his wisdom, reburied what was revealed to him in his proverbs, where he largely compares the wise (who had the Holy Spirit) with the foolish (who did not). When Solomon fell and it became apparent that the kings could not handle the power of the mysteries, the Holy Spirit and Understanding was withdrawn even from the kings.

It stayed like that for centuries, until the Holy Spirit came, in the sixth age of the Apostles. The apostles, especially Peter, John and Paul, gained very deep levels of understanding of all the mysteries, then they buried them again in their letters, using code and riddles which nobody understood – except their followers who also had received the Holy Spirit and with it, Understanding.

Meanwhile, the Serpent will release her own counsel, knowledge, understanding and wisdom to her own people through her own spirit, most of which is false, and none of it explains that she does not give any salvation to heaven to her followers. But it does bring great riches and pleasures while they live on earth. Just a reminder, the Serpent and the Moon is also known as Satan or the devil, the enemy, and other names. I use the name of the Serpent for continuity between creation and end times.

Modern times
So what is the relevance to us, today? As I have previously explained, in the last 2,000 years we have gone through another cycle with six ages of Darkness, and we have lost most of what we had. There is almost no Understanding today, so that we are back to where we were at the start of the sixth age, the age of the Apostles. Now, we are nearing the end of the sixth age. As before, the mysteries are being revealed in depth, but this time Yhwh has decided not to bury them again, but to publish them so they will be revealed to everyone with an enquiring mind. This has never happened before.

The purpose is so that we will understand and be prepared for the coming purge and passover, and the amazing age of Light which will follow it.

Now let's return to the story and read it in that light.

The Law of Moses – the ten commandments
Almost everyone has heard of the ten commandments, which are at the centre of the Law. Now that we know the purpose of the Law, let's look at them again.

Gabriel looked down at her people, and she was worried. She saw the spirit of the Serpent in almost everyone, and how it would manifest as soon as the authority of Moses was questioned. Gabriel needed to introduce laws to supress the spirit of the Serpent, and she needed the Serpent's spirits to know that the laws were targeted on them, not Yhwh's people. After all, law and punishment were always meant for creatures of Darkness, not Light.

She came down onto a mountain, allowing herself to be seen and making a great display of her force and power, speaking in the hearing of the people with the terrifying sound of angelic thunder and trumpets, with fire and lightning. It was a deliberately frightening display and as she expected, the people were in fear of her. Especially, the spirits of the Serpent who she needed to be trembling. They were all too scared to hear her voice again, so they cried out to Moses to hear on their behalf, which was exactly what Gabriel wanted them to do. Now, Moses would be the source of their spiritual knowledge, not the Serpent.

She called Moses to come up the mountain alone to be with her, face to face. She covered him in spiritual linen, the opaque spiritual covering of mercy which hid his sins and allowed direct contact between them. Then she spoke to him in words he could clearly hear and understand. She explained that she was going to lay down ten commandments and they would be written on two tablets of stone. Now the heart of the spirit of the Serpent was made of living stone. It was this that hardened the hearts of the people of Light, so that they became people of Darkness. So, by writing on tablets of stone, she would symbolically write these commandments on their spirits of the Serpent and on their hard hearts.

She explained to Moses that in the seventh age, when the spirit of the Serpent was no longer present in the people of Light, their spiritual hearts would be made of flesh. Then, she would write a new covenant of Light on their hearts of flesh, which was the covenant of mercy. At that time, their stone hearts would be gone, and the Law written on them and the old covenant of Law, would have served its purpose and be fulfilled. Until that time, the Law she was about to lay down would stand. This message about the coming change of hearts would be repeated many times after Moses, by the prophets to come – but no one would understand it until the Holy Spirit came.

The first tablet had five commandments, which if they were obeyed would lead to the inheritance of the earth and authority over Darkness. Hence these were commandments of blessing and mercy for her own people. The second tablet had five commandments of things you should not do, which if they were disobeyed would lead to no inheritance or authority, but instead they would serve the people of Light. These were all the things the spirit of the Serpent would wish to do, against the people of Yhwh, and if she did break the commandments to do them, there would be punishments. Serious punishments, including death. But these were aimed at the spirit of the Serpent, not the people of Yhwh.

Likewise, in keeping with the established principles of judgement, whatever commandments were broken by Yhwh's people if they arose from the temptation and influence of the Serpent, would fall on the Serpent. Not the sinner, but the person responsible for the sin. Also, now that they were written on their hearts, there was no excuse for not knowing about them and not obeying them. All of these commandments therefore deflected punishment to the spirit of Darkness resulting in them being acts of mercy for the people of Light. That is why the commandments were written on two tablets of five each. Why? Was it because the writing was too big for one stone? Or one stone was too heavy for Moses to carry?

No, this is a mystery hidden in the number code. We will look at this in more depth in Book Two, but if you look at Appendix One at the end of the book, you will see that five is the number code for mercy, and two is the number code for Yhwh and her way of Light. You will also see that 10 is the number of judgement and one is the number of the way and Law of Darkness. So, when you put these numbers together, they tell you a story. If you look at all **ten** commandments in **one** set of laws, then this is a set of Laws from the way of Darkness (1), which would result in judgement (10) and fire for whoever is under these laws. This applies to the spirit the Serpent in the people, since it is the spirit of Darkness under the Law and punishment. Therefore, every sin which originates from the Serpent will be judged and punished on the Serpent.

However, if you look at **five** commandments in **two** sets, the numbers tell us that these are actually a set of laws for the people of the way of Light (2) from Yhwh, which lead to no judgement (10), only mercy (5), for the people of Light. If they commit sins by breaking these commandments, the sin will either fall on the Serpent or it will be redeemed by the Messiah. That gives a completely different purpose for the Law.

The people may not have understood this, but Moses did, and the Serpent certainly did.

Gabriel knew that the biggest threat to her people was idolatry. She would tell Moses to emphasise this over and again in his teachings, and she placed idolatry at the very start of her laws. This message would be repeated by the future prophets too. There was a good reason for Gabriel's concern – every person who committed idolatry was worshipping, and sacrificing offerings to, the Serpent, not Yhwh. That meant that the divided house of Israel was losing numbers from Yhwh's side and gaining numbers on the Moon's (or the Serpent's) side. It is one thing to have the spirit of Darkness from birth through no fault of your own, but it is much worse to freely choose to worship the Serpent and reject Yhwh. You really would not want to switch sides from two tablets of mercy to one tablet of fire.

Gabriel knew this, and she also realised that most of the people did not realise that they were following and worshipping the Serpent. Without spiritual understanding, how could they? And that is where the Law comes in. You don't need to understand why you shouldn't commit idolatry, you simply obey the law. She knows that her people are going to go through a torrid time in the remaining ages of Darkness, and this is how she can help them get through it.

There are very many laws, which all have the same objectives, but here are the first four of the ten commandments as examples:

The first commandment forbids anything that puts any god above Yhwh, which includes idolatry. *'I am Yhwh your supreme God who brought you out of the land of Egypt, out of the house of slavery. You shall have no other God before me.'* It implies that Yhwh has just freed you from the slavery of the house of the Serpent in Egypt, so why would you put yourself back into its slavery?

The second commandment expressly forbids idolatry. *'You shall not make for yourself a carved image, or any likeness of anything that is in heaven above or that is in the earth beneath or that is in the water under the earth. You shall not bow down to them or serve them ...'*

Then it goes on to explain why they should stay on her side of the divided house of Israel, *'... for I, Yhwh your Supreme God am a jealous God, visiting the iniquity of the fathers on the children to the 3rd and 4th generation of those who hate me, but showing loving mercy to thousands of those who love me and keep my commandments.'* Those that hate Yhwh are on the Serpent's side of the house of Israel, who will receive punishment up to the end of the fourth age. (The fifth age is the first age of mercy, when Jesus comes.) Those that love Yhwh are on her side of the house of Israel the house of Mercy. The description of 'a jealous God' is because idolatry is like having an adulterous affair with another false god.

The third commandment concerns the spirit and Holy Spirit of Yhwh which (like Adam) you reject in favour of the spirit of the Serpent if you follow the Serpent and especially when you commit idolatry. The consequences are to lose your forgiveness and salvation. *'You shall not take the name of Yhwh your Supreme God in vain, for Yhwh will not hold him guiltless who takes his name in vain.'* Actually 'name' is a code word which always means 'spirit' and vain means 'desolation and ruin'. So this commandment means do not remove the spirit or Holy

Spirit of Yhwh leaving your spiritual self desolate and empty, and ruined. When you lose this spirit you lose the spirit of Light and you lose your mercy and especially your holiness and salvation, and so you will not be held guiltless, and your guilt will remain.

The fourth commandment is straightforward. *'Remember the Sabbath say, to keep it holy. Six days you shall labour and do all of your work, but the 7th day is a Sabbath to Yhwh your Supreme God. On it, you shall not do any work, you, or your son or your daughter, your male servant or your female servant or your livestock or the sojourner who is within your gates. For in 6 days Yhwh made heaven and earth, the sea, and all that is in them and rested on the 7th day. Therefore, Yhwh blessed the Sabbath day and made it holy.'* The whole point of the Law is to get to the seventh age as a person of Light, filled with the spirit of Yhwh and her Holy Spirit when it comes. Then you will not be judged and you will be saved to heaven because you are Holy. In fact, the whole age is Holy. It is 'blessed' to ensure that you will receive your promised inheritance. The 'work' is the work of Darkness which will not be done on the seventh day of Light. This extends to your whole household, for which you are responsible. However, on the Sabbath day, the people of Light will be working hard to bring salvation. The rest of the ten commandments, and indeed the whole of the Law and the prophets that comes with them, continues in this vein. For example, the law also looks forward to when the Hebrews will be freed from slavery and all covenants will end, in a 'Jubilee year', referring to the coming age of mercy and Light. Also, all the festivals look backwards to celebrate key events, but they also look forward to cycles of these same events in the future, specifically judgement day and the new covenants with the new law of Light. For example, there will be many Passovers to celebrate in the future, not just the one that happened in Egypt. Jesus dies to redeem sins on the festival of Passover, and redemption is an example of a Passover event. Also, the festival of Pentecost celebrates the giving of the Law by Moses, but it is also when the Holy Spirit is released in the sixth age, and the

Holy Spirit comes to fulfil and replace the old Law with the new, as we will see later.

The law is detailed and takes up four books of the Bible. Rather than trying to summarise it here, let's hear how Moses and Jesus summarised it:

Quoting Moses, Jesus condenses the Law and the prophets into two commandments. He says *'You shall love Yhwh your supreme God with all your heart with all your soul and with all your mind. This is the great and foremost commandment. And a second is like it: You shall love your neighbour as yourself. On these 2 commandments depend all the Law and the Prophets.'*

We will see later that 'Neighbour' is a code word for the Messiah and specifically the Holy Spirit of the Messiah. So Jesus is saying that the people should love Yhwh and her Messiah. If you do, you will reject the Serpent and be a person of Light with everything that brings. Then they will love you back and bless you and forgive you and save you into heaven. Both these core commandments are saying that for the people of Yhwh, the Law and the prophets have nothing to do with fire, only love. That is correct, because what they don't say is that the fire of the Law is reserved for the Serpent.

The Golden Calf

The Serpent was furious and her hatred burned. Losing the battle of Egypt and her whole army was a deep blow, but she had already come up with a counter-attack, to spread her darkness in the house of Yhwh through idolatry. But now, these commandments were going to cause a real problem for her. She thought the insult of writing them on her heart was just too much. Moses had received a great deal of the Law from Gabriel over the last few weeks and he passed them down to the people who had gathered before him. The people swore to obey the Law, including the ten commandments. Then Moses and his assistant, Joshua, were called to the mountain to receive more law and the ten commandments written on tablets of stone, by the finger of Gabriel herself.

The Serpent had noticed that when Moses was not in authority, the people tended to grumble and argue and rebel as her spirit manifested in them. She fully intended to milk that weakness in the near future, and if she got enough supporters, she knew she could incite a full blown rebellion. The problem was that Moses kept a tight rein on his people and exerted his authority constantly. But while Moses was focused on receiving the Law from Gabriel, he wasn't focusing on his people. Actually, he wasn't even near his people. This was certainly the time to strike. But how could she start a rebellion which would spread?

She saw that Moses had left his brother Aaron in charge while he was away, and she knew that it was Aaron who heard the word of Yhwh for Moses when he was not face to face with Gabriel. And there it was, the solution to her problem. Aaron wasn't with Moses. Aaron, like virtually everyone else, had the spirit of the Serpent in him, but it was normally suppressed by Moses. Now, in his absence, it would manifest and when the Serpent spoke to him, he would hear her voice. But he would think he was hearing the voice of Yhwh, like normal. It was a simple enough deception for the Serpent, and she was very good at deceptions, especially pretending to be Yhwh. She set her plan in motion.

The Serpent told a few of her followers to gather around Aaron and tell him to make gods for them to go before them. 'To go before them', is like describing the cloud and pillar of fire leading them, so Aaron thought they were talking about making images to Yhwh, and that it was Yhwh speaking to them. Then the serpent spoke directly to Aaron and he thought it was Yhwh giving him instructions. He told her to go ahead and tell him what she wanted him to do.

The serpent was delighted, because she knew exactly what she wanted him to do. She told him that the gold from the people of Egypt was unclean and was causing problems for the people of Yhwh. For example, the earrings were speaking the word of the Serpent into the ears of the people. He must gather the gold from the people and cleanse it with fire, until it melted. Then he should engrave it into a figure of a golden calf, which she said symbolised herself, Yhwh, and in his role of the priest to Yhwh, he should make offerings to it to make right the wrongs the gold had done. So Aaron thought the calf symbolised Yhwh, but it was actually an idol to the Serpent. He made the golden calf and he made an altar before it and he said, '*Tomorrow shall be a feast to Yhwh.*'

The next morning he presented burnt offerings and peace offerings, and as he did, because the authority of Moses was gone, the spirits of the Serpent in the people manifested. They worshipped the idol and ate the meat of the offerings. They drank the sour wine of the Serpent and danced and laughed and played. As did the Serpent. The wave of the manifestation of the Serpent swept through the camp and the numbers of the people who turned from Yhwh to the Serpent reached many thousands. Once again, very soon after Yhwh had purged the Serpent, her people fell and followed the Serpent.

Gabriel saw it from the mountain, and told Moses to go down to his people because they were committing idolatry. She was furious and even considered destroying them all and starting again with Moses, but he persuaded her to relent, and he went down. He threw down the tablets and broke them, symbolising that the covenant with Yhwh was broken, a terrible thing. But it was not Yhwh that broke the covenant, it was her people who had turned from her to worship the Serpent through idolatry. The fact is that idolatry leads to breaking the covenant with Yhwh and establishing it with the Serpent. Sadly, we will see that happening again.

When Moses asked Aaron to explain what he had done, Aaron could not. He only said that he threw the gold into the fire and out came the calf. That didn't mean much to Aaron, but it did to Moses. The calf was a living thing of living gold and it was a creature of fire. Now it was out of the fire and free. The act of putting the gold earrings in the fire had released the Serpent, and Moses saw that the people with the spirit of the Serpent had broken loose too.

What had happened? The gold was not unclean, that was a deception. It was the gold of Yhwh and in the spiritual world, it worked as a spiritual covering over the people's ears, a bit like linen but stronger, like armour. While they wore the earrings, they could not hear the Serpent. As soon as they took them off they freed their spirit to hear the Serpent, and the rebellion took off. It looked like a rebellious people, but it was actually the work of the Serpent.

To limit the damage, Moses asked who was on the side of Yhwh, that is which side of the divided house are they on. Then the house of Levi, Moses's and Aaron's own tribe of priests, went through the camp destroying the rebels. Their spirits went to sleep in Sheol to be redeemed and released at judgement day, but the spirit of the Serpent in them was separated to be condemned. A balance was restored to the house of Israel. But both Yhwh and the Serpent had seen how easy it was for the Serpent to make the people commit idolatry. It would be the first attack of many, and they would become successful, especially in the next age, despite breaking the specific and repeated commandments of Yhwh.

The deceptions of the Serpent are very convincing, especially when she convinces people that they are doing the will of, fighting battles for and teaching the word and Law of Yhwh. Remember that it is the intention of the Serpent to extend the time of Law (Darkness) and also to turn it into the Serpent's corrupt Law. Then, by lying, to persuade the people not to accept the Holy Spirit of Light (again), which will be offered through the Messiah, and against which she has no hope. Until then, however, the Serpent can and will gather followers and wreak havoc.

The first attempt to take the promised land
Moses took another two tablets to Gabriel on the mountain, and the ten commandments were rewritten. More of the Law was given. The people built a tabernacle, according to the new Law of Yhwh, and this became a mobile temple to Yhwh. Yhwh had her people,

and they worshipped their God. But the relationship was fragile. The people prepared to set out towards the promised land, but Moses had to persuade Gabriel to come with them and lead the way. Gabriel had originally planned to dwell with Yhwh's people, staying in an inner part of the tabernacle or a place of meeting where she could meet Moses and Joshua, but she was concerned that her people were so rebellious that she would consume them with fire. But Moses convinced her to come with them.

When they did leave, pockets of rebellions did break out, some major, and they were dealt with by fire and pestilence. This was indeed an age of Darkness and fire. Eventually, they came to the promised land, and prepared to enter it. But the rebellions continued, and even Aaron and Moses's sister Miriam rebelled against Moses and both of them were punished. Gabriel called the people 'stiff necked', meaning they followed the Serpent and they did not turn their heads back to Yhwh. Nevertheless, a group of men from the 12 tribes were told to go into the land and spy it out to see the best way to take it. They went in and came back with reports that it was indeed a good land of milk and honey and grapes. The milk is the spiritual food for new spiritual people of Light, like baby food from Yhwh. The honey was the Law and the grapes were the Holy Spirit to replace the Law. The spies should have seen that it was the perfect place for them to be and grow into a great nation, and they should have trusted Yhwh to give it to them. Especially since Yhwh had even made a specific covenant with them to drive away the people who inhabited the promised land, such as the Canaanites and their branches.

However, they didn't. They refused to enter, fearing the people there. Yhwh was furious again, and once more threatened to destroy them and start again with Moses. But two of the spies, Joshua and Caleb, disagreed and said they would defeat the inhabitants, and they should enter and take the land. These two were younger men, from the generation after Moses.

Yhwh decided not to destroy them, but instead, told them that they must continue to wander through the wilderness for forty years. In that time, all the older, more wicked, generation would die out, leaving the new generation like Joshua and Caleb to enter the land. This was to represent the new generation of Light replacing the old generation of Darkness, and it became a cycle which will be constantly repeated. Even until today. However, it only works if the new generation (or cycle) is different to the old one, and something must make the difference happen. The difference is that the new generation must be brought up differently, they should be under the Messiah and Yhwh, and being taught their true law and covenant.

The teaching is done by Moses, using the spiritual food which Yhwh sends from heaven, including the Law. It's called manna from heaven, or bread of heaven. It tastes sweet like honey, because it has the blessings of the Law in it. In a much later age, the spiritual food will be the new covenant or law of Light taught by the apostles, using the bread of Jesus from heaven. In both cases, there are 40 years for the old generation to die out before the new generation enter the promised land. In the case of Jesus, the 40 years is the sixth age, between his death and his return at the battle of Armageddon.

When Gabriel leads them back to the promised land after 40 years, they are ready, and Joshua and Caleb command a strong and effective army. Moses is old by then, and he is a man of Darkness from the previous generation – a generation of Darkness. He is allowed to see the promised land, but not to enter it. He dies in his old age, a remarkable man of God whose life transformed the lives of many millions of people, both then and now.

The job of taking back the promised land is given to Joshua and Caleb, who are a well-hidden mystery. They are Moses's two secret sons, from his wife Zipporah in Midian. They are from the next generation, but we are still well within the 10 generations of Moses, in the third age.

Chapter 11

Joshua and Caleb take the Promised Land

The angelic armies

Before we carry on with the story, there is another spiritual principle we need to understand. One of the most important mysteries hidden in scripture is the angel armies, or the angelic hosts, from heaven. Their existence is not hidden very deeply, but their different forms and functions are hidden somewhat deeper. The chosen people are about to take the promised land by force and Yhwh has promised that she will lead them and make them victorious. She does so by using angel armies. I could simply say that when Yhwh sends her angelic army, her people will win, but equally importantly, when she doesn't, they will lose. We are just about to see that principle being demonstrated. However, there is much more to these angel armies, and their role is essential in all the battles to date and in the future. Including Armageddon, which we do still need to understand better. So I will go just a little bit deeper here and hopefully, what is about to happen will make much more sense.

It is comparatively easy to imagine a large angelic army covering the spiritual world like invisible locusts. We can probably even understand that when our spiritual eyes are opened so that we can see 'the other side', the angel army becomes visible to us. This will happen a little later. But angel armies of water and the sea are harder to understand. We have already seen the armies of the 'waters' in the 'seas' of Noah's flood, and the parting of the Red Sea, and we can probably just about understand that these 'waters' can flow over the spiritual earth too, overcoming armies such as the Egyptian army. It might help if you understand that there are two types of armies, fire and water, for Darkness and Light. The locust types are warriors of Darkness and the waters are warriors of Light.

But the angel armies don't stop there. There are also water armies in rivers, not just the sea. These form defensive boundaries around areas of land, to protect the people of the land. Hence the river Jordan is a boundary of the promised land, and the warriors of Light that make up the Jordan in the spiritual world are actually a form of guardian angels, who will stop the armies of the Serpent from crossing it. There are other such boundary rivers in the region, including the Nile and the Euphrates. You can describe these guardian angels as forming a 'wall' of water angels around the chosen people. That's what happened in the Red Sea crossing. Thus we have already seen that they stop the people who are not meant to cross, but they open up for the people who are meant to cross.

Are all guardian angels water angels of Light? No. Most are righteous angels of Darkness. These, as always, have souls of spiritual stone rather than water. When these guardian angels of stone surround the people they are protecting on the earth, they form 'walls' of stone. When they surround cities, they are the city walls. But try to remember that these are describing the spiritual world, not the physical world, although what happens in the spiritual world may be reflected in the physical world too.

These spiritual principles should help us to understand what happens next. First, the crossing of the Jordan, when the waters part to let Joshua and the chosen people cross; and second, when the walls of Jericho come tumbling down.

Joshua and the people enter the promised land
Gabriel looked around her and she remembered. Forty years ago, on behalf of Yhwh she had made a covenant with the people. She said she would do marvels that had never happened before in all of

the earth. The people would see her at work, and they would see an awesome thing. She had then covenanted to drive out the tribes occupying the promised land before her people, so long as they did not break their part of the covenant, especially idolatry. When she said that it would be her who drove out the tribes, she meant it. Her and her angel armies.

She had summoned her angel armies, and she looked at them. They were indeed a marvellous and an awesome sight. They were invincible. Forty years ago she had prepared them to go to war, but when the people disobeyed her and refused to enter the promised land, she stood them down. Foolishly and against the command of Moses, when the people realised that they would all die in the wilderness, they tried to take the land anyway. Without the support of Yhwh's angel armies, they quickly lost. Now, 40 years later, the armies were prepared again, and this time, so were the people. They were the next generation. Moses had died, and Joshua was their leader, a great leader and warrior, like his father, Moses.

Guided by Gabriel, he led the people to the bank of the Jordan. When he was ready, the priests entered the waters with the ark of the covenant. This was a large, sealed, box which could be carried by priests, who inserted long carrying poles or handles into it. The ark contains the tablets of the Law, and it is the resting place of the spirit of Yhwh, that is Gabriel, when she is not in the tabernacle. With such precious cargo, it was treated with reverence and was well guarded, so that neither would be lost. Where the ark was, the spirit of Yhwh was, and this would bring victory.

She already had the authority over the army, so Joshua didn't need to raise his staff. Immediately the ark entered the river Jordan on the shoulders of the priests, the waters moving downstream, from well above the crossing place, rose up in a 'heap' of guardian angels, forming a wall and holding back the waters behind them so that the people could cross on dry land. All of Israel crossed over, beside the ark. And when the ark was finally brought over too, the waters continued on their way. In the spiritual world, they were ranks of angels marching along the boundary. By the way, later on, when people will be baptised in the river Jordan, it is these angels who wash them clean of their sins. As you would expect, water angels are angels of Mercy for the people of Yhwh.

The people stopped opposite a city called Jericho. They camped nearby.

Jericho

So did the angel army, waiting patiently and obediently. Jericho had a high and a strong city wall, and it was closed up tightly. Nobody was going in or out and it seemed to be impregnable. Then Gabriel told Joshua that she had already given the city to him, and gave him some very strange instructions about how to get past the wall. His army was to march all the way around the city wall and do so for six days. Then, on the seventh day, seven priests, each with a trumpet, would lead the army to march around the walls seven times, as they blew their trumpets. Then, there would be a final long blast of the trumpet and all the people would shout loudly. As they do so, the wall would fall down.

Joshua does so, and exactly as Gabriel promised, the wall fell down. What happened? All the guardian angel warriors in the wall of Jericho, had watched as the army of Israel marched around them, but they also saw the heavenly angel army marching with them. They knew exactly what would happen on the seventh day and what the seven trumpets and the war cry of the people meant, and they had no intention of fighting against Yhwh, where they would certainly be defeated. They knew that on the seventh day there was to be a change of authority as Light overcame Darkness, so the angels of Darkness simply accepted the fact and surrendered to the army of Light. They 'fell' from the high positions of authority where they stood, to lie below the army of Light, and therefore under the command of Yhwh and her Messiah. They welcomed the people of Israel and offered to serve them.

This sequence of events was, of course, a symbol of the six days of darkness giving way to the seventh day of Light. It is this sequence that will be followed in the lead up to the final battle of Armageddon, as described in Revelation. The city walls that will fall then, are the walls of the old, and by then corrupt, Jerusalem, as Jerusalem and the temple is destroyed. The Serpent will be purged before and during Armageddon, and it is the angel armies that will make the purge.

Ai

The next city was Ai, which was a smaller and easier objective, with only few inhabitants. On the advice of their spies, Joshua sent only about 3,000 men to take the city. They attacked, but to their surprise, they were defeated and fled from the people of Ai. What happened? One of the men of Judah had taken some of the objects of idolatry from Jericho. As we know, this is a major problem for Yhwh, so she needs to make a point. The man had broken their covenant, so as she warned, Yhwh did not send her angel army and did not lead her people. That is why they lost. Joshua repented, the man and his household were dealt with severely, and that closed the matter. They attacked Ai again and with Yhwh's support, they captured it.

The rest of the promised land

Joshua spent the rest of his life fighting the occupants of the promised land, and taking it back for Israel. He had great success, especially at the beginning, but Yhwh had been clear in her covenant that they must not engage with the existing peoples who survived the battles, in any way. They all practiced idolatry and they were all under the Serpent, and they would quickly lead Israel into following their practices. It was like mixing with a people who had a very infectious pestilence. Unfortunately, Israel never managed to clear the land completely, and they did mix to an extent with the inhabitants, so their practices, especially idolatry, spread throughout all Israel. The Law of Moses was neglected, and things went from bad to worse. As the idolatry grew, so did their defeats, until there was a period of almost continual fighting with an enemy that could not be defeated.

Towards the end of Joshua's life, Yhwh allocated the promised land to the 12 tribes, including the land which had not yet been taken. Joshua repeated the strong warnings of Moses against idolatry, and like Moses, he laid out the consequences if they did, specifically exile from the promised land. The spiritual principle is that the promised 'earth' is the place of the people who are covenanted with Yhwh. If they break this covenant and turn to the Serpent, especially through idolatry, they cannot stay in the covenanted earth.

When Joshua died, there was still a considerable area which had not been taken. Sadly, within one generation of his death, all the warnings had been ignored, and idolatry became rife throughout Israel. The taking of the promised land ground to a halt.

One of the unconquered areas was the land of the Philistines. There were regular raids between Israel and the Philistines, for many generations. Including the time of King David, whose battles against them rose to fame in biblical history. But before then, Yhwh introduced an important cycle to demonstrate to the people what had gone wrong and how to fix it. Here is the cycle:

The people turned from Yhwh and were conquered by their neighbours, becoming enslaved by the Serpent. Their suffering increased until they cried out to Yhwh for help. She heard them and brought them a saviour in the form of a warrior leader, who was also their judge. The judge would restore their peace, typically for a period of 40 years, when the people could either continue with Yhwh or turn back to the Serpent, like a test. If they turned back, then the cycle was repeated with a new judge. Like all cycles, if the people in the cycle learned from it, it would get better. But if they didn't, it could get worse. Much worse.

This cycle was actually the thinly disguised story of the six ages of Darkness followed by the Messiah Saviour and judge, who defeated the enemy and brought in the age of Light with its peace and salvation.

The cycles were called the time of the Judges.

Sadly, it turned out that after each success of the Judge and the period of peace that he brought, the people always failed the test and turned back to idolatry and the Serpent, and the cycle continued on to another judge, getting worse each time.

Chapter 12

The Time of the Judges.
Samson and Delilah.
The Greatest Love Story Ever Told

Yhwh and Gabriel were in despair. There had been 12 judges and things were getting worse, not better. The cycle was in a downwards spiral. What would it take to break this cycle? Yhwh's anger was raging, and her fire was growing. But it was not aimed at the people, it was aimed at the Serpent who was causing the suffering of her people. The other side of Yhwh wept for her people, and her mercy flowed. She loved them so much, with the love of a mother for her children, but how could she show them how much she loved them, and how easily they could come back to her, through her way of love? Then Yhwh told Gabriel what to do.

Yhwh decided that the next cycle would still tell the story of the seven ages but this time it would be told differently. It would not be a story of battles and victory or defeat, it would be a love story. It would not be just any love story, it would be the story of her own sacrificial love for her people, even when they rebelled against her. It is the true love story behind the whole seven ages of mankind. From fallen Adam to the sacrifice and redemption of Jesus to the purge of Armageddon to come. In fact, the story of the life of the next judge would be a summary of the story of God's and her Messiah's, sacrificial love for their people and you don't get a stronger love than the original and eternal love of God – which is why I say it is the greatest love story ever told.

Surely her people would see the message of her love for them, and love her once again.

Therefore, the whole story of Samson is a riddle, where everything has another meaning, and to understand the hidden meanings, you need to solve the riddle. This is our first serious riddle of very many to come, and although most of them will be revealed and solved in the next books, this riddle is relatively simple, being about the seven ages, and it is a good example of how to solve the riddles to come. So, I am going to summarise its core meanings here, but I will go into more detail in Book Two.

To reveal that the story of Samson and Delilah hides the love story of the seven ages of the sons of man, I am going to have to reveal some of the key events in the ages yet to come. Especially to uncover that what happens to Samson foretells what will happen to Jesus. Therefore, it comes with a spoiler alert for those who wish to learn about the future ages only when we come to them. They may prefer to come back here, after they have read the whole story. That, I'm afraid, is one of the problems we have with cyclical learning, when you can only understand the beginning when you have understood the end, and vice versa. Anyway, there is a summary of all the seven ages to refer to if you get lost. It can be found in the appendix at the back of the book. I will label the ages as we come to them in the riddle.

You may well be surprised at the accuracy of the description of the events to come, even though they were written and hidden in ancient manuscripts, hundreds of years before they happened. It's difficult to explain that if there is no spiritual world! But it does give us a sense of comfort that although we don't know what is going to happen, God already does.

1. The birth of Samson
The hidden meaning of the story starts right at the beginning, at the creation of the first Adam. Here, Samson represents Adam in

the first age. Now a mystery which we have already revealed, is that Adam had the Messianic spirit of the Sun, so to confirm this, we start with the birth of the Sun. The hidden message in the riddle is that Samson was the Messianic Sun on earth, as was Adam. 'Samson' means 'like the Sun'.

Gabriel chose an elderly married couple, who represent Michael and herself at the birth of the Sun, at the start of the long awaited day of Light during the ages of creation. True to the cycle of the original story, the wife was old and barren and had borne no children while she unknowingly waited for the age of Light. Gabriel came down to her and promised that she would give birth to a son, just like she did to Abram and Sarai before the birth of Isaac, who also had the spirit of the Sun. The son in this story was going to have the strengths and weaknesses of the first Adam, who was also the Sun, but who failed to receive the Holy Spirit in the garden. Thus we will finish up with a man with the spirit of the Sun but no Holy Spirit.

So the old woman's son would have no power or wisdom from the Holy Spirit, but he could gain strength through numbers. He could become a king with a kingdom of followers. The more followers he had, the stronger he would become. There is an important spiritual principle to understand here. In the spiritual world, an angel leader has spiritual connections to all his or her followers. The connection is a spiritual line from the follower to the head of the leader (the place of authority), and it looks like a hair. The followers become the angelic army of the leader, under his command, and it is they who are his strength. So he is the authority, and they are his power – just like the Holy Spirit would have been. If he has a lot of hair, he has a large army and much strength. However, if it is cut off, he is cut off from his followers and loses his strength, making his authority worthless. Baldness in the spiritual world is always a sign of being enslaved.

Now a strange part of the Law of Moses is called the Nazarite vow. A man can make an oath not to drink any wine or strong drink, and not to cut his hair. Therefore, he would become like the first Adam. With no spiritual wine he would not have the Holy Spirit, but he would not have the spirit of the Serpent either, or at least it would not manifest if he did. By never cutting his hair, his followers and his strength would only grow. So Gabriel told the mother to be, that she and her son must not drink any wine or strong drink, and no razor should touch his head. The boy was born, and he was called Samson, 'like the Sun'. He represented the first age of Adam. So far, so good. But what was missing? Adam had 'woman', who although she had been separated from him, she was beautiful and was his first love. She carries the Messianic spirit of Yhwh which became the house of Israel. But she fell and was lost to him, although he never fell out of love with her and wanted her back. Samson (the Sun) is incomplete without her.

2. Samson seeks a beautiful wife

Israel was occupied and under the control of the Philistines. When Samson grew up, he sought a wife. She was a Philistine woman but she was beautiful and Samson loved her. She was, in his eyes, the woman he was missing in his life and who would make him whole, even though she had fallen to become a Gentile under the Serpent.

This represents the second age of Noah. The missing wife is the house of Israel which fell when Canaan, the youngest son of Noah, fell. They became the gentiles, here represented by the Philistines. However, the Sun never forgot the lost Israel, and never stopped loving her or wanting her to be his covenanted 'wife'. She represented Eve in the second age and the following ones too.

3,4. Samson kills a lion

Since the fall, she had been enslaved by the Serpent, so Samson went to set her free and to marry her. This mirrors the third age when Samson represents Moses (who also had the spirit of the Sun), who came to free the chosen people from the Pharaoh, a 'king of the earth'. In the Spiritual World, a king of the earth is a lion. As Samson was going to meet his bride to be, he met a young lion, roaring at him. He killed it with his bare hands, revealing his strength. This represents the purge of the firstborn sons of the Serpent and the defeat of the Pharaoh and the Egyptian army. His strength was the victorious angel armies, under the authority of the Sun (like the staff of Moses). So Samson had plenty of followers and plenty of 'hair'.

A few days later, he passed the carcass of the lion, and saw there was a swarm of bees and honey in it. Honey means the sweet side of the blessings of the Law, and the bees with their stings were the angels who enforced the bitter side of curses and punishment if you break the Law. The most powerful enforcing angel is a large hornet. Samson took the honey without being stung and gave it to his family to eat. This is when Moses laid down the law to the Hebrews, also in the third age, after he had set them free from Egypt.

Samson makes a riddle to hide a mystery

Seven days before his wedding, Samson made up a riddle and gave it to the Philistines in the wedding party. He challenged them to understand it within seven days, and if they could do so he would give them new linen clothes. This represents the writing of scripture from Gabriel to Moses, along with the Law. It will be known as 'the prophets' and usually linked as one with the Law – becoming known as 'the Law and the Prophets'. It contained the mysteries, hidden in riddles, which can only be understood by receiving the Holy Spirit from the Messiah in the future ages. Therefore, the riddles were not supposed to be generally understood until the seventh day, hence Samson's challenge.

When the seventh day came, they would be given salvation, hence the white linen coverings. Using the number code, 30 confirms it is from the Messiah (3). On the seventh day, Samson reveals the meaning of the riddle to his bride to be, but it is only for her, not the Philistines. It is only for the people of Light and must be hidden again from the people of Darkness. This is what the apostles will do in the sixth age.

He tells her. The riddle is '*Out of the eater came something to eat. Out of the strong came something sweet.*' The basic meaning is that the strong eater is the lion and sweet thing to eat is the honey. However, the men forced her to tell them the meaning and Samson is angry. Not with her, but with the Philistines who intimidated her.

They cheated, so he refuses to give them the spiritual linen covering, and he strikes down 30 of the Philistines and gives their clothes to the wedding guests instead. They do nothing to hide their sin, so they do not receive salvation.

5, 6. Samson fights back

Meanwhile, the story continues, 'after some days', which means we skip some days, that is, ages, and we move to the fifth and sixth ages. The status of his bride, Israel, does not change in the rest of the third age and the fourth age – she is still fallen and enslaved under the Serpent. This time the problem is widespread idolatry which is to worship other gods. In the story, Samson still loves his bride, but she has been taken from him and given to the best man, a Philistine, and is still enslaved. Samson now represents Jesus in the fifth age, and he comes to win her back and to marry her and 'go into her'. That means for his Holy Spirit to enter her in the salvation of the Holy Spirit. This is not permitted because she is still under the Serpent and the Holy Spirit is not released yet.

So we continue into the sixth age and what the riddle describes as the time of 'the wheat harvest'. In the riddles, a harvest means salvation, which can either the grape harvest of the wine, which is the salvation of the Holy Spirit, or it can be the wheat harvest of the bread, which is the salvation by redemption. Here it is the salvation of redemption which happens at judgement day, at the end of the sixth age. The sixth age is the age of the apostles, which was an age of great conflict between the Messiah and the Serpent. The Serpent was pushing her own corrupt word and evil ways, through her own corrupt religious leaders and false prophets which lead to death. The Messiah was pushing his true word and good ways, through his own apostles and true prophets which lead to salvation. It was a tough age, fuelled with the Holy Spirit of fire.

In the story, Samson is angry with the Serpent and her people. In a strange passage, he captures 300 foxes and ties their tails together. This describes the conversion of the people of the Serpent in the sixth age. The foxes are the fallen people with a spirit of Darkness (1) in their tails, and he ties them into pairs to make them spirits of Light (2). Then he takes torches, which are the Holy Spirit of fire, and attaches them to their tails. This is when the spirits of the Serpent are cast out and replaced by the Holy Spirit. These are the early converts who hear and preach the word of Yhwh and go out to do so.

They take on the corrupt word of the Serpent directly, and they overcome it and persuade others to join them, and they do so with their Holy Spirits, which are actually the very powerful Holy Spirit of fire. In the story, they destroy the stored grain (spiritual knowledge) of the Serpent, by fire.

The Philistines retaliate and burn Samson's bride and her father, to the fury of Samson, so the conflicts continue. Samson attacks with a great blow on their hips and thighs, meaning the powerful Holy Spirit of fire against the spirit of the Serpent.

7. The final battle

This part of the story concludes after a break, with a great battle against the Philistines, where Samson uses the jawbone of a donkey to strike them down, and he is victorious. This is the start of the seventh age when Jesus returns to win the battle of Armageddon. He fights with his own army of followers (his hair) but he has the alliance of the guardian angels of Ishmael, the Muslims, fighting together with him. They are symbolised by a jawbone because they are a resurrected army, having died and been redeemed. In the Bible Ishmael is known as a wild donkey, which is a compliment, and denotes that he is stubbornly loyal and obedient to God. Samson's own army are also redeemed and resurrected. (The break is significant, because this is when he redeemed them.)

That concludes the story of Samson's first bride. He saves her from her captors and she is redeemed and saved along with the people of Ishmael. But she does not receive the salvation of the Holy Spirit.

Next, the riddle of Samson reveals the story of the people of Judah rather than Israel. It repeats much of the previous story, but from a new perspective, and this technique of multiple views is commonly used in the riddles. Not least in Revelation.

5, 6. *The gates are moved*

It starts with a very strange event. Samson comes to a stronghold of the Philistines (Gaza) and he sees a prostitute and *'went in to her'*. Why would Samson, a righteous man, do this? Because this story starts at the end of the fifth day, when Jesus takes on all the sins of Israel on their behalf and dies for them. The prostitute is Israel who is engaged in idolatry, but Samson still loves her. When he went into her, he received her spirit of the Serpent with all her sins, and he died and redeemed her.

Then, in his Messianic identity of the gatekeeper of heaven, the riddle describes how he outsmarts the Philistines and moves the city gate of Gaza to the top of a hill at Hebron. The symbology of this is that the gate on this hill represents the gate to heaven, but only for the righteous at the top of the hill. The gate at Gaza had been used to keep the people in, as slaves, but now they are freed by Samson and can leave. From the top of the hill, he calls them from their captivity to salvation. This is like the call of the Messiah to the exiles of Israel, to be saved.

We have now moved on to the salvation of the Holy Spirit, and this closes the second part of the riddle.

5. Delilah

We continue with the third part, which tells the story from the perspective of Judah, and we rewind to the fifth age of Jesus, during his ministry and before he dies. At last, we move on to the famous story of Samson and Delilah, and we are looking at how she is offered the salvation of the Holy Spirit, but she rejects it.

There is a woman who lives in the valley of Sorek, which means 'choice vines'. That means she is one of the chosen people who is entitled to receive the wine of the Holy Spirit if she so chooses. Samson loves her, and this time she has a name. It is Delilah which means feeble and languishing. If she had the Holy Spirit she would be strong and busy! He knows that she has turned to the Serpent and idolatry, and that she hates him and will betray him, but he loves her anyway. All he can see is his first love, the most beautiful woman in the world, and he is simply not complete without her. His is the undying love of a husband for his wife. Gabriel looks down and her heart goes out to Delilah as she weeps tears of love and forgiveness. Hers remains the undying love of a mother for her children.

They are both determined to prove their love for her, whatever it takes, and they hope that they will be loved in return.

Samson lives with her in her house, and the Lords of the Philistines want to capture and kill him, but they know he is too strong for them. They represent the religious leaders of the fifth age, the corrupt Pharisees and high priests. They offer to pay Delilah 1,100 pieces of silver if she will betray him and tell them how to overpower his great strength, so he may be captured and killed. She accepts. She knows that all he wants is to show his love for her, so she asks for the secret of his strength and how he can be subdued. He tells her three ways to bind him and she does so, three times, setting men in ambush to capture him. But he easily escapes from her traps. She pleads that he should not mock her or lie to her. She doesn't understand that he, representing Jesus, is not mocking her or lying to her, and for three years of his ministry he has been telling the truth, but he is accused of lying because it is not what the Serpent has been telling them. For three years, the Serpent has been trying to kill him, aided by the deceived and lost people of Judah and their religious leaders, but the Messiah has carefully escaped their traps. He has always known that this is the plan of the Serpent yet even so, he does not hide from it. He always offers the option for the people to reject the Serpent's plan and to follow him. Each year he gains more followers, and his hair grows thicker and longer, as his strength grows with it.

Then, on the fourth attempt, she asks him how he can say he loves her, when his heart is not with her? At this, his heart breaks and he knows that the time has come. He tells her the secret of his strength so that he can be captured and killed, and he willingly sacrifices his life for her. She cuts off his hair and all his followers are scattered, and he is captured. As Jesus, he will take on the sins of the people, his disciples will scatter and he will become enslaved to the Serpent, as is shown publicly to the spiritual world by his baldness. Then he is crucified at the end of the fifth age, and he suffers the punishment of their sins. But his spirits live on regardless and are imprisoned in hell.

Samson is also imprisoned and his eyes are plucked out as he loses his Holy Spirit and his ability to see the spiritual world. We will see how Jesus heals the spiritually blind so they can spiritually see, but when he takes on the sins of the people, he himself is made blind. In both the cycles (of Samson and Jesus), it looks like a victory to the Serpent, but it is not.

6. *The destruction of the temple – Armageddon*

We have now entered the sixth age, when the resurrected Sun is imprisoned for 40 years, and his apostles spread both the word and the Holy Spirit on earth, gaining very many followers for Jesus. In the previous story, this is the break. In the cycle of Samson, his hair grows back while he is in prison, and his followers and his strength returns. He goes to the corrupt temple of the Philistines, and using both his hands (armies of Light and Darkness) he topples the supporting pillars so that the temple falls to the ground and is destroyed. The corrupt leaders of the temple are also destroyed.

In the cycle of Jesus, this is also the climax. The apostles preach his gospel, and Jesus gains more followers and his strength grows as his army builds. The Holy Spirit is released and fills most of his followers, casting out the spirits of the Serpent who go to their death. Then after 40 years in prison, his sentence has been carried out and his strength has been restored. We will see that there are other sources of followers too, as Sheol is opened and the dead are raised to form an enormous angelic army. Then, Jesus returns to earth, but in the spiritual world, and he fights with both hands, the right for the army of Light and the left for the army of Darkness, both under his command because he is the Sun who rules day and night. Jerusalem and the temple have become corrupted by the Serpent and they are both destroyed in AD 70. This final act and final victory is the battle of Armageddon.

The numbers of the dead spirits of the Serpent were enormous, or as the story of Samson says, more than Samson had killed during his life. On the contrary, the people of Israel were redeemed and became sin free, so they were saved and received eternal life in heaven. Jesus then moves on from the spiritual world of earth, to take up his throne in Heaven in the seventh age, as the king of kings and Lord of the Sabbath.

So the riddle of Samson finishes, not with a terrible defeat, but with a glorious victory. But to Yhwh and the Sun, what was important was the salvation of their loved ones – who finally loved them back.

7. *The sabbath age?*

And what happened to Samson in the original story and riddle? He was buried in his father's tomb, so that his father's whole house would rest with him. Why would they all rest at the end of the sixth age?

Because his father's house was the house of Elohiym/Michael, the original house of righteous Darkness. Remember at the beginning of the riddle I explained that his father was very old and represented Michael at the beginning of creation? He was always planning to rest on the sabbath day to make way for Yhwh and Gabriel as Light replaced Darkness. In the riddle, this is confirmed to us because Samson's father is called Manoah, which means 'rest'.

That concludes the story of the seven ages as revealed by Samson, his first bride, and Delilah. Although there is a long way to go before this is fully revealed by the events in the rest of the Bible. At least we can see that there is a happy ending to come. That is a message that Yhwh would constantly give to her people throughout the difficult ages of Darkness, through the prophets, to give them hope and keep their faith alive.

Civil War

That riddle is over, but the time of the judges doesn't finish with Samson, it moves on to the next cycle and the next generation. Surprisingly, Delilah had a son called Micah, which means 'who is like God'. Delilah continued in her idolatry and used some of the silver she had been paid, to make idols, which she gave to Micah when he grew up. He made a shrine and other household gods, and he made one of his sons his priest. There was no king in Israel, and everyone was without guidance, doing what they thought was right, and they slipped even further into Darkness.

The final story in the series is one of the most terrible in the whole of the Bible. As we know, the Serpent was targeting the Messianic spirits in the chosen people, which meant Judah who had the spirit of the Sun, and Benjamin who had the spirit of Yhwh. They had both fallen, and Benjamin in particular, had fallen to the greatest depths, despite the efforts of his father, Israel, and his brother, Joseph which I described earlier. Up to now, the judges' purges of the Serpent had been in the surrounding nations who were attacking Israel. This time, there was no attacking nation, instead, the Serpent was working through Benjamin, so the purge was to be of the tribe of Benjamin itself. It was to be reduced to a remnant so it would not be completely lost, but the purge was a terrible blow to Yhwh as she accepted that her house of Israel had not been just divided, but it had been overcome by Darkness. She had no option but to carry out the purge.

For there to be any judgement, there had to be a witness and a judge. Yhwh sent a special Levite who had the Messianic Holy Spirit, to try to bring the people of Yhwh back to her. Through a horrific living parable and riddle, he witnessed the tribe of Benjamin's persecution and abuses of the people of Yhwh, and he judged the whole tribe of Benjamin guilty. Yhwh sentenced them to be purged, and all of the people, except Benjamin, were outraged by what Benjamin had done.

Who would carry out the sentence? Yhwh decided it should be Judah, the house of the Sun Messiah. The result was that the chosen people had been split into two. On one side was the Messianic house of Judah and on the other was the Messianic house of Benjamin, the house of Israel. The result was nothing less than full blown civil war between the strongest of the tribes. It was the first example of Judah versus Israel, but it would not be the last. The chosen people would soon be split into two great kingdoms of Judah and Israel, with their own kings, and civil war would become the norm.

For this battle, Yhwh knew that Judah and the other tribes were not innocent and had also been infected by the spirit of the Serpent, and so this civil war was to purge them as well, although to a much lesser extent than Benjamin. The losses would be truly terrible, and Yhwh's heart would be broken. But her anger was directed at the Serpent, not her people, as she knew perfectly well who had caused the rebellion.

The Time of the Judges. Samson and Delilah

Benjamin was attacked by Judah and they fought back fiercely, killing 22,000 men of Judah. Judah asked Yhwh if they should attack again, and she said, '*Go up against them*'. Judah attacked a second time and 18,000 of them were killed, totalling 40,000. That number tells us that they were spirits of the Serpent, and that by 'going up' they were being raised from their fall. Nevertheless, the slaughter of the chosen people through civil war was shocking.

They asked if they should attack a third time, and Yhwh told them to go up again, but this time she would give Benjamin into their hand. The battle was hard, but Benjamin was defeated and 25,100 of their men were killed. Only a small remnant of Benjamin remained.

As always, Yhwh's people were redeemed and slept in Sheol, but still she wept and wept and wept. She knew that this was only the first in a series of divisions and civil war between Judah and fallen Israel. '*In those days there was no king in Israel. Everyone did what was right in his own eyes.*'

But she looked at the rainbow around her and she kept on going, through the ages of Darkness and ever moving towards Light. The third age was at an end and the fourth age was starting. This was still an age of Darkness, and it would be very tough for her people, but she would fight back hard against the Serpent. She was going to bring the Messiah Sun to earth as a mighty warrior and a great king.

She was going to bring king David, the Messiah king.

Chapter 13

The Fourth Age – The King of Israel

Gabriel took a deep breath and reviewed the situation around her. It was a mess. The Serpent's targeted attacks on the Messianic spirits in the people had been largely successful, and her introduction of idols for the people to worship the Serpent rather than Yhwh had been exceptionally successful. The laws against idolatry had been broken, and the warnings had been ignored. Yhwh's chosen people had chosen the Serpent and turned to Darkness. But neither Yhwh nor Gabriel had any intention of giving up. They loved the people too much, and they remembered the rainbow and the seven ages which would bring victory. It was only a matter of time before the age of Light came.

So Yhwh decided to restore the lines of the three Messianic spirits, so as to lead her people towards Light. The old lines of Darkness would need to be ended, and replaced by the new lines of Light. First she would restore Judah and the Holy Spirit of Joseph.

Boaz and Ruth
This is the mystery of how the Messianic spirit of Judah was reinstated after the earlier fall of Judah. You may recall that Judah was the son of Jacob who had the Messianic spirit of the Sun on earth, and he started the line of the kings which would lead to king David. But he fell straight away, when he lay with a prostitute called Tamar. Tamar means judge, because she was the Serpent and judge over Darkness on earth, and so Judah's line turned to Darkness. She fell pregnant with twins, and to fulfil this cycle, which had started in creation, the twins fought in the womb for who would be the

firstborn and receive the inheritance of the Sun. One twin started to be born and the midwife tied a scarlet thread onto his arm as it emerged. However, his brother pulled him back so that he was born first. His house carried the inheritance, and he was called Perez. It was true that he was in the line of Judah, but the Messiah king, David, could not come from his line because it was fallen.

Then, many generations later, it was time to put things right. Gabriel caused a great famine in Israel, so that the old spiritual food and spiritual knowledge of the Serpent would dry up, and the people would be hungry for the new spiritual knowledge. A man and his wife and their two sons moved to the land of Moab, but the famine was just as bad there. The sons married two of the local women but had no children. First the father died, followed by both the sons, leaving three widows. Therefore, the line of this family had ended. This line was not straightforward, the Bible says, '*They were Ephrathites from Bethlehem in Judah*,' which is itself a riddle.

The mother decided to return to her homeland, where she had heard that the famine had ended, and the harvest time had come. One of the young widows decided to stay in Moab, but the other young widow, called Ruth, set off with her mother-in-law. They were going back to the homeland of the family, to a town called Bethlehem, which means 'house of bread'.

The bread of Bethlehem is very important, because it is the clean spiritual knowledge of Yhwh for her people of Light. Bethlehem is a town in the land of Judah and it will become famous as the birthplace of Jesus. The bread of Jesus is the bread of Bethlehem, and it is so vital that it becomes the first half of the Christian ritual of communion. The second half comes later and it is, of course, the wine of the Holy Spirit. Therefore, we can see that it is no coincidence that the new line will come from Bethlehem.

Now let's look at the line of this family, '*They were Ephrathites from Bethlehem in Judah*.' So we can see that there are three identities in one family. Three in one. Bethlehem is the word of Yhwh, Judah is the Sun and King, and Ephraim is the Holy Spirit, since he is the son of Joseph. Each tribe had fallen to the Serpent, therefore, the line that died out is the whole of the old and fallen Messianic line. The three spirits had ended, and the famine had removed the old and corrupted spiritual knowledge. Now, Gabriel and Yhwh have to replace the old spirits with a new line, and provide the new spiritual knowledge, or bread.

Where do the new spirits come from? Ruth is the young woman from the next generation who is going to provide the new line of the Messianic Holy Spirit of Light, but not from this family, she is from Moab, so it is the line of a man called Lot. He represented the Messianic Holy Spirit in the time of Abram, and this is where the new line of Light comes from, in Ruth.

All we need now is a new man from the original house of Judah before it fell, that is from Bethlehem in Judah.

When Ruth and her mother-in-law arrived in Bethlehem, the famine was over and the harvest of good grain was in full flow. The rest of the story is about 'sojourners' (from 'the other side') and shows us what is happening in the spiritual world.

Ruth went into the field of the house of her mother-in-law, to glean what was left from the harvest, and there she met a man called Boaz. He was a 'kinsman redeemer'. He could buy the original land of his kinsfolk if it had been taken over by someone else. He was, of course, the Messiah redeemer, the Sun.

Boaz was the tenth generation after Abraham, and he brought in the fourth age, with a new Messianic line and a new start. The famine was the purge of the old spirits of the Serpent and this story is about the salvation that always comes after the purge.

Boaz noticed Ruth and fell in love with her. This is the intense love between Judah and Israel and between the bridegroom and the bride of the Holy Spirit, which we will see more of in the new testament. He redeemed the house of the old widow which now included the widow of her daughter, Ruth, so they came under the shelter of his angelic 'wings'. The people prayed that Ruth would be like Rachel and Leah, wives of Jacob, which was a significant and accurate prayer. Leah bore Judah and Rachel bore Joseph. They also prayed that their house would be like the house of Perez, which was the house which held the inheritance of Judah. Except that this time, the house which would lead to king David would be a house of Light. Then, the Messianic spirits of the Sun in Judah, and the word of Yhwh in Bethlehem, and the Holy Spirit in Ephraim, will have been restored.

Then Boaz married Ruth and she bore a son called Obed. Obed fathered Jesse, and Jesse fathered David, that is king David. David was the tenth generation from Perez hence he was the start of a new age of the Messiah king of Judah.

Yhwh has not given in one little bit to the Serpent. She is about to fight back hard, with her warrior king, redeemer and saviour, David, the Sun on earth, in the fourth age. He would have the toughest job so far, because the fourth age is the age of the Moon, which comes after the age of the Sun. The battles between the Sun and the Moon would be severe.

Samuel

Gabriel then turned to her own Spirit, 'the word of Yhwh', which is in the prophets. The old line of prophets had also turned to Darkness, and their line was to be ended in the prophet Eli and his two wicked sons. They would be replaced by Samuel, a prophet of Light. Now this was still the time of the judges, before the kings, and Eli was a judge and a priest. Samuel would also be a judge and a priest, but he would not be a king. Instead, he would be a prophet of Yhwh so that she could guide him to be a great judge. In practice, that meant that Yhwh would be the judge, working through Samuel, and this method would work well. However, when the time came for kings to take over from judges, Gabriel will provide prophets to guide the kings indirectly. But the question is, would the kings listen to their prophets?

Soon it was the time for Samuel to be born as a prophet in the new fourth age. There was a man from Ephraim who had two wives. In the now familiar story of bearing a child of Light after the ages of Darkness, one of them was barren and she longed for a child. She wept and prayed, but her womb remained closed. Year after year she went to a city called Shiloh, where the ark of the covenant was kept, and the annual sacrifices were made at the temple. Jerusalem was not a city of the Hebrews at that time. One year, Eli and his two sons were in the temple and Eli saw her praying. She swore an oath that if Yhwh would give her a son, she would give him to Yhwh to serve her all his life. She swore that no razor would touch his head, so he would be a Nazarite. She did not touch wine or strong drink. Eli went to her and prayed that Yhwh would grant her prayer.

She returned to their home in Ramah and at the right time, she conceived and bore a son, Samuel, and he was to be a great man of Light. When he was weaned, she took him to Eli and dedicated him to the service of Yhwh.

Eli had two sons, corrupt priests who bent the law and their authority to suit their desires, and Eli chastised them but did not prevent what they did. Another prophet came to Eli and through him, Yhwh said that he and his two sons would soon die, and their house would never have an old man in it. Meaning no one would live long enough to grow old.

Gabriel's main problem was that the old line of prophets were from the line of darkness in her divided house. That meant they could hear the Serpent but not Gabriel or Yhwh. She needed to test and confirm that Samuel was from the side of Light and could hear her. So one night, Gabriel called quietly to Samuel. Would he hear the voice of Yhwh, even during darkness, or not? Samuel heard the voice, but Eli did not. So Samuel learnt directly from Yhwh what she was about to do to the house of Eli. Samuel grew up in the temple,

The Fourth Age – The King of Israel 201

serving Yhwh, and sure enough Eli and his two sons died. Eli had judged Israel for 40 years, and the cycle of the judges continued to Samuel.

The first thing Samuel declared to Israel, was that if they were returning to Yhwh with all their heart, they would have to discard all their idols and structures of idolatry and serve only Yhwh. Then she would deliver them out of the hand of the Philistines. So they did. Soon afterwards, the Philistines gathered to attack Israel and the people were afraid. Samuel cried out to Yhwh, who answered him. As the Philistines drew near, the voice of Yhwh thundered with a mighty sound and threw the Philistine army into confusion, and they were defeated. This is actually an example of the cycle of the judges which I described earlier, continuing as promised. Yhwh continued to be against the Philistines all the days of Samuel, and they were subdued and did not again enter the territory of Israel, and the cities they had taken were restored. Peace reigned, even with the old enemy, the Amorites. This peace and security is a feature of the short-term sabbath age.

Yhwh had clearly demonstrated that through her judge, she could do everything that a great king would do and there was no need for an earthly king. But the people of Israel disagreed. Samuel's sons were not like him and they had become corrupted, so the people insisted that Samuel should appoint them a king like the other nations, to judge them. Samuel was displeased, but Yhwh told him to do what the people wanted, because they had not rejected Samuel, they had rejected Yhwh. It was Gabriel who should be displeased, and she was. All she needed was for her people to have a little faith in her, because she had already lined up an even better Judge to take over from Samuel, in the line of Judah, and she had no intention of appointing Samuel's sons. In fact, she did not want a king from the house of Israel, which was the rebellious house, she wanted a king from Judah, the Messiah Sun, who she had already prepared through Boaz.

But she told Samuel to warn the people about what they would get with a king they chose, like the other nations who had kings of the earth. They would take a tenth for themselves, and the best of everything, and appoint people to be his commanders to run the kingdom for himself, the people working for him as slaves. In other words, their king would fall to the Serpent, and life would be awful. Why not stay with Yhwh and her choices?

They refused, saying that they wanted a king to go out and fight their battles. So a king of Israel was chosen to rule the whole kingdom of 12 tribes, just as they asked for. He was the most handsome man in Israel, and he was called Saul. He was from the remnant of the tribe of Benjamin, the divided house of Israel. Although he could start on the side of Yhwh, it was very likely that he would fall to the side of the Serpent, as had nearly all of his tribe before him. Yhwh prepared him and he was crowned the first king of Israel. The people cheered. But Gabriel didn't.

King Saul

Saul's reign started well. The Ammonites gave notice that they were going to attack a region of Israel, and Saul mustered his armies. Israel had 300,000 men and Judah had 30,000 men. On the day the Ammonites gathered to attack, Saul put his army into three companies and came into their camp, striking down the Ammonites until the heat of the day. Those who survived were scattered. The use of the number three, three times, indicates that this this was an army under the Messiah and you can assume that an angelic army was included, under the command of the Sun. That is why the battle took place in the morning and until the heat of the day.

Samuel was by now a very old man. He spoke to the people and made it clear that although they had done a wicked thing in demanding a king against the wishes of Yhwh, all would be well if they and the king obeyed the commands of Yhwh. But if they did not serve Yhwh faithfully and with all their heart, then they would be swept away, both them and their king. Although even then, she would not forsake her people.

Then things started to go wrong. Saul's son Jonathan was a great warrior and commander too, and he defeated a garrison of the Philistines. The Philistines mustered a large army and prepared to counter-attack Israel. The men of Israel were afraid and followed Saul in trembling. Saul needed input from Samuel, and a meeting was appointed after seven days. But when he was late, Saul made sacrifices and offerings himself. This was a terrible mistake, because it was against the commandments of Yhwh. Only priests can made sacrifices, and Saul was not a priest. So the unauthorised offering did not go to Yhwh, it went to the Serpent. When Samuel arrived, he told Saul what he had done wrong. If he had obeyed Yhwh, she would have established his kingdom over Israel forever, but now his kingdom will not continue, and a man 'after her own heart' would be prince over his people. This was David, who was still just a boy. From this moment, Saul's time as king was limited.

The Philistine army was still threatening Israel and had to be dealt with. But it was not defeated by Saul, it was defeated by a clever raid by Jonathan, who pretended to be Philistine royalty. This started a wave of confusion which grew until there was a collapse and the Philistine army fled in confusion. This victory was actually delivered in the spiritual world by an angel army of Yhwh, and this tactic of confusion backed up by a heavenly army became a common strategy thereafter.

Samuel continued to give Saul the word of Yhwh, and he continued to have victories against Israel's enemies. But on one occasion against the Amaleks, a particularly fierce enemy tribe, Yhwh, through Samuel, told him to destroy everything that belonged to them, and he refused to do so. He spared their king even though he was a king of darkness. Then he set up a monument to himself. It was now obvious that he had turned from his obedience of Yhwh, to follow the will of the Serpent. Samuel told Saul that he had rejected the word of Yhwh, so that Yhwh had rejected him. The kingdom would be removed from him this day, and given to a neighbour of his. The neighbour is a code word which means the Messiah (David). Samuel did not see Saul again until the day of his death.

The fall of Saul was not a small issue, because as king, he had authority over his whole kingdom and in turn, the people followed him. So when Saul followed the Serpent, they all followed her too. That is why there was so much urgency to remove his authority and his kingdom from him that very day. He was now only a king by title, but he had no kingdom.

David is Prince

Yhwh told Samuel to go to Bethlehem and anoint a son of Jesse to be king. He turned out to be his eighth and youngest son, still a boy, and he was a shepherd. He was called David. He was handsome and had beautiful eyes and he was ruddy, like Adam. That's because he was a son of Adam, that is a son of Man, the fourth one. As he was anointed with oil, the spirit of Yhwh came onto him, or more specifically, the spirit of Counsel of Yhwh. This is represented by olive oil, which is poured over the recipient, not drunk inside like wine.

Meanwhile, back at the court of Saul, he was now a man of Darkness and so the spirit of Yhwh in Saul had left him. Thus, the spirit of the Serpent started to manifest. To prevent this, Yhwh sent him a spirit of darkness and fire, which works like a thorn, which is a spirit buried in the flesh and continually temps and irritates. But this thorn was not under the Moon, it was under the Sun who had the greater authority. Thus, it stopped the Serpent's spirit from taking over.

Saul's servants knew what was happening to him and suggested that he call on a man who was good at playing a lyre. In the spiritual world, a lyre is a living spirit of Darkness, used during judgements. It speaks through songs, and the songs are the judgements of those who play it, if they are judges. It is a normal feature of the righteous way of Darkness. The servants say they know of such a man, and he turns out to be David. He is brought to Saul's court and immediately Saul loves him. This is the love of Judah and Israel, which still exists at this time, but it is fast fading. The point is that David is the Messiah Sun on earth, and he is the judge. The harmful spirit is under his authority and his judgements or commands. We can safely assume that David's commands are for the harmful spirit to stop harming Saul. When he plays his lyre, the spirit listens and obeys. So when David is playing to ease the torment of Saul, the spirit stops. Then, when Saul is not with David, it manifests again. The consequence is that David is welcome to stay in the court of Saul. Yhwh's plan is working.

David and Goliath
The army of the Philistines is mustered and returns to threaten war with Israel. Israel's army is also mustered and stands opposite them, with a valley and a river in the middle. There is a standoff, and both sides taunt each other. Then the taunting becomes more severe, with the arrival of Goliath, a great and fearsome warrior. He is the Philistine's champion. But he is more than that, because what happens next is set in the spiritual world, and there, Goliath is a powerful warrior angel, armed with living angelic armour and weapons, made of bronze, who represents the angel army of the Serpent herself. When he speaks, he is speaking the word of the Serpent. The story of David and Goliath is actually a living parable of the greater story of the battle between the Serpent Moon and the Messiah Sun.

His taunt is that Israel's army has nothing that can match him. They have no champion. And he is right, because nobody has dared to accept his challenge. Goliath has said that if Israel's champion can fight and kill him, then the Philistines will be the servants of Israel and will serve them. But if Goliath beats him, then Israel will be their servants and serve them. This is exactly why the Serpent and the Messiah are fighting, and it applies even to the battle of Armageddon. All of Israel were afraid to take him on. Even when Saul offered to enrichen the man who kills him, and give him his daughter in marriage, and make his father's house free in Israel. The challenge is very serious because it means that whoever wins the fight wins the inheritance of the earth and his father's house will be made free. Either the Sun or the Moon. You could say that Goliath is a mighty king of the earth of Darkness, and David is a mighty king of the earth of Light, so the fight is for who will be the king of kings.

The riches mean little to David, but the marriage to the daughter of Saul means a lot. That's because she is the princess of Israel and he is the prince of Judah, so this is literally a match made in heaven, to unite the kingdoms of the next generation.

David is present when Goliath makes his challenge, and he is told what the king will offer. David is offended and asks who does he think he is, defying the armies of the living God? He goes to Saul and offers his services, saying that Goliath is no different to the beasts he dealt with who were threatening his flock when he was their shepherd. That's true, because David is describing what is happening in the spiritual world, where the flocks are the lost sheep of Israel, he is the good shepherd who is watching and looking after them, and the beasts are the kings and chiefs sent by the Serpent against them and their shepherd. This battle has been going on for hundreds of years, not only the time of David!

After some scepticism, Saul let him go and gave him his own armour. Now that is a problem, because in the spiritual world, armour is a living spirit which protects the wearer spiritually. Actually, it is a defensive Holy Spirit, just as the weapons of an angel are offensive living Holy Spirits of fire. The problem is that Saul's armour is, by now, like him fallen and under the Serpent, and it will do nothing to protect David in the spiritual world. Therefore, David could not go when he was wearing them, and he removed the armour and rejected Saul's sword. Because David already had the spirit of Yhwh on him and the two are incompatible.

Instead, he took a sling. Now, in the spiritual world, a sling is an important angelic weapon. It is used to throw the very best angel warriors into a specific and high value target. They are the heavenly special forces. These angels have wings, so the sling simply gives them greater speed, but they find the targets by themselves like a guided missile. They never miss. However, a sling without a warrior is useless, and David cannot sling himself.

And that's where the river in the centre of the valley comes in. As we know, rivers are a description of marching ranks of angelic warriors. They are the army of Yhwh, commanded by the Sun, and David is the Sun on earth. David looks for the most experienced and well trained warriors in the river, and he chooses five of them, all with hearts of stone. They are very experienced and battle hardened, and they have been around for so long that they are worn smooth. They will do nicely, and David puts them in his pouch. Now, he cannot lose. Certainly, these five are warriors of mercy (the meaning of the number (5)) for the people of Yhwh, but only one will be enough to defeat the forces of darkness (the meaning of the number (1)).

David approaches Goliath who taunts him for his youth. However, as we know, the old generation of Darkness will rest and the new generation of Light will take the inheritance, so this is not a taunt to David, it is a declaration that he will win. Full of confidence, David says that *'he comes in the spirit of Yhwh of the angelic hosts, the supreme God of the armies of Israel, whom you have defied. This day, Yhwh will deliver you into my hand and I will strike you down and cut off your head.'* He goes on to promise that the Philistine armies will be struck down so that all the earth will know that Yhwh is supreme God and that she does not save with the sword and the spear, for the battle is not his, it is Yhwh's. This is David's way of saying that the salvation of Yhwh is not through weapons of fire, but mercy. Of course, he is hearing and speaking the words of Yhwh through her spirit.

So David slung his first stone and it entered the forehead of Goliath, and he fell face down on the ground before David. Thus, the champion of the Serpent fell, losing his position of authority, to take up the position below the Sun, as a servant like he promised! If you imagine what this scene looks like in the spirit world, he is actually bowing deeply, in submission. This is what David called 'struck down', or fallen from authority to servant.

It is also the victory that will take place at Armageddon and in every purge when there is a reversal of authority. Then taking Goliath's sword, he cut off his head. Now the head of the angel is whoever's authority he is under. Here, his head was the Serpent. But separating his body from the Serpent, in the spiritual world he has not killed the angel, he has freed it from his master. We will need to wait a long time, but eventually, this is going to happen to the whole Philistine army, and it will be freed and turn to follow the Messiah.

Conflict between Saul and David

Following David's success, Saul placed him in charge of the army, and he had great victories wherever he went. It became apparent that Yhwh was with David and not Saul, which of course was correct. Quickly, Saul became jealous of David and an escalating series of conflicts arose between them. Although it was always initiated by Saul, and David refused to harm Saul even when Saul was trying to kill him. All these series of conflicts represented the conflicts between the Serpent and the Messiah. To start with, David was able to subdue Saul with his lyre, but as the spirit in Saul became more rebellious, David's authority was ignored and he could no longer subdue Saul. This will happen in the wider and future conflicts, when the Serpent will rebel, ignore authority and need to be subdued by force, involving large spiritual armies. When I keep repeating that in the lead up to Armageddon nobody should rebel against authority, because nobody has to die, this is what I am talking about. You do not want to be on the side that is subdued by force!

David struck up a strong friendship with Jonathan, Saul's son, and he loved him. Initially, Jonathan was able to persuade Saul not to kill David, but eventually, Saul even turned against Jonathan. We come to realise that Saul represents the fallen and rebellious part of the divided house of Israel, and Jonathan represents the next generation of Israel, on the side of Yhwh. The old, wicked generation always represents the generations of Darkness, and the next generation always refers to the generation that turns to Light and follows the Messiah. That is why the love between David and Jonathan is so strong – it is the love between Judah and the Light side of the house of Israel.

At one point, when Jonathan realised that his father was determined to kill David, and would kill him too, he made an important covenant with David. *'Do not cut off your mercy from my house forever, when Yhwh cuts off every one of the enemies of David from the face of the earth.'* Jonathan is describing the situation at judgement day, when the enemies of David, that is the spirits of the Serpent, are cut off from the earth of Yhwh. David will be the judge. Jonathan is concerned that, at that time, his house will have fallen people who have not followed the Messiah into redemption and salvation. Therefore they will still be filled with the spirit of the Serpent, and treated as an enemy. So Jonathan seeks to protect them by asking David to have mercy on them and to redeem them too. David agrees and this covenant becomes binding. David will indeed remember it, and as a result, even those people of Israel from the next generation who do not follow Jesus, will be redeemed and saved. But it is not the Holy Salvation given to the followers of Jesus.

Then, much later, in a moment of repentance in the spiritual world, Saul will ask David to do the same for his house, the older generation of Israel. David accepts this covenant too. These two covenants are easily missed, but they will be crucial for the fate of

Israel at judgement day. The deeper meaning of Saul's repentance is well hidden but very far-reaching for Israel.

The conflicts get steadily worse, as Saul's jealousy turns to uncontrolled rage and hatred. Despite David's continuous victories against their enemies, Saul goes out of his way to find him and kill him. But David always evades him. When David finds Saul, he hides and does nothing to harm him. He continues to treat Saul as Yhwh's anointed, and he is indeed the anointed one of Israel, despite his fall to the side of Darkness, while David is the anointed one of Judah. The point is that David has nothing against Saul and the house of Israel, his enemy is the Serpent in them.

Meanwhile, in desperation, Saul used a spiritual medium to contact Samuel, who had by this time died and was resting. Samuel's spirit was called, and he was not pleased! Saul, in great distress, asked him why the Philistines were warring against him and why God had turned away from him, and doesn't answer him anymore. Samuel replied that it was exactly what he told him when he said the kingdom has been torn out of his hand and given to his neighbour, David, because he did not obey the voice of Yhwh.

Moreover, Samuel said that tomorrow, Yhwh will give Israel into the hand of the Philistines and Saul and his sons will be killed.

The next day, the Philistines overtook Saul and his sons as they were defeated and fled from the battle, and they were killed. And that ends the rule of Saul, the king of Israel.

Chapter 14

King David

We have just seen the power struggles between the Moon in Saul and the Sun in David, when David was only a prince and a threat to the Saul's throne. But these struggles are nothing compared to what will come next. Far from giving up at the death of Saul, the Serpent throws everything she has at David. This will be a power struggle like no other. There will be a magnificent warrior king, with great bravery and many victories, followed by a fall, corruption of power, the resulting fall of a family dynasty, deception, manipulation, secret scheming, lust for power, betrayal within the royal family, murder, revenge, rebellion, civil war, rape of a princess, a prince's coup to steal the throne from his father, great battles between the armies of the kings, injustice and the underlying sense of guilt of the man who started it all.

They will make modern cinema and TV epics look tame by comparison. The story of what comes next could have come from the scripts of the greatest of these dramas, but actually, it's the other way around. This drama came first, because it is rooted in the first power struggle of them all, the heavenly fight between the Moon and the Sun, even before the creation of mankind. Where the Moon desperately wants the Sun's kingdom and will go to any length to get it. We said that the story of Samson was the greatest love story ever told, but here we are going to see that the story of David is the greatest power struggle ever told. Not the original love of God for her people, but the original hatred of the Serpent/Moon for her people and the original and never-ending battles between the Messiah and the Serpent/Moon for the throne and the power.

And the cycles that were started from these battles in one form or another, are still happening today. They are mostly described as the struggles between good and evil, but it is really the struggle between the two great houses of Light and Darkness in the spiritual world, and whether the prince or the princess will take the succession of the throne of heaven and earth. What makes this story special is that it is not fiction, it actually happened, and it keeps on happening.

King of Judah

When David heard of the death of Saul and Jonathan he wept and mourned for them, and he wrote a moving lament to them. When it was time to move on, he asked Yhwh if he should go to stay in a city of Judah, and Yhwh replied, that he should go to Hebron. When he was there, the men of Judah came to him and anointed him king over Judah. David realised that after Saul's death, he needed to unite Judah and Israel into a single kingdom, and he approached the men most loyal to Saul to convince them that he would be a good king to Israel too.

But they were not the problem, the obstacle to unification was not the people of Israel, it was the commander of the army of Israel, Abner. Judah had a commander over their army called Joab, and both commanders knew that in a unified kingdom there was only room for one commander. They knew that although the king held the authority, it was the commander of the army that held all the power. Abner wanted the power, but he expected King David to choose Joab, and he wasn't going to let that happen. So Abner made a surviving son of Saul, Ish-bosheth, king of Israel and he remained his commander of the army of Israel. The kingdom was therefore divided into Israel and Judah, under two kings and two armies.

Now the feud between Israel and Judah continued, but it was not the feud of the kings, it was the feud of the commanders. One day it came to a head and the armies were mustered against each other. Twelve champions were chosen from both sides, but when they fought, they were evenly matched, and all 24 died. The armies then engaged each other, but Judah had the edge and defeated Israel. As Abner was fleeing the battle, he was bravely pursued by a brother of Joab, but Abner killed him with his spear. Joab continued the pursuit until Abner took a stand with the people of Benjamin and called him to stop. He said there had been enough bloodshed and asked if the sword would devour both sides forever? Joab agreed and withdrew. But he hated Abner for the death of his brother, and the fire of an eye for an eye was kindled.

The civil war raged on, and David grew stronger while the house of Saul became weaker, but Abner increased his personal strength within the house of Saul, until eventually he rebelled against Ish-bosheth, the king. He approached David for the two of them to make a covenant together. This was not a covenant with the king of Israel, but a covenant with the commander of his army, and the deal included that he would bring the army of Israel with him. He already had the agreement of the tribe of Benjamin, and he could bring the rest of the tribes too. They met face to face, and David agreed to the proposal, but as Abner was leaving in peace, Joab saw him and realised what was happening. He concluded, correctly, that David had secretly agreed to make Abner the commander of the united army, and he was not going to allow that. He summoned Abner to return, and when he did, he murdered him. To avenge the killing of his brother, and, of course, to secure his own position regardless of whatever deal that his king had just struck.

But David was angry with Joab and he deeply mourned Abner, who he described as a great man who had fallen that day. So all the people and all Israel were pleased with David and saw that it was not him who put Abner to death, but that he had treated him kindly.

Then two of King Ish-bosheth's men murdered the king and took his head as a trophy to David, expecting a reward. But David was horrified and had the men executed publicly. David was seen by

Israel to be a just king, and with both their king and their commander murdered, their resistance faded. They needed a shepherd.

The people of all the tribes of Israel remembered how David had won so many battles in the time of Saul. Also, that they were brothers because before they fought, they were all sons of Jacob. They came to David and asked him to be their shepherd. So David made a covenant with them and was anointed king over Israel. The two kingdoms were therefore united under King David.

David, King of the United Kingdom of Israel and Judah

David had been king of Judah at Hebron for seven years and six months. Now he sought a bigger and better capital city. He set off to take Jerusalem, and he called it the city of David and the stronghold of Zion. He reigned from there over the united kingdom for 33 years.

David fought the Philistines with the consent of Yhwh, and he defeated them. But he knew very well that his success was not due to his own army, but to Yhwh's angelic armies. The first victory he put down to 'Yhwh has broken through my enemies before me like a breaking flood.' This described the angel armies of the waters, like Noah's flood. The second victory was when Yhwh told him to wait until he heard the sound of marching in the tops of the 'weeping trees', for then Yhwh has gone out before him to strike down the army of the Philistines. As before, the angel armies are the key to victory.

Next, he had the ark of the covenant, where the angel of Yhwh (that is Gabriel) resided, delivered to Jerusalem. And David was made complete in his city, Jerusalem. After his victories, Yhwh had given him a period of rest from his enemies. During that time, Yhwh told David that Yhwh was to build him a house, meaning a line of his offspring and his inheritance. This house and his kingdom shall be made sure and his throne shall be established forever. That means the Messianic line of the Sun and the kingdom of the Sun has been made certain, and he would rule it as king.

In practice, this means that the Sun is David, and he will be the first of the three Messianic spirits of Jesus. In the future, he will be the Messianic identity who will return to fight the angelic war of Armageddon, with the commanders of his armies. Then, he will take up his throne in heaven, forever.

Soon, the period of rest was over, and the cycles of conflict continued. David won more and more victories against the Philistines and many other enemies. The fame of David and Joab as great military commanders spread. Over time, David's enemies were subdued and became David's servants. All of this reflects the coming change of authority from Darkness to Light.

Everything was going very well for King David and Yhwh, and her chosen people. David was their king and Yhwh was their God and all of Judah and Israel were united as her people. The Serpent was being thoroughly defeated and subdued. This had always been the plan and now, at last, it was happening. It was the best of times.

And then, everything went wrong.

David's fall

The Moon looked down and she saw that something dramatic was needed. She knew the Sun from the beginning of creation, so she knew his strengths and it was no surprise to her that he was doing so well. Then again, she knew his weaknesses too. His biggest weakness in the eyes of the Moon was his love for the house of Israel. The name 'David' means 'beloved' because this love is mutual. But although you can't presently see the split, the fact is that the house of Israel is divided and split into Light and Darkness, and the Sun's love extends to the fallen side of Darkness too. He loves the lost sheep just as much as the righteous people of Light. That is what the Moon sees as a weakness, and she intends to exploit it.

We will see that the Moon's plan for the fall of David is actually the continuation of the cycle of the fall of the Sun which originated in heaven before mankind was created. First, we will see all of the original elements then we will see how the cycle and its consequences pass on to the next generation while David, the Sun, looks on with terrible guilt.

The Moon knew from personal experience, both in heaven and earth, that the Sun could not resist her beauty. So she arranged another meeting of the spirits of the Sun and the Moon, this time on earth. Just as David was the spirit of the Sun on earth, the Moon put her spirit in a woman on earth. She called her Bathsheba which means 'daughter of seven'. She was incredibly beautiful, and from the house of Israel, but she had fallen into the side of Darkness. The name 'seven' is another deliberate deception of the Moon, because it sounds like it signifies the seventh age of Light, but it is also the number of the spirit of darkness and fire, with its seven sub spirits.

The Moon's plan had the same ingredients as the original plan for the fall of the Sun, which was to have Bathsheba seduce David and become pregnant by him. David would be filled with her spirit of Darkness, and he would fall like Adam in the Garden. When he fell, his whole house would fall with him and his household would manifest the spirit of the Serpent in them. But that was just the beginning. As in the previous cycles of the offspring of the Sun and the Moon, this was a scheme where the firstborn of Darkness would inherit the inheritance of Light, forever. The moon was going to contrive that the union would be unlawful and she would do everything she could to ensure that the punishment for the Sun's crimes would be his death. Her plan had worked before, so she expected it to work again.

Bathsheba

One afternoon, as David was walking on the roof of his house in Jerusalem, he saw a very beautiful woman bathing naked below him. He was utterly smitten and asked about her, only to discover that she was married to a soldier in his army, a righteous and obedient Hittite called Uriah. Ignoring her marriage, David sent for her to be brought to him, and he lay with her. As in the previous cycles of the conception of the offspring of the Sun and the Moon, it was the wrong time of her monthly cycle. She became pregnant with the prince and heir, but secretly, this firstborn was the heir of Darkness, a son of the Moon/Serpent. She informed David that she was pregnant.

David tried to hide what he had done by arranging that Uriah would return from the wars to lie with his wife so it would appear that Uriah had made her pregnant. But he was a very righteous man and did not spend time with her while his brothers in arms fought on the battlefield without him.

Then David planned to marry Bathsheba, but first he had to remove Uriah. He sent him back to the wars and instructed Joab to place him where he would be killed in the battle, effectively murdering him. Uriah was indeed killed. David married Bathsheba and she bore him a son.

The Moon had achieved all of her objectives. David had fallen, he now has the spirit of the Serpent in him and that is the voice he hears, because he has lost his spirit of Yhwh. Accordingly, when he listened, he murdered and deceived and abandoned his army and his wars, to be with Bathsheba, and the penalty for murder, according to the Law is death. Then, worst of all, his inheritance will go to the firstborn, a son of darkness with his mother's spirit.

Yhwh is, to say the least, displeased with David. But now, because he cannot hear her voice, she sends a prophet, Nathan, to speak to him. Through Nathan, she tells him what he has done and what he has lost, and she says that his punishment from her will be fourfold. First, that the sword will never leave his house, second, that evil will be raised up against him in his own house, and third, that his wives will be given to his neighbour in plain sight before Israel and the Sun. However, Nathan says that once punished, his sin has been put away by Yhwh, and he has not been given the death penalty. That makes his sentence an act of mercy. Fourthly, Yhwh says that his son, borne by Bathsheba, shall die.

So Yhwh has managed to limit the damage done by the Serpent, in particular, David avoids the death penalty. Bathsheba is forgiven too, and she and David are in love and are married. This union is very important because Bathsheba had represented the fallen, dark, side of the divided house Israel, but now she has turned to follow the Messiah Sun, and so she is forgiven. She now represents the side of Light in Israel, and she is redeemed and saved. Yhwh has put things right, not by punishment, but by the power of Love and mercy. The significance is all the greater, because Bathsheba's beauty means she carries the spirit of Light, and this is the inheritance that she will pass on to her son. It is the Light that David wants to pass down too, so his blessing would be given to his son by Bathsheba, not his previous wives who did not have the spirit of Light.

The Moon had planned to take the inheritance through Bathsheba's firstborn son, but he has died so the inheritance of Light will fall to the second born. Bathsheba, now forgiven, gives birth to another son, and his name is Solomon. David promises Bathsheba that his inheritance and his throne will go to Solomon rather than any of his previous sons by other wives. That is his blessing, and it stands, whether his other sons like it or not. David will prepare Solomon to take his throne and rule his kingdom as a united kingdom. However, he did not warn him of one thing. To beware of any beautiful woman with Sheba (seven) in her name, especially if she was a queen who was charming and flattering and gave him great riches. That omission is going to shatter his kingdom forever.

Meanwhile, David's house, before Solomon, has fallen, and everything that Nathan has prophesied must be fulfilled while David looks on, realising that they are the consequences of his sins. Now he knows that this cycle from heaven is going to continue, and the Serpent will visit the next generation too.

David doesn't have to wait long.

Here is a list of David's children with their mothers in brackets, to help you follow what happens next:

King David 219

1. Amnon (Ahinoam of Jezreel)
2. Chileab (Abigale)
3. Absalom (Maacah daughter of Talmai, king of Geshur), and his sister Tamar
4. Adonijah (Haggith)
5. Shephatiah (Abital)
6. Ithream (Eglah)
7. Unnamed child who died when seven days old (Bathsheba)
8. Solomon (Bathsheba)

Tamar and Amnon's fall

Tamar was the name of the woman who caused the fall of Judah, by pretending to be a prostitute. Her name means a judge, and the judge of the people of darkness is the Moon. Now, in this generation, a very beautiful daughter of David is called Tamar. Through Tamar, the Moon is about to strike again, using the same cycle which started in heaven, against the next generation, the sons of David. The eldest son of David, Amnon, is tormented by his passion for her, his half-sister. With the assistance of a 'very crafty man', who was part of the conspiracy, he arranges for her to look after him while he pretends to be sick, and she bakes special cakes for him. When they are alone in Amnon's room, he tries to lie with her, but she refuses him. He then rapes her. As soon as he does, he receives her spirit of the Serpent and he does not love her, he hates her. Tamar leaves the toom, crying aloud with ashes on her head, looking for her brother to complain to and ask for justice.

Her brother, Absalom, is David's third son, and when she tells him what has happened, he hates Amnon and decides to take vengeance on him. Fire for fire. He hid his hatred for two years, then he arranged a visit away, with his brothers, and he had Amnon killed.

Absalom's fall

Absalom fled while his brothers returned to King David, weeping. David and all his servants wept bitterly, and David mourned for his murdered son. Absalom went to a city called Geshur and was there three years. After his mourning, David's spirit longed to go out to him.

Encouraged by the advice of Joab, David sent for Absalom to return to Jerusalem, but only on the condition that he lived apart from David and did not enter his presence. He returned to Jerusalem for two years, until his patience ran out and he demanded to see Joab. When Joab ignored him, he set fire to his field to get his attention, and Joab agreed to find out if David would see him. He did, and Absalom bowed before David who reconciled with him and kissed him.

But Absalom had plans to rebel against his father and take his kingdom and all its wealth and power – a typical temptation of the Serpent. He put himself forwards to the people of Israel, as their unofficial judge, to settle disputes, saying the king has not designated any man to hear their complaints. He was adding petrol to the smouldering fire between the two kingdoms. He flattered them and won their favour and stole their hearts – just like the Serpent does.

Then, after four years, he went to Hebron, where David was first anointed king by the people of Judah, and there he planned his revolt. He sent secret messengers to all of Israel, saying that when they heard the trumpets sound, they should declare him king at Hebron. He even persuaded David's trusted advisor to join him. The conspiracy grew strong.

David heard about the rebellion, and he knew that Absalom would come to Jerusalem to take his throne by force. He decided to leave Jerusalem immediately. Not to give up, but to plan his return on his own terms, when he was ready. He left 10 concubines behind. David left with his loyal personal guard, and also 600 Philistines from Gath, the city of Goliath. They had decided to join him during the wars, and they had sworn allegiance to him. This signifies the change of sides of the Philistines that I mentioned following the beheading of Goliath.

David had not lost his cunning as a great warrior. He sent a handful of loyal officials and advisors into Jerusalem, who pretended to have changed sides. Also, during his journey away from Jerusalem, he was met by many people along the way, and it became apparent who were his friends and supported him, and who were his foes and opposed him.

Absalom called his rebellion and marched into Jerusalem, to find it empty of David and his people, except for his 10 concubines and the handful of David's loyal advisors. Absalom gathered all his advisors together, to determine what to do to capture David. He first asked David's ex-advisor who had betrayed David, and he came up with a good plan which had a good chance of success. He advised Absalom to go out immediately with 12,000 men to find David and strike only him down. The rest of the people would then come back to Jerusalem. But then Absalom asked David's still loyal advisor who was pretending to have changed sides. He rubbished the original plan, saying that David was too good a commander to be caught out like this, and he would not be with his army, but hiding elsewhere. His armies would fight Absalom's army valiantly, and word would go out that Absalom had not defeated David. Instead, he counselled that Absalom should command his army of Israel in person, to fall upon David where he hid. Absalom decided to go with the second plan. Meanwhile, he accepted advice to lie with all 10 of David's concubines so everyone could see what he had done to despise David. This had been prophesied by Nathan and so it was fulfilled.

David's advisor got word of the plan to David, through brave and skilful spies who were nearly caught, but evaded the enemy with the help of a loyal local woman. When he heard the plan, David immediately crossed the Jordan and waited some distance ahead, where he received food and shelter from the locals loyal to him. Absalom also crossed, and he set up camp for the night.

In the morning, David mustered his men and separated them into three companies, each under their own commander. He wanted to lead them himself, but his men told him he was too valuable and he must not come, but leave it to them. David agreed but commanded them to deal gently with Absalom, his son, and everyone heard him say so.

The army went out and engaged Absalom's army in the forest of Ephraim. This forest is important because it is the angelic army with the Holy Spirit of fire, fighting on the side of David. Israel was defeated with heavy losses and the battle spread over the whole country. But *'the forest devoured more people that day than the sword.'*

Absalom was captured by the branches of a thick oak and Joab was informed. He commanded the men who had seen him held in the branches to kill him, and offered them silver, but they refused to disobey the orders of David. So Joab killed him himself, with 10 of his armour bearers.

Messengers were sent to tell David the news. First that he had won the battle and his enemies were defeated. But David pressed for news of his son. He was told that he was dead, along with his other enemies. But David could not see him as his enemy, only as his son, and he knew that it was his sin that had resulted in his son's death. He went to his chamber and he wept, saying, *'O my son Absalom, my son, my son Absalom! Would that I had died instead of you, O Absalom, my son, my son.'* Five times he had called him his son, and three times by his name. These were no empty words, rather, the Sun had once again pledged to die for all of Israel and redeem them, including his sons. Meanwhile, David mourned bitterly for the son he loved so much. (You might ask why it is significant that he called him his son five times and by name, three times. This is using the number code to reveal that he will give salvation to Israel in both ways, firstly the baptism of water and mercy (5) for redemption, and secondly the baptism of the Holy Spirit (3) for holiness.)

The rebellion continues

David prepared to return to Jerusalem, but he had been rejected as king during the rebellion, by both Judah in Hebron, and by Israel. Now that this rebellion was over, there were great arguments about whether Judah or Israel would take the positions of power after he had returned. He badly needed to reconcile the divided kingdom. Not least, who would be the commander of a combined army?

But the rebellion is not over yet. David sent out messengers to Judah, offering that they be the first to come to return him to his throne in Jerusalem. Then he fired Joab and placed the commander of the army who had rebelled against him as commander of his army in place of Joab. He was called Amasa. Judah accepted, and sent word to David that he should return to Jerusalem and they would bring him over the Jordan. As he journeyed, those who had cursed him when he left Jerusalem, fell down before him and much to the displeasure of his loyal officers, he pardoned them, saying that nobody would be put to death on this day. As he went, all the people of Judah and half the people of Israel came with him.

Then all the people of Israel complained that it was Judah who had brought him over the Jordan, and it should have been them. An argument ensued about who was the more loyal, and it was apparent that Judah and Israel were still divided.

Then a man of Benjamin rose up against David, and his name was Sheba, the son of Bichri. Yes, Sheba, meaning seven! He declared that Israel had no portion or inheritance in David, who was from the tribe of Judah, so Israel should not make him their king. The implication was that they should make Sheba, a Benjamite like Saul, their king. Therefore, the rebellion against David continued. All the men of Israel then withdrew from David and followed Sheba. David was rightly worried about Sheba, and he told Amasa, his new commander, to gather the men of Judah to him in three days. But he did not return on time, and David told one of his previous commanders, Abishai, who was a brother of Joab, to go after Sheba. He went, and he took Joab with him.

On their journey, Amasa came to meet them. Joab went to greet him with a kiss, saying, 'is all well with you, my brother?' Then he ran him through with his sword and killed him. Joab is continuing to make his power plays to be restored as the commander of the armies, and reluctantly, the men of the dead Amasa followed him. They pursued Sheba and caught up with him in a city, which they besieged and started to batter down the wall. A woman of the city called Joab to explain his actions, and he said he only wanted Sheba, nobody else. She threw Joab his head, and that was the end of the rebellion. Joab took command of all the army of Israel, and returned to David at Jerusalem. Under one army, the kingdom was reunited.

The end of the days of David

By now, David was old and weakening. Despite the united kingdom, the Serpent continued the conflicts against David. There were attacks by the Philistines once again, and David was nearly killed in one of them. His men insisted once more that he did not come to the battles, and his mighty warriors took over. They even defeated a mighty giant called Goliath from Gath, and three other giants from Gath who taunted Israel. The circle of David had almost completed a full turn as a new generation of warriors took over the fight – including Goliath again. There was no sign of it ending.

Right up to David's death there was conflict, with external battles and internal rebellion. The final stories of David become stranger and harder to understand, but that just means that the meanings are buried deeper. What happens next is a good example, and although the meanings are hidden, they are not very difficult to understand when you realise their context. I will explain the hidden meanings as we get to them this time, so you can see how they are buried and how they are revealed.

Near the end there was a judgement and a purge on David's people, which was brought about by Yhwh. But as always, there followed hope through the salvation of the next generation.

The judgement and purge came when Yhwh told David to 'number' Israel and Judah. To number or measure people is to judge them, but at the same time the number code reveals hidden spiritual truths. Here, the numbers and the judgement revealed the sins of the people that were the consequence of David's own fall and sins. David saw them and said, *'I have sinned greatly in what I have done.'* The code also revealed that Israel's sins would be redeemed so they would be resurrected, and that Judah's sins would be forgiven by the salvation of the Holy Spirit through the Messiah. The enormous burden of the sins of the people was therefore shown to David and it was too much for him to take. His reaction was to ask for personal forgiveness. *'But now, O Lord, please take away the iniquity of your servant for I have done very foolishly.'*

But it's not that simple, because this is about David redeeming his people, so he will not be forgiven. The problem is that if there is to be justice, somebody needs to pay for the sins of the people. If David doesn't accept the punishment but asks for forgiveness, then there is no redemption and the people must suffer for their own sins. But to take on the punishments for the sins of the people is voluntary and cannot be forced on anyone. David has just rejected the burden of his redemption, so Yhwh responds by offering David three options for the punishment of the people, which they must bear by themselves. He is the judge, and he must decide the punishment. He decides on three days of pestilence for Israel, the tribes who were to be redeemed. Seventy thousand men died.

David saw what he had done and he was mortified. Watching the terrible suffering of his people was too much. He realised that it was his fall that had brought about these sins, so it was he who had sinned, and he was wrong to ask for forgiveness. He asked that Yhwh would direct her punishment on him, so they would be redeemed.

'*Behold, I have sinned, and I have done wickedly. But these sheep, what have they done? Please let your hand be against me and against my father's house.*' Yhwh accepted his decision. David was required to make offerings under the law, and when he tried to buy the animals to sacrifice, the owner offered to give them to him for free. But David said, '*No, but I will buy it from you for a price. I will not offer burnt offerings to Yhwh my Elohiym that cost me nothing.*' And the plague was averted from Israel.

This story is important because it covers the future redemption and resurrection of Israel at judgement day, when the Messiah king makes good his promise and suffers the sins of the lost sheep of Israel and Judah. He becomes the sacrifice and the offering personally, and he bears the full price.

That deals with the salvation by redemption, but what about the salvation of the Holy Spirit and the Christian Church in the next generation? There follows a short story where David is dying and cannot get warm. His servants bring a beautiful young woman, a Shunammite, to attend to the king and serve him and lie in his arms to warm him up. This woman of the next generation represents the early Christians who are holy. As he deals with their sins so the Holy Spirit can enter them to make them Holy, he burns with fire (like the Sun) and this warms him up rather than damaging him. They can then enter his presence and serve him. They do not die, spiritually, but they receive eternal life.

Now, David has ensured that the cycles of the two types of salvation for the seventh age will continue (that is redemption and resurrection, or salvation by the Holy Spirit), and they are not broken. All that remains is to make sure that it is his son Solomon who takes over his throne for Light, and not a choice of the Serpent for Darkness.

Right to the end, the Serpent attacked David, trying to divide the kingdom once again. The family rebellions continued. As David neared his end on earth, his fourth son, Adonijah, tried to take his throne instead of Solomon. Joab supported his bid, as did a priest called Abiathar who had previously been loyal to David. Adonijah made sacrifices by the 'Serpent's stone', his choice of location confirming that he had fallen to the Serpent. When Bathsheba and Nathan the prophet went to inform David on his deathbed, he confirmed that Solomon should be king and told them to have Solomon ride on David's donkey and be publicly anointed as king, and take his seat on David's throne. They did this, and all the people said 'Long live King Solomon and rejoiced with great joy'. Adonijah gave up his rebellion.

Soon afterwards, after warning Solomon to stay obedient to Yhwh if his throne was to continue, David died. The story of David's life on earth is truly remarkable and inspirational, but what is even more remarkable is the hidden story that his life is a long series of cycles which do not just repeat during his life on earth, but continue in his life in heaven, where he is the Sun. We are not going to review them here, but they span from creation to the end of scripture, and so in the story of his life you can see all the cycles that have happened before and will happen in the future. His battles on earth reflect the continuous cycles of conflicts between the Sun and the Moon, including his fall and recovery and his pledge to redeem his people. And, of course, his final victory of Armageddon.

Most of these events are deeply hidden in symbology and riddles, so what I have described here is not easy to see in the simple text. For example, David's exit from Jerusalem in the face of a coup, followed by his triumphant return, represents the future cycle when Jesus dies, only to return later to defeat the Serpent. The people who either cursed David or were loyal to him when he left, represent future people and nations who will also be present and repentant (or not) on his return. Even the spiritual ancestor of the great apostle Paul is included! Yet all of this was written hundreds of years before Jesus came and returned. We will look in more detail at the cycles and the riddles and the symbology in the second book, and you will see what I mean.

Chapter 15

King Solomon, a Short Age of Light

Solomon's wisdom

Solomon came after the successful battles of his father, and as we have seen, after a purge of fire there is a time of salvation and mercy. Solomon was a king of Light who followed Darkness. Rather like Noah was a man of Light after the Darkness of Adam. After Solomon's kingdom was established, he did not use the sword or fire, he ruled by a different way. So instead of conquering Egypt, he made a marriage alliance and took Pharaoh's daughter as his wife, bringing her back to Jerusalem. Solomon loved Yhwh and walked in the statutes of David his father. It was a good start.

The marriage to the princess of Egypt (and many others to come) is like making mutual alliances through marriage rather than the defeat and submission of war. Both ways bring valuable tributes to the greater king (or king of kings) but one way is the way of the great warrior king who brings death, and the other way is the way of the peacemaker who ends the wars, bringing wealth and cooperation and harmony and extensive trade and riches throughout the new empire. Trade that brings mutual wealth and benefits is a good alternative to war.

Then, like Noah, in the time of Light after Darkness, he was entitled to receive the Holy Spirit and all its gifts, to help him rule. Noah drank the wine of the Holy Spirit, and so could Solomon. When, in a dream, Yhwh asked him what he wanted from her, she was delighted when he asked for understanding, so that he could discern between good and evil when he governed the people. This is a vital gift which had been lost since the time of Adam. Understanding comes with the Holy Spirit, and with the Holy Spirit, Solomon would not need the input of prophets and nor would he need the law of Moses, he would simply know what to do. It was a giant step towards the way of Light. And with the Holy Spirit and Understanding, also came the spirit of Wisdom, for which Solomon will be famous. Wisdom is the gift to know what to do with the spiritual mysteries that you have understood or the advice (or Counsel), which you have received.

He quickly demonstrated his new gift when he was settling disputes in his capacity of king and judge. Two young mothers appeared before him, and one of their babies had died while the other still lived. Both mothers claimed the living baby as their own. Solomon commanded that the living baby be divided in two, with each mother receiving a half. One mother accepted the judgement, but the other was horrified and begged that the baby was kept alive and given to the other mother. She was the true mother and Solomon restored her baby to her. In fact, this story is a riddle with a deeper meaning, and it comes as a test for the future, to see who has true understanding of the meaning of the story. The deeper meaning actually tells the story of the divided house of Israel. There are four peoples involved, and you can use the number code to help to reveal them. The two mothers represent both sides of the divided house of Israel, (1) for Darkness and (2) for Light. One side follows the Moon (4) who intends to destroy both sides of the next generation, and the other side follows the Messiah King and the Sun (3) who saves the side of Light in both generations. The understanding of this hidden mystery is much more important than the simple story of the wisdom of Solomon.

This was a time of peace and security and wealth for Israel, a glimpse of what should happen in a time of Light. Israel had dominion over the whole region, which is what happens when Light takes authority over Darkness, and they all gave the king tributes and more wealth. Then, having demonstrated that he would use the power of the Holy Spirit properly, Solomon received great wisdom and understanding. It surpassed all the wisdom of the people of the east and the people of Egypt, which describes the false wisdom of Darkness, from the spirit of the Serpent.

Solomon spoke 3,000 proverbs and 1,005 songs, where he spoke what he had learned through the Holy Spirit, but buried the true meanings in riddles and code. He understood the basic hidden spiritual meanings of trees and walls and beasts and birds and crawling things and fish. People from all nations came to hear about them and other examples of the wisdom of Solomon, because the gifts of the Holy Spirit provoke much curiosity and stimulate enquiring minds. This time of the rule of Light was a great time for Yhwh and the people of Light, and the Serpent was effectively supressed through the rule of King Solomon. For a while, anyway. This age of Light is something that our next generations can look at and aspire to after the coming purge, but also to learn vital lessons from. Especially how to prolong it and avoid its ending in a fall to the Serpent.

Solomon's temple and palace

Solomon is also famous for building a magnificent temple to Yhwh, and a palace for the king. These represent the houses of the people of Light for both Yhwh and the Messiah king, which will be built up in the seventh age. That is why they are built by Solomon rather than his father David, a man of war and fire. But Solomon's temple will also serve as an amazing temple to Yhwh in Jerusalem, during the remainder of the fourth age of Darkness, where the priests will carry out the rituals of the law of Moses. The temple is full of accurate symbology and codes of spiritual mysteries, which come directly to Solomon from Yhwh, without a prophet. It took seven years to build, then the Ark was brought into it, and Yhwh (as Gabriel) resided in the temple, in the midst of her people, and as their God.

When Solomon dedicates the temple to Yhwh, he warns the people about the coming exiles from the promised land if the people

King Solomon, a Short Age of Light 231

sin, which was first declared by Moses and then Joshua. But he relies on the mercy of Yhwh, asking for forgiveness and compassion, if they repent. Soon, Yhwh replies to this prayer by repeating her strict warnings. If the people turn to idolatry and serve and worship other gods, she will not just cut off Israel from the promised land, the temple which Solomon has just built will become a heap of ruins. *'And when people pass by the ruins and ask why Yhwh did this to the land and the temple, they will know that it was because they abandoned Yhwh and worshipped other gods.'* It could not be clearer, but sadly, as we know, it will happen at the end of the age of this story, the fourth age.

However, for now, everything was going very well for Solomon and his kingdom of Light. Then Solomon was to learn an important lesson, which is just as important to all of us now. The seventh age of Light, the Sabbath day, is a cycle. It remains a day of Light for as long as there is no Darkness. For as soon as there is a fall to the Serpent, the Sabbath ends, and the days of Darkness begin again. We have seen this happening many times in previous ages after a purge, for example the age of Noah, and we are about to see it again, here in Solomon's time.

It is an important lesson for us because the age of Light which came after the first Armageddon purge in AD 70, was not permanent on earth. What was built up then, including the great house of the Christians, fell to the Serpent and we entered a new cycle of seven ages. The seventh age is nearly here again, and we must be better prepared, to make sure it lasts.

Let's look at how Solomon's age of Light failed, to see if there are any lessons for us.

Solomon's fall

The queen of Sheba heard about what Solomon was doing and she came to him to test him. Yes, she was not just Sheba, meaning seven, like Bathsheba who caused the fall of David, but she was the queen of Sheba. This was the spirit of the original Moon, and her intention was to destroy the kingdom of the Messiah, starting with the King. First though, she had to find Solomon's weaknesses. So she quizzed him on matters of deep spiritual knowledge and understanding, and he was able to answer every question. Solomon showed her all his wealth and all his religious structures including the temple and palace and its gold and silver, and his hierarchy of servants and priests and rituals and sacrifices. They were perfect.

So she flattered him and befriended him and offered him gifts from her country and from everywhere else that she asked for. He accepted her offers. Then she returned to her country, leaving her gifts behind. And although he didn't know it, Solomon was doomed. She had totally deceived him.

Unfortunately, all her gifts were living spiritual gifts, from her own nations of Darkness, and they were poisoned with her venom. She left Gold which was supposed to be a spiritual covering like armour to protect whatever it surrounded, but this armour gave no protection to Israel, only to the Serpent. Solomon had accepted 666 talents of this gold yet he did not understand what that number meant. It is the number of the Serpent, also known as the dragon or the beast or Satan, the enemy. It is all Darkness (6) and no Light. The fact that he did not understand the number meant that he had already lost his Understanding from the Holy Spirit of Yhwh, and this is a sign that it had already been replaced by the spirit of the Serpent. In other words, Solomon had already fallen. The gold went into the shields of the army, and it would not shield the soldiers from any spiritual attack at all. He overlaid his throne with the gold so it blocked the Counsel of Yhwh coming from the throne, but allowed the Counsel of the Serpent. And so on.

Then Solomon accepted more and more chariots and horses as gifts from countries of the Serpent so that the army of the Serpent infiltrated his own army, growing until it outnumbered it. They never changed sides.

And Solomon had many foreign women as his wives and concubines, who brought the ways of their people to Israel. Including idolatry. These marriages had been specifically banned by Yhwh for that reason. When Solomon became old, his wives turned his heart from Yhwh to other gods. He engaged in idolatry and went after the goddess of the Sidonians and the abomination of the Ammonites, and the abomination of Moab, and he did what was evil in the sight of Yhwh to satisfy his wives. Solomon had well and truly fallen.

Yhwh tore the kingdom from Solomon, as she had from Saul, but for the sake of David, she deferred it to the next generation. Yhwh raised up adversaries against Solomon, as she had done in the time of the Judges. The age of Light was well and truly over.

The key reason behind Solomon's fall

What was it that made Solomon fall so far and so quickly? The queen of Sheba had discovered that Solomon did not properly understand the concept that everything was a cycle. He and his people thought that they had reached the time of salvation in the seventh age, which they thought was eternal, and they didn't appreciate that they were only in the fourth age and had centuries of Darkness to go before the true sabbath age of Light. Without the protective armour to protect Solomon, the Queen was able to use the wives and concubines of Solomon to wear down his faith, giving him progressively more corrupted versions of the purpose of the cycles. Even doubting that there would be salvation in the end, especially if the Serpent won the victory of Armageddon.

The Serpent persuaded Solomon that he had been deceived by Yhwh and perhaps it would better to turn to the Serpent and let her look after Yhwh's people? Solomon became depressed and disillusioned and eventually he wrote down in a book, that he had concluded that all of life was in vain. He started with the famous passage about there is a time and a season for everything, which was a simple description of cycles but then he went on to say that there was just one cycle after another, endlessly repeating what had come before, so it was pointless and there would be nothing new under the Sun. Maybe, he implied but never wrote, there would be something new under the Moon? He never mentioned the seven ages or the seven sons of man or the rainbow which ended in salvation. So he went after other gods.

He died a broken man, having rejected Yhwh, with his hope destroyed and with no kingdom and no future to look forward to.

What are the lessons to learn?
- Don't be proud and show off your riches and what you have. You will reveal what you don't have.
- Recognise the Serpent
- Recognise her temptations
- Recognise her deceptions
- Recognise her poisoned gifts
- Ensure you never lose your Holy Spirit and its wisdom and protection and become naïve
- Always trust Yhwh and the Messiah
- Be patient and never trust fast riches or pleasure

Chapter 16

The Kings of the Divided Kingdom and the Prophets

Solomon's son, Rehoboam, reigned after Solomon, but Yhwh fulfilled her word to Solomon and stripped the kingdom from Rehoboam rather than him, and divided it into two. Ten tribes of Israel were given to a man called Jeroboam, a servant, and he became the king of the kingdom of Israel. The throne of Israel was established in the city of Samaria, thus the king of Israel could be called a Samaritan. (Something we should remember for when we get to the time of Jesus). The tribe of Judah remained in the line of David and Solomon and Rehoboam, and their offspring became kings of Judah in Jerusalem.

There were 20 kings of both Israel and Judah before the end of this fourth age. None of the kings of Israel did what was right in the eyes of Yhwh and only a couple of the kings of Judah were good kings. The remainder did not do what was right in the eyes of Yhwh either. The kingdoms degenerated into idolatry and wickedness until the Serpent had effectively enslaved all of the chosen people. They were the lost sheep of Israel, and they were 'lost' because in the kings and the religious leaders, they had no good shepherds to guide them.

Yhwh sent many prophets to guide the kings and the people back to Yhwh, however they had little success, were largely ignored, and many were killed. Yet the prophets and their messages are useful to demonstrate how Yhwh continued to pursue her lost people and never gave up on them despite their rejections of her. They also show the continuing conflicts with the Serpent in action.

Earlier, we saw a pair of prophets and priests in the time of the judges, in the third age, called Eli and Samuel. We saw that Eli was the end of the line of Darkness who was replaced by Samuel. Then in the fourth age, there is another pair of prophets and priests – Elijah who was a man of Darkness, and he was replaced by Elisha, a man of Light. This pair are important because you will see that their spirits will reappear in the fifth age too, in another pair of prophets and priests. Elijah is in John the Baptist, and Elisha is in Jesus who replaces him. You will see that Elisha's life foreshadows much of the life of Jesus. These three pairs are three cycles which demonstrate the transition of Darkness to Light. Here, we can take a brief look at Elijah (with his enemy Queen Jezebel) followed by Elisha. John the Baptist and Jesus will come in the next chapter.

Elijah and Jezebel

The story of Elijah reveals how the Serpent was able to make use of the authority of the kings, by using their queens to influence and often to control them. One of these was a woman called Jezebel, and she was particularly evil. She manipulated her husband, King Ahab, giving him her advice like a prophet, and she got her own way. The advice she gave came from the word of the Serpent, so she was, in fact, speaking as a prophet of the Serpent, in direct opposition to the prophets of Yhwh. This was the Serpent's strategy against the prophets. She also had a large number of priests who carried out the rituals of idolatry, rather than the rituals of the law of Moses, and they heard and obeyed the voice of the Serpent too.

Jezebel hated Yhwh's prophets and priests, so much so that she had them all killed. That is all except a prophet called Elijah, who was the last of them. On the other hand, Jezebel had 450 prophets of Baal and 400 prophets of Asherah. There was one against 850, so the odds were not looking good for Elijah. But Elijah was a prophet, and he could hear the word of Yhwh, so he knew what to do to defeat them.

To prove who was stronger, the Sun or the Moon, Elijah arranged a duel before the king. Him against the prophets of Baal. Ahab accepted. They set up two altars for a burnt offering, but did not light it. The challenge was to light the wood with spiritual fire, bearing in mind that fire was the speciality of the Serpent. Baal went first, and as the day progressed, the prophets produced no fire at all and had to give up. Elijah mocked them, asking if their god had to take a rest, or a break to go off to urinate. Elijah came next, and he poured water on the wood to make it harder to burn. Immediately, fire came down from Yhwh and lit the wood and the offering. Elijah had won, and he took the prophets of Baal and executed them. They had fought with fire and died by it.

Why did Elijah win against people of fire? Because he held the contest in the middle of the day, when the Sun was strongest, because the Sun rules the day. The moon, was indeed resting as Elijah had taunted them. He was implying that unlike the sweet water of mercy that Yhwh pours on her people as the rain from her tears, the Moon only has her bitter urine to pour on her people. But the result of the defeat was that Jezebel hated Elijah and declared that she would kill him that night. He took the threat seriously and fled, because the Moon ruled night and so at night, she had the greater power.

Much later, Elijah is taken up to heaven without dying, as Elisha, his student, watches. He is in fact, a descendent of Enoch and Nimrod, a man of darkness doing the will of Yhwh then being taken up to heaven alive. In heaven, as always, his spirit will wait patiently for his next task. In due course, his task will be to return as John the Baptist.

But the Serpent has a long memory and even more hatred, so when Elijah returns as John the Baptist she is waiting. The queen of the time is a descendant of Jezebel and with the assistance of her daughter and her seductive dance, she persuades her husband, King Herod, to have John killed and give her his head. And he does, but only after John had prepared the way for Jesus, as Light takes over from Darkness. Here though, in the time of Elijah, it is Elisha who takes over.

Elisha

Before Elisha sees Elijah taken up to heaven, he had requested a double portion of Elijah's spirit. That means he requests a spirit of Light (2) from a spirit of Darkness (1), and that is what he received. Immediately he receives it, his spiritual eyes are opened, which is a feature of the Holy Spirit of Light. He then sees the angelic horses and chariots of fire which take Elijah up. He knows what they are and cries out, *'the chariots of Israel and its horsemen'*, which they are – the heavenly army.

Later, Elisha and his servant are surrounded by an army of the enemy, out to kill them, and his servant is scared, but Elisha is calm. When asked to explain his confidence, he replies that there are more with us than with them. Then he asks Yhwh to open his servant's eyes and he saw that Elisha was surrounded by horses and chariots of fire – the heavenly army.

This is just one example of Elisha performing what Jesus will do later. Both Elisha and Jesus can see the spiritual world around them, and both of them can open the eyes of the blind so that they see it too. In the next book, we will look at many more such similarities between the work of Elisha after Elijah, and the work of Jesus after John the Baptist.

Israel and Judah are exiled from the Promised Land

As they neared the end of the age, the prophets warned explicitly that the people would be exiled from the promised land, just as Yhwh had previously warned them through her prophets. They sought repentance and an end to idolatry, but it did not come. Then, as promised, Yhwh exiled the 10 tribes of Israel, followed soon after by Judah. Israel was taken to Assyria by the king of Assyria and Judah was taken to Babylon, by the king of Babylon.

The Kings of the Divided Kingdom and the Prophets 239

Yes, the same king of Babylon, that we have seen before, coming from the east, a king of Darkness doing the will of Yhwh. He is the descendant of Enoch and Nimrod, and Nimrod founded the empires of both Babylon and Assyria.

Now the king of Babylon at that time was called King Nebuchadnezzar. He was a great warrior king and ruled a great empire as he had been promised. As they descend on the promised land, the armies of both Assyria and Babylon are described as 'waters' which will sweep through and cover the lands – like a great flood. That is, like Noah's flood and the flood of the Red Sea over the Egyptian army. Not only the promised land, but also he defeats Egypt and Tyre, and the Philistines and many other nations which have become the strongholds of the Serpent. He will also destroy the corrupted city of Jerusalem and the corrupted temple of Solomon, full of the venomous gifts of the queen of Sheba.

However, he conquered Judah in two stages. At first he left Jerusalem intact and merely imposed tributes or taxes on the people, leaving a king to keep order. However soon afterwards, the people and the king rebelled against him and his taxes, so the army of the Babylonians returned to complete the exiles and destroy Jerusalem and the temple. This is an example of avoiding rebellion to avoid destruction and death. The next such cycle will be Armageddon, just after the end of the sixth age, where the people of Jerusalem rebelled against the Roman army, which put down the rebellion with great force and destroyed Jerusalem and the Temple once again.

All this is the purge of the end of the fourth age to cleanse the land of the spirit of the Serpent. Of course, Nebuchadnezzar secretly has the Messianic spirit of the Sun, and so under his rule, the people of Yhwh are in safe hands. Through her prophets, Yhwh had commanded her people to submit to Nebuchadnezzar so that nobody should die. Now we can see why. In fact, the exiles can be seen as a Passover event, an act of mercy, so that Israel and Judah will escape the purge. So what does happen to them?

The 10 tribes of Israel are dispersed throughout the region of Assyria and then further afield, and apart from a few, they do not return, but make new lives among the foreign peoples. However, through her prophets, they are under a promise from Yhwh that there will be a call from the Messiah, so they can turn and be saved. There will be a path or a way to their salvation in the new Jerusalem, the Holy city in heaven, and the new lands of their inheritance in heaven, when they physically die. This will be the new way of Light after their lives of Darkness and Law. Although the call comes in the next age, the fifth age, it comes towards the end of the age, so it is still centuries away.

Meanwhile, their previous lands are given to other nations by the Assyrians, including Samaria. Thereafter, to be a Samaritan will be an insult to a Hebrew.

However, the people of the tribe of Judah will, after some 70 years in Babylon, be allowed to return from Babylon to the old Jerusalem to rebuild it and the temple and resettle there. Many do, and after many centuries of growth, this becomes the Jerusalem and surrounding land of Judah that John the Baptist and Jesus will come to, to make their call to the lost sheep of Israel.

Chapter 17

The Fifth Age – John the Baptist and Jesus

Introduction

We have moved on to the new testament, which is quite different from the old testament. That's partly because it describes mankind's long-awaited salvation to heaven, which will happen soon. Therefore, it is a good idea to refresh our understanding of salvation before we start. I know that many readers get somewhat confused between the two types of salvation, so let's look at them again. I am only going to consider the people who receive salvation here, although not everybody does.

Then we will go on to see that the real difference between the old testament and the new testament is the release of the Holy Spirit on earth, and everything that means. The Holy Spirit changes everything.

Redemption and resurrection

This is not the preferred route to heaven, but it is very common. It applies to the people of Yhwh who have the spirit of the Serpent in them when they physically die, but are promised for redemption. That includes all the lost sheep but not the bad shepherds who have chosen to reject Yhwh in favour of the Serpent, and who lead her people astray. Having the spirit of the Serpent is a real problem when it comes to salvation, because, as Yhwh said to Adam and Eve, it leads to death, not life.

The first problem is that nobody can go to heaven with the spirit of the Serpent in them, and the second is that having it means that they are people of Darkness and subject to judgement when they die. Therefore, even Yhwh's fallen people must be judged and punished for their sins, and for most of us, that would be a terrible punishment in the fire, ending in the spiritual death of the person. This is the aim of the Serpent, but Yhwh simply cannot allow her people to go through it.

Therefore, she deals with the problem in this way:

First, salvation through redemption can only apply after the people have physically died, because when they are alive they are bound to the spirit of the Serpent in their body. But when they die, the spirits are separated. However, Yhwh must avoid their judgement when they die, because their sins would lead to their spiritual death immediately. So, she defers their judgement until the end of the sixth age, judgement day, and in the meantime, they sleep in Sheol.

Second, while they sleep, she and the Sun take on the sins of the people of their own houses, Israel and Judah, and they suffer them personally on their behalf. This entails many long and painful years in the fires. This pays their 'debt' of sin and is called redemption. It is like a redeemer paying the unpaid debt or ransom of a slave to free them. The result is that the person is set free from the Serpent, their sins are fully punished so that the Law is not broken, and they are deemed to be righteous. Redemption must happen before judgement day, and when the person is redeemed, they are given a spiritual covering of white linen so that they are sin free.

Third, at judgement day their soul and spirits are woken up, leave Sheol, and are resurrected to heaven in their white linen. There they are judged by Jesus as the Sun, but not as we would have thought. The judgement is simply whether they are spirits of the people who were redeemed, or whether they are spirits of the Serpent, which are now separated from the other spirits. If they are the redeemed people then they are deemed righteous, so they stand and enter heaven as angels of Light. If they are spirits of the Serpent, then they are judged for the sins they have caused and are punished in the fire or drowned in the sea. They never enter heaven.

Thus, the Hebrews and the people of Ishmael who were promised this redemption in the time of Abraham, are redeemed and resurrected to heaven. They enter on the eighth day, the day of resurrection, which is the first day of the new week in heaven.

Because Jesus died carrying the sins of the people, including the spirit of the Serpent, he was resurrected using this method, on the eighth day, the day after the sabbath. Unfortunately, this has led to misunderstandings among many Christians, who believe that this method is the only route to heaven, and because it happened to Jesus after his death, it will happen the same way to them too. But that is not so. It misses the essential point that Christians should achieve salvation through the Holy Spirit, and it happens while they are still alive. They are not redeemed, resurrected and deemed righteous after they die and sleep in Sheol, instead they are made holy and given salvation while they are still alive, so they do not go to Sheol.

Salvation of Holiness

The preferred route to heaven is through becoming holy. This was the option given to Adam and Woman in the Garden of Eden, but was rejected. This method is quite different to redemption and resurrection.

This time, the spirit of the Serpent is cast out while the host is still alive, and is replaced by the Holy Spirit of Light. That makes the host a person of Light, and it also makes them Holy. Any future sins and uncleanliness will be immediately removed by the Holy Spirit, so that the sin-free state of holiness is permanent – unless the host rejects the Holy Spirit, and it leaves them.

When a holy person physically dies, their angelic being goes straight to heaven. They do not sleep in Sheol. They are not judged, because they are holy, and they enter heaven as a righteous and sin free person of Light.

While they physically live on earth, they also receive many powerful gifts and talents from the Holy Spirit, such as Counsel, Understanding and Wisdom. They have their spiritual eyes opened and they can hear and speak the word of Yhwh. They are guided by Yhwh and their life changes substantially and for the better. This is the state that was originally planned for Adam and Woman and all their descendants – and it still is.

The Holy Spirit is only available to followers of the Messiah, Jesus. If you reject Jesus, then you reject the Holy Spirit. However, you can receive the Holy Spirit simply by having faith in Jesus and asking him to fill you with it, and if you mean it and expect to be saved, you will get it. (To describe this process of salvation, Jesus will soon say, '*Ask and it will be given to you*' in the context of receiving good gifts from God. The rest of Jesus's statement, when fully understood, is that you can then '*seek*' and find the kingdom of God when your eyes are opened to see, and you can '*knock*' on the door to heaven and it will be opened to you.)

There is one problem to overcome, however. Originally, when Adam and Woman were supposed to receive the Holy Spirit in the Garden of Eden, they were innocent and sin free so they could safely receive the Holy Spirit. But now, when the spirit of the Serpent is cast out at the beginning of the process, the host is usually covered in sin and is very unclean. If the Holy Spirit enters at that point, they will probably be killed as the sins and uncleanliness are instantly removed by it. Yhwh deals with this problem as follows:

There are three stages to being filled with the Holy Spirit after you have asked for it, and after the spirit of the Serpent has been removed. They take a few seconds, and they just happen, you don't need to ask for them. They are described as Love, Peace and Joy and you feel these emotions intensely as they happen.

1. Love and Mercy are the same things, and they are your washing and cleansing by Yhwh. You feel waves of powerful Love over your whole body as it happens. It is a beautiful experience and you come to realise just how much Yhwh loves you – as she loves all of her people. You have shown faith and expectation (or hope) but without this love and mercy you will not be saved.
2. Peace is not the absence of conflict, it is the peace you get when you are at peace with God. It happens immediately after stage one, when you are clean, sin free and deemed righteous. You feel completely relaxed in the presence of God and you have an overwhelming feeling that everything is OK and God is taking care of every problem, so there is nothing to worry about, now or in the future.
3. Joy is not the simple gladness that you can feel when you realise that you have been redeemed. It is a dramatic feeling of total joy as the Holy Spirit enters you. You feel like you could not be happier. Observers have described the effect as behaving as if you are drunk, but it is the spiritual wine of the Holy Spirit which makes you so joyful.

Usually, there is then a period of a few minutes when you want to take it all in and come to terms with it. This is often when you have your first spiritual communication with Yhwh, and you simply know things that you didn't know a second ago. You can ask questions and receive an answer. It's just the start.

Later, you will be able to lay your hands on somebody who asks to be filled, and you will feel the Holy Spirit flow from you into the person and witness the effect it has on them.

To finish this lesson on the principles of salvation, we will look at the similarities between redemption and the Holy Spirit and ask if the Holy Spirit salvation is only for Christians. Especially since the new testament we are just about to look at, is not read by the Jewish and Muslim people as their scripture.

You will see that the first two stages of being filled by the Holy Spirit are similar to redemption. The Love and washing clean is like the baptism of water from John the Baptist, for everyone who repents and turns back to Yhwh. It is the same as continually asking for and receiving the mercy of God.

The peace is what is given to the redeemed when they are washed sin free and deemed righteous. This peace means you have been saved, and that is why it is prayed for constantly (even if you don't realise it) when you wish peace on someone, like a greeting of 'Shalom' which is the Hebrew for peace, or 'peace be upon you', with the response of 'and on you' which is the Islamic greeting. This well embedded greeting confirms that redemption is available to the Jewish and Muslim people. They are both people of Law and fire, so they can expect to be judged, and therefore rely on and seek the deemed righteousness of redemption. They seek the water of mercy, constantly.

Without getting ahead of ourselves, we will shortly see that Jesus will regularly emphasise the universal spiritual principle that 'you will receive what you give', or 'do as you would be done to'. So if you give fire you receive fire but if you give mercy you will receive mercy. These greetings are a great example of what Jesus meant. When you wish peace on someone you are giving them mercy too, and immediately they give you mercy and peace in return. The next step is for us all to do what we say! To put out fire you need to pour the water, not just say it, even if it is a tough thing to do. We will see that it can lead to lasting peace.

Gladness can be felt by the redeemed, but intense Joy is reserved for the salvation of the Holy Spirit, given only through Jesus. John the Baptist came to offer the baptism of water, but he made it clear that this was only to prepare the way for Jesus and the baptism of the Holy Spirit.

The arrival of the Holy Spirit

We started this story with the rejection of the salvation of the Holy Spirt (the tree of life) in the Garden of Eden. We will finish it with another chance to receive the Holy Spirit and its salvation, so that we can be restored to the original plan, before the fall of mankind. Why is this so important? Is it only about salvation to heaven? No. The arrival of the Holy Spirit changes everything on earth too. You can say that the Holy Spirit is the answer to every problem.

For example:

- How do we get to heaven? The Holy Spirit
- How do we become sin free and freed from the Serpent? The Holy Spirit
- How do we see the spiritual world? The Holy Spirit
- How do we talk to God? The Holy Spirit
- How do we hear her reply and other messages? The Holy Spirit
- How do we spread her teaching to others? The Holy Spirit
- How do we understand the mysteries? The Holy Spirit
- How do we obtain the wisdom to know what to do with it? The Holy Spirit
- How do we cast out the spirit of the Serpent? The Holy Spirit
- How do we calm the storms and conflicts around us? The Holy Spirit
- How do we get the talents we need to fulfil our part in the plan? The Holy Spirit
- How do we have the might to defeat the Serpent? The Holy Spirit

And so on.

In the first four ages we saw how bad life could be without the Holy Spirit. In the next three ages we will see how good is can be with the Holy Spirit. And that is the essential difference between the old testament and the new testament. That is what you should look out for when you read the rest of this book.

We will see that the number of people filled with the Holy Spirit are important. A few people can be overwhelmed, but a large army filled with the Holy Spirit is invincible. So the next question is 'Who can receive it? Is it really only for Christians?' The new testament is crystal clear that both Hebrews and Gentiles are people of Light and entitled to receive the Holy Spirit through Jesus, but it is a personal choice. The Jewish people do not accept that Jesus is the Messiah, so by rejecting Jesus they reject the Holy Spirit and all of its gifts, and remain people of Darkness, people of the Law and fire. Nevertheless, all of the chosen people are entitled to receive the Holy Spirit, because it has always been the plan that they would have it, and it still is. Many were filled in the time of Jesus and the apostles, and joined the church at its beginning. Jesus is calling them, even now, and it is up to them, as individuals, if they answer the call or not. But it was the gentiles who filled the churches, and the two religions diverged when they really should have joined together. Remember that the gentiles were the original chosen people in the second age of Noah.

The position of the Muslims is different, but equally important. The mysteries of the Bible tell us that Muslims can be confident that they will achieve salvation through redemption. They show us that Muslims are on the side of God and that they are an essential part of God's plan for the future. I will come back to that later.

I said at the beginning of this book that it would help us prepare for the coming battle of Armageddon, but more importantly it would help us prepare for the seventh age which follows it. The best preparation you can have is to be filled with the Holy Spirit so that you will be personally guided what to do. Not with your own limited ideas, but with the wisdom of God, no less. Certainly, that will ensure the victory in the spiritual battles ahead, but it is more about what happens after that.

The age of Light will be an age of security, where people will live in harmony, without wars, and mercy and forgiveness will dominate. That seems difficult for us to accept in these times, but with the power of the Holy Spirit driving it, it will happen. Actually, the challenge is not about whether it happens or not, because that is up to God and the Holy Spirit, but rather how long can we make it last, because that is up to us.

Let's continue into the new testament and see how salvation unfolds for the Hebrews and the gentiles as the Holy Spirit is first demonstrated and then released and offered to them both.

The New Testament

The fifth age is the age of mercy. Although it is still one of the six ages of Darkness and fire, the spirit of the son of Man, the Messiah, in this age has become a holy spirit of Light and mercy in a time of Darkness. Looking at the rainbow sign of the seven sons of man, we have moved from red to blue (the fifth colour of the rainbow), which is from fire to water. The fifth son of man is Jesus and the change he reveals from Darkness to Light is dramatic and far-reaching. There is universal agreement that the 'new testament' and the 'old testament' are quite different in their messages, with the old testament being blood thirsty and full of wars, and the new testament being full of forgiveness and kindness. This is why.

As we know, the Messiah has three spiritual identities in one. So as well as being the Holy Spirit of Light, Jesus also has the identity of Gabriel, the 'word of Yhwh', and the Sun. So when we see Jesus at work, we will see all three of his identities working together.

Firstly, he will deliver the word of Yhwh, preaching and teaching about the coming kingdom of Light and the way of mercy, the inheritance of Light over Darkness, and the salvation to heaven. Secondly, he will apply the authority of the Sun to make commandments to the spirits of the Serpent which they must obey.

But thirdly and essentially, the Holy Spirit we see at work is the **divine** Holy Spirit of Yhwh, whereas the spirit of the Serpent only has the lower **angelic** authority and power. Why is that so essential?

Because until now, the Serpent has been able to ignore or get around the higher authority she faces from the Sun. If the Sun commands her spirit to leave a person, she will simply refuse and there is nothing he can do about it. That means that the spirit of the Serpent can only be separated from the person by their death, when all the spirits are then released from the 'clay vessel'. Therefore, the purges of the spirit up to now have usually involved mass deaths and warfare. However, from now on the Holy divine Spirit of the Messiah does not only outrank the Serpent's spirit, it overpowers it too.

In practice, that means that if the Serpent's spirit refuses to obey the Sun's authority, she will be forced to comply by the power of the divine Holy Spirit. This is a fundamental change, which Yhwh has waited four long ages to achieve. Now, Jesus has the authority and the power to command the spirit to leave a person, and it must go. In other words, Jesus can cast out the demon spirits. It is no longer necessary for the Sun in Jesus to use his sword. From now on, his command has taken over the work of his sword, as if his sword is in his mouth. Indeed, to illustrate this point, when we see Jesus later, in his angelic form in the spiritual world, he will have a sword coming out of his mouth.

Although casting out the spirit of the serpent is an essential role of the Holy Spirit, it has many more functions. In fact, the arrival of the divine Holy Spirit is the most important thing that happens in the new testament. Jesus will carefully demonstrate all the gifts of the Holy Spirit as it replaces the spirit of the Serpent which is cast out from people. He will make the blind see, then through the spirit of Counsel, the deaf will hear the word of Yhwh, and the dumb will speak it, and the lame will spread it. He even demonstrates what it means to have understanding and wisdom, although this will not reach his disciples in this age. Almost everything Jesus says concerns deep mysteries which are buried in spiritual code and riddles and parables, so it will only be understood after his death, when the Holy Spirit is released to the people who accept it.

But most important of all, the Holy Spirit will cleanse away sins, and the visible effects of sins such as spiritual leprosy, and make people Holy so they can go to heaven and stand before God without sin. In other words, it brings salvation through casting out the Serpent and replacing it with the Holy Spirit, without having to die first. This can be called the salvation of Light, because the spirit of Darkness has been cast out and replaced with the Holy Spirit of Light.

Jesus will also demonstrate how he can bring salvation to people who do not receive the Holy Spirit, though his redemption and resurrection. To remind you, this is the first form of salvation, when he takes people's sins upon himself, then, when they physically die, he brings them back to spiritual life, without the spirit of the Serpent, by resurrection to heaven. There, they will be sinless, deemed righteous, and able to stand before God without being punished by fire. This can be called the salvation of Darkness because the spirit of Darkness is still in people when they die, so they die in Darkness but are resurrected to Light. The key point to understand is that the spirit of the Serpent cannot enter heaven, so it must be removed one way or the other. Either after physical death, or after it is cast out.

Because this is a spiritual or angelic event, we do not normally see resurrection taking place, but when Jesus demonstrates it on others, he will allow witnesses to see it. Obviously the most famous example is when he himself dies a man of Darkness and was resurrected as a man of Light. Then, all three of his spiritual identities will become visible to some, as angels.

Since Darkness comes before Light, John the Baptist (a man of Darkness) will demonstrate the salvation of Darkness without the Holy Spirit, and he prepares the way for the Salvation of Light through the Holy Spirit, available only through Jesus the Messiah. The salvation of John the Baptist will be called the baptism of water and the salvation of Jesus will be called the baptism of the Holy Spirit.

Because the Holy Spirit is the wine made from the grapes of the vine, the tree of life, it is not a surprise that the first miracle of Jesus is that he starts with water then turns it into wine. At the risk of repeating myself, I cannot emphasise enough how important the Holy Spirit is going to be in the rest of the story of the Bible.

John the Baptist

To set the scene, after the purge of Nebuchadnezzar, the remnant of Judah who returned from exile to rebuild Jerusalem, were determined to obey the commandments of Yhwh and stay as righteous as they could. The practice of idolatry was, at last, stamped out and is no longer a problem to the Jewish people. However, the kings and the religious leaders, including the parties of the Pharisees and the Sadducees (the latter did not even believe in an afterlife) remained under the Serpent. They remained the bad shepherds, and instead of guiding the people to Yhwh, they taught false interpretations of the law which guided them towards the Serpent. They are a real problem to those on the side of Yhwh, constantly opposing and trying to kill Jesus, and they are targeted by John the Baptist and then Jesus, who both tried to turn them back to Yhwh, but they are particularly stubborn, and they prevent many people from turning too. Yhwh calls these stubborn people 'stiff necked' because they do not turn their heads back to Yhwh. John the Baptist calls them a brood of vipers, and Jesus calls them hypocrites.

The empire of Babylon has gone, but the people are now under the empire of Rome. That is not such a bad thing, because Rome has introduced a great civilisation which is based on a rigid system of law and order, and which is for the most part, a just system. As you probably expect by now, the emperor of the Roman empire is a spiritual descendant of Nimrod, and so the chosen people remain in good hands. In particular, the Romans separate the religious laws from their civil laws, so the law of Moses is permitted to continue. No other nations or kings of the earth are able to withstand or overcome the Roman army, so the situation has been stable for a long time. The problem will be that the internal politics of Rome will be corrupted by the Serpent, so revolts and new leaders installed by the Serpent will replace the good emperors installed by Yhwh. But that will happen after the age of Jesus. The worst of these emperors will be Nero, who persecutes and kills the early Christians, and he will be known as the anti-Christ.

John is born to elderly parents from a long line of priests. His mother was childless and barren, in the manner of many others who had to wait a long time for the right time to come. In fact, John is the end of an old line of priests and prophets, the line of Elijah, but he now serves Yhwh not through the old way of sacrifice and offerings, but through repentance and turning to Yhwh, bringing forgiveness, redemption and salvation to heaven. Everything that was needed to prepare the way for Jesus and the Holy Spirit. When Gabriel foretells his arrival to John's father, she specifically states that '*he will go before him in the spirit and the power of Elijah.*'

When John grows up, he lives in the wilderness and wears a garment of camel hair and a leather belt, eating locusts and honey. That means he is living like an animal of Darkness and eating the spiritual food of the law of Darkness (honey) as you would expect in his line. However, this Law is the true, uncorrupted, law of Moses, and specifically the sweet side of blessings and inheritance. His preaching was special, because he called for repentance not just routinely, but because '*the kingdom of heaven is at hand.*' That means he was preaching the blessings of salvation to heaven, and that the long awaited seventh day of Yhwh was near. The people didn't have to wait any longer, because his baptism today would give them salvation at judgement day, which although they didn't know it, was only one generation away, which came after them.

Many people did come to him, and they did repent and were washed clean in the Jordan, baptised in water, and redeemed. But they were not filled with the Holy Spirit. Even the religious leaders came to see what was happening, but they did not repent and were not baptised. John recognised them for who and what they were, saying, *'You brood of vipers! Who warned you to flee from the wrath to come?'* That means judgement day. Since they were filled with the spirit of the Serpent, they were like the Serpent's offspring, or brood, and they were lined up for the fire to be given to the Serpent, not the mercy to be given to the people. Unless they repented and changed sides, that is. John's baptism and this comment summed up judgement day. We will see that the lost sheep will be saved, but the bad shepherds who led them astray would be condemned.

John then explained what he was preparing the way for. He said, *'I baptise you with water for repentance, but he who is coming after me is mightier than I. He will baptize you with the Holy Spirit and with fire.'* The Holy Spirit is for the salvation of his followers, and the fire is also from the Holy Spirit, but for the purge of the spirit of the Serpent. More significantly, John explains that it will be Jesus who will judge and decide who will go into salvation and who will be purged. He will *'gather his wheat into the barn, but the chaff he will burn with unquenchable fire.'* You would think that would be enough to persuade the religious leaders to repent, but the problem is that they don't know they are working for the Serpent, they are deceived and convinced by the Serpent that their teaching is correct and that it is the teaching of John which is wrong. So they ignore him.

John became famous, and popular with the people, since he was a saviour. Clearly, he was not so popular with the Serpent, who wanted him dead. I mentioned when we looked at Elijah and the king and queen, that it was not just the religious leaders who were under the Serpent, but the kings too, and sure enough, King Herod had

The Fifth Age – John the Baptist and Jesus

him arrested and imprisoned. John, being a righteous man of the Law, had told him that he could not lawfully be married to his wife Herodias, because she was still married to his brother, another king of the region, Philip. Herodias has the hallmarks of a descendent of Jezebel, and is capable of getting whatever she wants from her husband – or husbands. In fact there are many similarities with the actions of Jezebel in the time of Elijah (in the fourth age). She is a 'false prophet' of the Serpent and fed the king with evil advice. She is opposed to John because he gives the king good advice from Yhwh and John seeks to have her removed. She seeks to kill John because he is a true prophet to the king.

Herod had only imprisoned John and not executed him, because he feared the people who correctly held him to be a prophet. Herodias had no such qualms. As a birthday present, her daughter danced seductively for the king and he foolishly offered her anything she wanted. This is another example of a foolish king doing a foolish thing for the benefit of the Serpent, then being stuck with it because it cannot be rescinded. It is a cycle which started with the covenant of Darkness entered into in heaven by Michael with his daughter the Moon. To promise to do anything that was requested, means he has in practice delegated his royal authority to the Serpent, a terrible mistake, much like the original one. Prompted by her mother she asked for the head of John, which he was obliged to give her because of his oath, even though he regretted it.

Thus John dies, but we have not heard the last of his spirit, Elijah, who is taken to heaven but will soon return.

The virgin conception of Jesus
Shortly after John is conceived, Gabriel visits a woman called Mary to explain that although she will stay a virgin, she is going to conceive and give birth to the Messiah. The important thing to realise about this birth is that Jesus is going to be the new Messiah, replacing the old. The old is the first Adam who fell and rejected the Holy Spirit

of the Tree of Life. Jesus is the new Adam who will not fall and will bring the Holy Spirit with its salvation. Therefore, like the first Adam, he will be made in the image of God, that is, he will be three in one. However, because he is the new Adam, a sin free man of Light, he must not have any of the fallen spirits of the old Adam of Darkness. That means nothing must come from Mary's husband to be, Joseph, and that is why this must be a virgin conception.

The first Messianic identity is 'the word of Yhwh', and this spirit is already in Mary and will be passed by her to Jesus in the womb. This will make Jesus a prophet who hears and speaks the word of Yhwh perfectly.

The second is the Holy Spirit which will come upon Mary and Jesus in the womb, and make him Holy, although this is the Holy Spirit of fire. It will turn to the Holy Spirit of water later in the life of Jesus, just before he starts his ministry.

The third is the spirit of the Sun or King David, who is the son of God. His mother is Yhwh, in Gabriel, and this spirit is already in the womb of Mary. His father is not Joseph, but Elohiym in Michael, a spirit of Darkness. He comes to Mary and he *'casts a shadow over her'* with his spirit of righteous Darkness. This is the spiritual conception of the Sun. That means that Jesus does have both a divine father and mother in the spiritual world, and that he is made in their image. Gabriel says to Mary, *'Therefore, the child to be born will be called Holy – the Son of God.'*

In summary, these three spirits make Jesus complete and new and sinless. If Mary's husband to be, Joseph, had been involved, his paternal spirit would have been descended from the old Adam after he fell. If you compare Jesus's birth to John the Baptist's birth, John had two old parents and he represented the old. However, Jesus had a new mother, a young virgin from the next generation, and no spirit from his old father, so he represented the new. Thus, Mary had to remain a virgin in physical terms, and her conception was pure and spiritual. It is the Holy Spirit which creates and which brings the breath of life, and it is the male and female side of God who gives their spirits to the Messiah so that he is made in their image.

Mary, the blessed one

One final point about Mary, and why she is so special. Her spirit is the original Messianic spirit of Yhwh (the word of Yhwh) which had been given to woman from the rib of Adam, when they were separated during creation. This is the pure spirit before the fall of Eve, so it is from the time when Eve was simply called 'woman'. Now we have the new Adam and the new Woman, neither of whom have fallen. This time, Adam and Woman will not fall and will not choose to reject the Holy Spirit in favour of the spirit of the Serpent. When they receive the Holy Spirit, they become the complete, sin free, unfallen Adam and Woman, both people of Light as was always intended.

Because they are people of Light they will inherit the earth. To inherit means to be blessed, therefore Mary is called '*blessed among women*'. Specifically, she has just been chosen and blessed by Gabriel, with huge consequences for mankind.

My final point regarding Mary is that she was not pure and innocent and blessed, before Gabriel came to her. Her name, Mary, means 'their rebellion' reminding us that she was part of fallen Israel, who was descended from fallen Eve, not Woman. Yet Israel were always the chosen ones and Gabriel calls her 'favoured one' to remind us of that. However, now, Mary has been spiritually transformed from a fallen descendant of Eve to the original unfallen woman, making her the mother of the **new** chosen people.

Jesus will make a point of calling her 'woman' which is not an insult, it is a compliment. He is saying that she represents the new chosen people who unlike Eve, did not fall. Mary will not be the mother of the new chosen people through Joseph her husband to be, who has fallen, but through her son, Jesus who has not. Perhaps this point explains the necessity of the virgin birth best of all.

The birth of Jesus

The result of all this is that when Jesus is born, he is perfectly prepared for his tasks. Apart from one thing. He is a tiny baby and very vulnerable, and the Serpent was looking for him, to find and kill him. So Gabriel and the Sun in the spiritual world, set about hiding and protecting him. It was widely expected that when the Messiah came, he would come from Bethlehem, like King David his forefather. That is indeed where he was born, so the best they could do for his safety was hide him in a place nobody would look. Not a palace fit for a king, not a nice room at a comfortable inn, but a stable full of animals, all creatures of darkness. But the animals were domestic and under Yhwh. Bethlehem means 'house of bread', and Jesus was himself the bread to come, where bread means the food of spiritual knowledge, especially for the lost sheep. Mary therefore laid him in a manger, where the animals go for their food.

His Holiness (called his glory) would be visible to angels, including those sent by the Serpent, so she fully wrapped him in swaddling clothes which were spiritually opaque. Jesus was therefore well hidden.

The shepherds

Then Gabriel set up angelic protection all around him, her own 'watchers' on earth, called shepherds of the lost sheep. They protected their flocks at night when they were prone to attack from the Serpent. She told them who Jesus was and where he was, so that they could surround and protect him, and they went. At the same time, she revealed a huge heavenly angelic army, who were on standby if required. The Christmas story assumes that physical shepherds are being described, but it is actually about the guardian angels in the spiritual world, both earthly and heavenly.

The wise men, or magi

Meanwhile, some of the Serpent's angels in heaven had seen the dawn of the Messiah of light, that is the rising of the angelic Sun, or the star of King David. She sent some magi to find him on earth. A magus is a magician and they are filled with the spirit of the Serpent, and practice divination and other spiritual gifts from the Serpent. They have been around since the magi of the Pharaoh in Egypt who performed minor miracles against Moses. They are wise, because of the wisdom of the Serpent, and they are therefore very dangerous. These are angels from heaven, so they come from the 'east', a code word for travellers from heaven. They sought Jesus and lied that they planned to worship him. Actually, they planned to kill him. Like all the magi, they were rich, and they carried spiritual riches from the Serpent which would cover their needs as they travelled.

They didn't know where Jesus would be, and had lost sight of the star of David, so they had nothing to follow and instead they went to King Herod in Jerusalem. He was a king of the Serpent and he also wanted Jesus dead, which they would have known. They made no attempt to connect with Yhwh or her people. Instead, Herod consults his priests who tell him the Messiah will be born in Bethlehem, and the Magi tell him when they saw the star of David leave heaven. So they have the place and the time.

As they left Jerusalem for Bethlehem, the star they had seen in heaven appeared to them again. Actually, he was right in front of them, and he blocked their way. The Sun had no intention of letting these magi get to Jesus. But in fear of the Sun, as soon as they saw him, they bowed down before him and therefore turned away from the Serpent (the Moon) to follow him (the Sun). As soon as they became followers, their spirits of the Serpent were cast out, then they were filled with the Holy Spirit and they 'rejoiced exceedingly with great joy'. You always experience great joy when you receive the Holy Spirit. Thus, the magi became the first to receive the salvation of the Messiah through holiness, and they followed him. At that point, Jesus was safe.

The Sun then led them to the stable in Bethlehem, and they fell down and worshipped Jesus. They gave him their riches from the Serpent, gold, frankincense and myrrh, and they were the first to do this good deed too. The giving of immoral riches will become a feature of turning from the Serpent to Jesus, especially in the age of the apostles. Now Mary knew that the myrrh was a valuable ointment which reduced the pain of burning in the fire, so she hid it and kept it for Jesus at the appointed time. She will use it on Jesus, just before he was crucified. Look out for a jar of very expensive ointment, applied by a woman called Mary, just before Jesus entered Jerusalem to be crucified. He knew it and his mother knew it, and his mother would do the best she could to help her son through his terrible ordeal. Not death, but burning in hell as he redeemed his people and suffered their sins on their behalf.

That night the magi had a dream from Yhwh, their first spiritual contact with Yhwh, through the Holy Spirit, which warned them not to go back to Herod. So they departed to 'their own country', heaven, 'by another way.' The other way was the way of Light, having turned from the Serpent's way of Darkness. 'The way' is what the early church of the followers of Jesus will be called.

The story of the magi is important, not because they praised and worshipped Jesus, but because they are the first to turn from the Serpent to follow Jesus and be filled by the Holy Spirit and receive the salvation it brings. Or if you like, they are the first Christians. Note that they turned when they first met the angel of the Sun. This is when the Sun first used his authority to cast out the spirit of the Serpent, using the power of the divine Holy Spirit, without killing the person. Up to this point, casting out the spirit has been impossible, since it requires the divine Holy Spirit, which is to be demonstrated in this age, then released in the next age. As soon as the spirit of the Serpent left them, they followed Jesus and received the Holy Spirit

The Fifth Age – John the Baptist and Jesus 261

to replace it. The deeper you look, you see that whole process of the salvation of Light is included, if you know what to look for!

Meanwhile Herod was furious when he heard that the magi had turned and failed in their mission, and he had all the male children in Bethlehem under two years old, killed. Just like the Pharaoh had done at the birth of Moses. He knew the age from the time that the magi told him they saw the star leave heaven, before their conversion. But having been warned by Gabriel, Joseph and his new family had already left, to hide in Egypt. But why Egypt? Isn't that a nation under the Serpent?

As we know from the times of Joseph and Moses, if you have the right Pharaoh in place, in the line of Enoch and Nimrod, Egypt is a good place to hide and grow. The Pharaoh is not identified here, but you can safely assume that he is Moses, come down to earth again to protect Jesus. Therefore, both of the secret weapons of Yhwh (Moses and Elijah, the law and the prophets) are working, as you would expect. Sure enough, they will both appear in angelic form with Jesus, towards the end of his ministry.

Jesus prepares for his ministry

Jesus grew up safely, and returned from Egypt. He showed exceptional knowledge and understanding of the Law, impressing his teachers greatly. He spent time in the temple and partaking in the rituals. He was very much a young, righteous Jew, and he embraced the Law. Thus for Jesus too, Darkness came first, and this explains why his Holy Spirit was initially the Holy Spirit of fire.

John the Baptist was already preaching his message of repentance and baptism in water, so Jesus went to him and was baptised. John was surprised, but Jesus knew that this was necessary to demonstrate the fulfilment of the time of righteousness under the law. The law would be replaced by the Holy Spirit, and that is exactly what happened to Jesus. Immediately after he was baptised in water, he received the Holy Spirit of Yhwh as a dove appeared and rested on

Jesus, and a voice from heaven said '*This is my beloved Son, with whom I am well pleased.*' A dove is the angelic soul of Yhwh, and because Yhwh was satisfied that he was worthy, Jesus had passed from the justice system of Darkness to Light. From old to new. From water to wine.

As soon as Jesus received the Holy Spirit of Light, he would have been full of the new spirits of Understanding and Wisdom of the way of mercy, and the new covenant was instantly written on his heart of flesh. He would need time to digest it all, without the distraction of the old teaching and doctrines, and so he went into the wilderness for 40 days and 40 nights. Even Jesus needed time to fully understand the hidden mysteries of scripture.

There, when he had finished understanding scripture, he was met by the Serpent, who tempted him, to test him. He tried three times, one for each identity, using the arguments of wealth and power and empires, that had worked on mankind since creation. Would he fall like the first Adam? No, he overcame the Serpent by using his new understanding of the true and hidden meanings of scripture, and quoting from it, to reject every temptation.

At the end of the trial, Jesus had passed, and he was ready to start his ministry.

The ministry of Jesus

The main purpose of Jesus was to teach and demonstrate what will happen in the coming kingdom of Light. You can split the ministry into three categories, one per Messianic spiritual identity:

- His preaching and teaching, which uses his prophetic gift, including his sermons and parables and riddles – Gabriel, the word of Yhwh
- His divine authority, which casts out the spirit of the Serpent – the Sun and King David, enforced by the divine Holy Spirit

- His healing miracles, which demonstrate the replacement of the spirit of the Serpent with the divine Holy Spirit.

Here, we will look at just a few of the more famous examples, but in Book Three, we will look at a greater selection and in more depth.

Changing water into wine

This is the first miracle of Jesus, taking place just after he started to gain his disciples. These twelve men are pre-chosen and important because there is one for each of the twelve tribes. They will follow Jesus during his ministry and gain a lot of knowledge from his teaching, but they won't understand much of what he says until after he dies, when they become apostles to the twelve tribes. At that point they receive the Holy Spirit and they then understand the ministry of Jesus and all of scripture too. They spread the teaching of Jesus and the Holy Spirit to all of Israel, with mixed results. Later, Paul will spread them to the Gentiles. Thus, after they have received the wine of the Holy Spirit, the disciples will be instrumental in turning the water of mercy into the wine of the Holy Spirit and salvation, which Jesus is now about to demonstrate.

This miracle is full of spiritual symbology which is easy to miss, but it reveals important mysteries in the story. There is much more to this than simply turning water to wine. We could keep it really simple and repeat that Jesus is transitioning from the water of mercy to the Holy Spirit and the Tree of Life. However, to show you an example of the wealth of information hidden in the stories, we are going to look for the hidden messages, sometimes line by line. We will see that this simple story is really a riddle with many levels of meanings. It's a glimpse of what we will see in the next two books, but we won't go too deep here.

There is a wedding at Cana in Galilee and Mary, Jesus and the disciples are invited. Now weddings are an important feature in the new testament. That's because when the Holy Spirit fills you it is like a marriage bond, and when a follower of Jesus receives the Holy Spirit through him, they become 'married' to him. At the wedding, there was wine to drink, which represented the old wine of the Serpent, because at this stage, the people are the old people of Darkness, and all of them are fallen. Then the wine ran out (like a famine or a drought), and Mary commented to Jesus that they have run out. This is to represent the time in the future when the spirit of the Serpent will be purged, rather like a famine, ready for the Holy Spirit to replace it.

Mary knows that Jesus's ministry is to replace the old wine with the new wine of the Holy Spirit, but that first there must be cleansing with the water of mercy. She also knows that it is time to start. Jesus disagrees and he says, '*Woman, what does this have to do with me? My hour has not yet come.*' It is apparent that Mary is prophetic, and that Jesus is not hearing Yhwh directly, only through Mary, who he calls 'woman', for the reasons we have looked at. This is showing us that, like in creation, Mary is 'woman' who was Adam's prophet or Yhwh's 'word' to Yhwh. Without the spirit of the word, Adam could not hear Yhwh, and neither could Jesus. But he could hear woman.

Mary does not argue the point, she has already passed on the message, so she has done her job. However, she commands the servants, who at that time are obeying her, 'Do whatever he tells you.' At that moment, Mary has handed over her authority over the servants to Jesus. This is representing the time when Gabriel will hand over her authority over the divine Holy Spirit to the Sun, king David. From then on, he has both the full authority and power of God. You might say what authority is Mary handing over here, and why does she have authority over the servants at this wedding and why is it relevant? This little mystery is hidden in a little riddle, and the key is the location.

Cana means 'place of reeds' and reeds are righteous guardian angels in the waters of, and under the authority of, and serving, Yhwh. Remember the upright reeds in Egypt and the Red Sea?

The Fifth Age – John the Baptist and Jesus

These are the servants at the wedding feast. They are an angel army, all around the room and the town, full of the power of the Holy Spirit. That shows the level of authority which is being passed over. Jesus is taking control of the hidden angel army around him, even at the very beginning of his ministry. Mary has authority over the servants because she has the spirit of Yhwh in her, who is doing the talking.

Moving on, in the room are six empty stone water jars, Their purpose is to provide the water used in the purification rites under the law, which cleanse people who have become unclean. It's like an early form of the cleansing water of baptism. Jesus tells the servants (now under his authority) to fill the jars with water, which they do. But this water is from an old ritual of the law, and Jesus needs to replace it with the new wine, which will fulfil (or complete) its role under the law. So, he turns it to wine and tells the servants to take a sample to the master of the feast. When he tastes it, he called the bridegroom and said, '*Everyone serves the good wine first, and when the people have drunk freely, then the poor wine. But you have kept the good wine until now.*'

It is true that the good wine has been kept until now, but only because it had been rejected by Adam and Woman in the Garden of Eden. Now, at last, the new Adam (with the approval of the new Woman) is accepting it and distributing it to all who would drink it. In the wedding ceremony to come in the seventh age of salvation, Jesus will be called the bridegroom, and it is he who will have ended the bitter old wine of the serpent, and changed the waters of Yhwh to the good new wine of the Holy Spirit. And he has the full authority over it, to use its power as he sees fit, as he starts his ministry.

That completes the riddle of the first miracle.

The sermon on the mount

This is the first sermon of Jesus, delivered to the house of Israel, the lost sheep. He is giving a message of hope, about turning Darkness to Light, and saying that it is they who are the people of Light, and that they will inherit the earth in the coming kingdom of Light. But they must turn away from Darkness, especially judgement and punishment, and turn to Light, especially mercy and forgiveness. He gives some memorable examples. Especially, he says that if they show mercy they will receive mercy, but if they judge they will be judged, and if they give punishments then they will receive punishment. It's a very long sermon, which we will look at in depth in Book Three, but let's look at the key points here.

Jesus starts by listing some qualities of the people who will inherit the earth – the people of Light:

- The people of Israel are poor in the spirit, because they are still blind to the spiritual world and do not have the Holy Spirit
- They mourn the dead, but they will be comforted when they experience everlasting life through the Holy Spirit
- They are meek, whereas the people of the Serpent are proud, which are features of the Holy Spirit or the spirit of the Serpent
- If they hunger and thirst for the true spiritual knowledge of Yhwh, they will receive it and be satisfied. Hunger satisfied by bread and thirst satisfied by wine, the Holy Spirit. But if not the wine, then they will receive the water of mercy
- If they are merciful, they will be shown mercy, leading to redemption
- They will be pure in heart because they will be sin free after their redemption
- If they lead others to the peace of righteousness through redemption by the son of God, they will be called the sons of God. This is because they will carry the spirit of Jesus, and will be called a spiritual brother of Jesus. If you are a brother of the son of God, that makes you a son of God too. (The apostles will call all those filled with the Holy Spirit the brethren.)

- The people of Light will be persecuted by the people of Darkness, even to becoming martyrs, but they will be rewarded in heaven, through salvation.
- They are the Light of the world, and their example should be seen by others. Then the word and Holy Spirit of Light will spread.

Next, Jesus deals with the old law and the prophets. It is true that he will replace them with the new way and the Holy Spirit, but not yet. Only after judgement day. Until then, the law and the prophets will continue exactly as before, but after then, in the seventh age of light, the law and the prophets will have served their purpose, and will have been fulfilled. The new covenant will replace the old covenant, and the places of the covenanted are heaven and spiritual earth. So when they are replaced, the old heaven and earth will pass away, and will be replaced by the new heaven and earth of the new covenant. Later we will see this happening and it is described as the old heaven and earth being rolled up like a scroll – which is the scroll of the old law.

Then Jesus describes some examples of the system of Darkness that most people will not have realised are Darkness. You must avoid them or you can be caught in a trap of Darkness and receive fire.

- To be angry with your brother means you have judged him. If you judge, then you are on the way of Darkness and you will be judged in return.
- To call someone a fool means you must think you are wise, and in the absence of the Holy Spirit, the wisdom comes from the Serpent.
- Do not resort to the courts to settle disputes, since the courts are a feature of Darkness, and if the judge of Darkness (the Serpent) gets his hands on you then he won't let go until you have paid every penny you owe, not just what you are

disputing. That's because the legal arguments you use against others will be used against you, because you too are far from righteousness in any system of Darkness. Rather avoid the judge and be reconciled with your accuser before you get to court, because that settlement will involve forgiveness to an extent, even if it is not deserved, and then you will receive the same. In other words you will be showing you are on the way of Light, not Darkness, and will receive the forgiveness of Light.

- Don't make an oath at all, just do what you say you will do. If you break an oath, you can expect punishment from the person or thing you use as a pledge. So especially don't swear an oath by God.
- Don't live by the law of an eye for an eye and a tooth for a tooth. It simply leads to the escalation of fire. The alternatives are clever ways of outwitting the serpent, such as turning the other cheek, or walking the extra mile, which we will look at in Book Three. In many ways, when you understand them, these are the most important examples in the whole sermon. If you struggle to outwit the Serpent then ask Yhwh, because she does it every time and she will give you her own wisdom!
- Don't just love your neighbour but love you enemies and pray for those who persecute you.
- Love is the best answer to hate, and it is what Yhwh uses. Her mercy extends to everyone, like the rain falls on both the just and the unjust, friend and enemy. So must yours if you want to experience the rain too.

The guidance continues at length and in the same vein. All of it is meant to tell people how to leave their life of fire under the law, and turn to a life of mercy. We will see all of the points made in this long sermon, including the Lord's Prayer, in Book Three. They also reveal an amazing hidden spiritual structure to the sermon, which reveals that Jesus is a special prophet who delivers pure scripture, even when he is simply speaking, not when carefully preparing a written text. That's because it's the word of Yhwh in him who is speaking.

Then, having explained about the way of mercy, Jesus will live his life by it, as a demonstration to us all. For example, even when he is dealing with the religious leaders who are firmly against him and out to kill him, he is calm and gentle in his teaching, showing no sign of judgement or fire against them. He merely explains why they are hypocrites, and attempts to correct them. Until finally, when it is time for his own death, he judges the hypocrites, knowing that means he will be judged in return, and sentenced to death.

The parable of the good Samaritan
Parables are riddles hidden in stories. Some of the stories appear to be fiction with a moral message, while others are actually real lives being lived as a living parable. However, when you unravel the riddle, you see that they are all true stories about a greater mystery. Most of them have multiple layers of understanding before you get to the main point.

The parable of the good Samaritan is one of those. It is a very famous parable, short and to the point, and it is often used as an example of how Christians should live, showing behaviour of mercy and kindness, even when you are despised by everyone. Although that is true, there are deeper meanings which are relatively easy to unravel, so let's look at them here, to illustrate what I mean about the riddles. We will start with the basic meanings and then take a look at the progressively deeper ones. This is a small preview of what we will be looking at in the next two books.

Most people would recount the parable like this. A man was travelling on a road when he was attacked, robbed and beaten, leaving him half dead. A priest and then a Levite were going down the road and saw him, but passed by on the other side of the road. Then a despised Samaritan came to him and took compassion on him. He tended his wounds and took him to an inn, to take care of him. Then he paid the innkeeper to care for him while he was away and promised to repay any further expenses when he returned. Therefore, it was the Samaritan who showed him mercy and who was his neighbour, so we should be like him.

That seems to be the message, but it isn't. Let's look again.

First, why is Jesus telling this story? It is to answer a question from a man of the law who wants to know how to get eternal life in heaven. Therefore, this riddle is about salvation. Jesus asks the man what he thinks the law says, because the man is an expert on the law. He replies with the commandment of love on which all the law is based, *'You shall love Yhwh your God with all your heart and with all your soul and with all your strength and with all your mind, and your neighbour as yourself.'* That is a perfect answer and Jesus says that if he does this, then he will have eternal life. That could be the end of it, but the man asks, 'who is my neighbour?' He has understood the first part about loving Yhwh, and that is enough to receive the love of Yhwh in return, which means her redemption and resurrection to heaven. But that does not mention the Messiah or the Holy Spirit, so it will not lead to the salvation of the Holy Spirit given to the followers of Jesus. To get that, he needs to understand the second part, to love his neighbour. That is what the parable is all about – to answer his question, who is his neighbour? So let's look at the parable in that context.

To fully understand a parable, you have to understand all the symbology used by it, especially to reveal who the characters involved actually represent. The man in the riddle is on a road or a way which takes him away from Jerusalem, where Yhwh and the king reside. He is a man who lives by the way of the law, that is Darkness, but he has turned from Yhwh and is going further away from her. He was set upon by the people of the Serpent who hate him and who persecuted and beat him, stole his salvation, and so he was already half dead. This shows us that the man represents the lost sheep of Israel who Jesus came to save. He was going away from Jerusalem, so he was moving away from salvation.

Then two religious leaders came. They are the shepherds of the lost sheep, and they are meant to look after their flock, saving them from attack at night and healing them when they are hurt. The priest represents the Law, and the Levite represents the prophets. Moses and Aaron were Levites. They are meant to teach the true law and keep their flock on the right path, but these shepherds have fallen, teaching the corrupt law of the Serpent, and are now only hypocrites. They simply turn away and let their flock die. They represent the bad shepherds or the hypocrites, the fallen religious leaders of the Pharisees and Sadducees.

Then the Samaritan comes. Remember that Samaria was the capital of Israel and was where the king of Israel had his throne. Jesus is not just the Messianic king of Judah, he is the Messianic king of the house of Israel, through Gabriel. Jesus can therefore be properly described as a Samaritan. We also saw when we looked at the ten commandments that he was the neighbour whose wife and other possessions should not be coveted by the Serpent. So he is both the neighbour and the Samaritan. To give a complete description, he is both the old Samaritan of Israel and the new Samaritan of the gentiles who now live in Samaria. He wishes to give salvation to both groups of people.

Now let's look at what happens at that level of understanding. The story says that the priest and the Levite were passing by a coincidence, and had not intended to be there. But it is implied that the Samaritan came to the victim deliberately. He bound up his wounds, which symbolises overcoming and binding the spirit of the Serpent so it could not manifest any more. Then he poured on oil and wine. That's not normal medicine or healing, that is the Holy Spirit of Counsel (oil) and the complete Holy Spirit (wine). He has just symbolised healing the lost sheep and then baptising them in the Holy Spirit. This is the salvation of holiness, only available through Jesus.

The inn represents the early church and the inn keeper is the apostles. Jesus leaves them to care for the recently healed new converts, and he pays in full for their salvation, taking nothing from anyone else. Then Jesus promises to return at the end of the age, and to settle any additional debt that has arisen while he was away.

So when Jesus asks the man who is his neighbour, he correctly says, '*The one who showed him mercy.*' It is not the way of darkness that gives you the salvation of the Holy Spirit, it is the way of mercy, the way of Light. The principle is that if you show mercy then you will receive mercy. Jesus replies, '*You go and do likewise,*' telling him to show mercy and then receive it.

That is the end of the parable, but is this the whole of the mystery? No, there remains an unanswered question. What happened to the man of the law and the two priests who left the victim and did not care for him in the story? This is an example of the mystery being revealed in several pieces of a jigsaw. In the first piece we revealed that the parable is about salvation and how it is achieved through the mercy of Jesus, our good shepherd. We also saw that the bad shepherds did nothing to help. We assume that the two bad shepherds did not repent, because they continue on their way which is away from Jerusalem. So what does happen to them? Likewise, the man of the law, another shepherd, leaves with the knowledge of how to be saved, but he has a choice to make. Will he show mercy so he will receive it, or not?

The last words in the first jigsaw piece are '*You go and do likewise.*' Jesus will continue the jigsaw with another piece a little later (Matthew 25). The link between them is '*You go and do likewise.*' So let's continue, to see what happens.

Jesus will describe how, when he returns at judgement day, he will sit on his throne in heaven as king and judge. He says that like a shepherd, he will divide the spirits of the people he is judging into two groups. Those who are blessed and will inherit the coming kingdom, and those who are cursed and will not inherit. What is the test he will use to determine into which group the spirits before him will go? It is simply whether or not they showed mercy like the good shepherd did to the victim in the parable. This is therefore the link. If the man of the law had gone and done likewise, he would be in the group who were to inherit, which is the answer to his original question.

Certainly this is about the principle that if they show mercy then they will receive mercy, but this message goes a little deeper still.

This is what Jesus said, to those who were good shepherds and will inherit. *"'For I was hungry and you gave me food, I was thirsty and you gave me drink, I was a stranger and you welcomed me, I was naked and you clothed me, I was sick and you visited me, I was in prison and you came to me." Then the righteous will answer him, saying "Lord, when did we see you hungry and feed you or thirsty and give you drink? And when did we see you a stranger and welcome you, or naked and clothe you? And when did we see you sick or in prison and visit you?" and the King will answer them, "Truly, I say to you, as you did it to one of the least of these my brothers, you did it to me.'"*

The deeper message is that we all start as victims of the Serpent, but when we are healed we should become shepherds of other victims. The victims are the lost sheep of Israel, but when they are healed they are no longer lost and they become shepherds to guide the others to the way of salvation.

There is more. Jesus is the king of Israel at the head of the house of Israel, and he knows every one of his lost sheep. That's because spiritually, they are all his offspring and followers, connected to him like his hair, and so they are all part of him and together they are one. Therefore, whatever is done to them, is done to Jesus. And if you show mercy to them, you show mercy to Jesus. Then he will show mercy to you and redeem you.

Remember that Jesus is the king of Israel, and Samaria is the old capital of Israel, and that is why he is the good Samaritan. He is saying that everyone in his kingdom should be a good Samaritan. Jesus calls this group his sheep, but not his **lost** sheep, and he places them on his right, the side of inheritance. Whoever is on the right side is redeemed and saved. We can hope that the man of the law showed mercy and is in this group.

Hopefully you can already see that when the riddles are explained, the underlying messages are quite straightforward. They are all about love and mercy, water to put out fire.

Then Jesus has the opposite message for the other group of spirits on the left side, who do not inherit, but are cursed. These are the spirits of the Serpent who beat up the people of Jesus and make them their victims in the first place, and it includes the bad shepherds who then did nothing to help them. The same list of healing and mercy is used, but they did none of them. They are all purged and are not redeemed or saved. Instead, they suffer the fire that they have chosen.

Jesus said, '"*Depart from me, you cursed, into the eternal fire prepared for the devil and his angels. For I was hungry and you gave me no food, I was thirsty and you gave me no drink, I was a stranger and you did not welcome me, naked and you did not clothe me, sick or in prison and you did not visit me."* Then they will answer saying, *"Lord, when did we see you hungry or thirsty or a stranger or naked or sick or in prison, and did not minister to you?"* Then he will answer them saying, *"Truly I say to you, as you did not do it to one of the least of these, you did not do it to me."* And these will go away into eternal punishment, but the righteous into eternal life.'

This group are not identified as sheep but as goats. What's the difference? Sheep represent Israel and goats represent Judah. Yhwh is not saying that all of Judah is going to be punished, rather that these goats are the bad shepherds, the corrupt religious leaders of the temple of Jerusalem, and all of them are from Judah. The rest of Judah will be redeemed by the Sun.

There are other pieces of the jigsaw of judgement day, and all the examples have the same message. Whether it is between the good

The Fifth Age – John the Baptist and Jesus

shepherd or the bad shepherd; or between the sheep or the goats; or between the wheat or the chaff; or between the good wine or the sour wine, the spirits of Light are saved and enter the kingdom of heaven, and Serpent and the spirits of the Serpent are purged and punished by fire. And if you are worried about the coming judgement day, remember that the redeemed and the holy are not even judged.

Whenever you start to get lost in the mysteries, the one thing you need to remember is that to receive salvation to heaven, you only need to follow the Messiah, Jesus. He will sort the rest out. You will either be redeemed and resurrected or filled with the Holy Spirit, but he knows which is right for you. Alternatively, if you don't believe in Jesus, you can follow Yhwh directly and you will be redeemed, but you will not receive the Holy Spirit. What you should avoid is to choose to follow the Serpent and lead others astray. The best way to see the difference between the messages of the Serpent and the Messiah, is to ask yourself if they show love and mercy or not.

The Miracles

The arrival of the divine Holy Spirit changes everything, and the miracles are all about what the Holy Spirit will bring. Rather than just talk about it, Jesus demonstrates both the power of the Holy Spirit and the divine authority Jesus has over it – and the spirit of the Serpent that it replaces. In Book Three we will look at a few individual miracles in some depth. But here, rather than listing many miracles, I will split them into groups and explain the underlying spiritual meanings of each group, starting with the healing of leprosy. Then I will describe three examples of miracles in action.

Leprosy

Why leprosy? Because it is an infectious visible skin disease which looks similar to the spiritual appearance of the uncleanliness of sin on the flesh of people and angels, if you could see them in the spiritual world. When you 'expose your nakedness', which started with Adam and Eve in the Garden of Eden, God and Jesus and other angels can see your sins. It is these that are temporally washed off with the waters of Yhwh. But what Jesus is demonstrating is the next stage from washing, it is covering of sins with 'linen'. When your sins are redeemed, you lose your sins, and they will be taken by your redeemer and your punishment will be served by him. In the meantime, you are covered with a spirit called 'linen' which is spiritually opaque and hides your sins. Therefore, you appear to be sin free and this is called to be 'deemed righteous'. When you are judged at judgement day, your linen is a mark that you have been redeemed, you are treated as being righteous, and you will pass into heaven.

Linen is a spirit of mercy from Yhwh, but it is not the full Holy Spirit. It goes on you but not in you. So, in summary, Jesus is demonstrating the salvation of redemption and resurrection. When lepers approach him, you can see their disease, but when they leave, they are covered in 'linen' and they appear to be clean. In the spirit world they are sin free and deemed to be righteous. However, the spirit of the Serpent in them is not cast out, it is suppressed and bound up by Yhwh's spirit of mercy, so that it cannot manifest. The final point is that when Jesus the good Samaritan, bound the wounds of the man, he used linen to bind them.

Other miracles demonstrate the full Holy Spirit in the followers of Jesus, which replace the spirit of the Serpent. There are seven sub-spirits in the Holy Spirit, each with their own function or gift.

Deaf and mute

You can only hear Yhwh speak and then speak what she tells you, through the Holy Spirit of Counsel (called olive oil in the spiritual world). Without the Holy Spirit you are therefore spiritually deaf and dumb. However, if you receive the spirit of the Serpent then you receive the Counsel of the Serpent through it, and you can hear and speak the word of the Serpent. Yhwh usually intervenes and makes you completely spiritually deaf or dumb so you hear neither voice.

When you are filled by the Holy Spirit, the spirit of the Serpent has been cast out and, through the spirit of Counsel with Yhwh, you can hear and speak the word of Yhwh, and you are no longer spiritually deaf or dumb.

Lame

It sounds strange, but the position in the body for the Holy Spirit is the legs and the feet. It's because this is the lowest position and the Holy Spirit has the lowest authority, being a spirit of service to those with higher authority. That is why the ground around a holy angel becomes holy ground. When the spirit of the Serpent is in your legs you become spiritually lame, so you will not spread the word of the Serpent. Even a whole nation who are filled with the spirit of the Serpent will become sedentary. But when you are filled with the Holy Spirit you spiritually leap up in joy, and move around, prophesising and spreading news about what has happened to you, to everyone you meet. Another way of looking at this is that when you receive the spirit of the Serpent you fall to the lowest position, and crawl like a crawling serpent, so you lose the use of your legs and can only move slowly. When you 'leap up' you are rising to your proper position. This is symbolised in a miracle when a lame man is lowered from the roof to the floor then he is healed and he is told to get up with his bed. Why does he take his bed? Because his place of rest rises with him, and he will never rest on the floor alongside the spirit of the Serpent again.

Knowledge and Understanding and Wisdom

Hearing the teaching of Jesus is eating the bread of Jesus, and bread is raw spiritual knowledge. It comes before the Holy Spirit fills you, so it does not include spirits like 'Understanding'. Instead, you hear the word and receive the knowledge of it, but you can't unravel the riddles or understand the code, so you miss the deeper meanings. When you receive the Holy Spirit, you receive the spirit of Understanding and this is called 'yeast' or 'leaven'. Unleavened bread has knowledge but no understanding of it. But when you eat leavened bread you understand it. Wine is fermented so it always has yeast in it.

Before the Holy Spirit came, you could only eat unleavened bread. That is because the spirit of the serpent has leaven too, but it is false understanding, so you understand only what the Serpent wants you to understand. You may have some true spiritual knowledge, but your interpretation of it will be wrong. You are better off not understanding anything, and simply obeying the word (bread) and the law (honey) from Yhwh, blindly, without understanding it. That is why Jesus will warn his followers to beware the leaven of the Pharisees when his own leaven is to be released to them.

Therefore, when you are filled with the Holy Spirit, you receive knowledge and personal guidance through Counsel, which you understand, including all the deep mysteries of scripture. Then you receive Wisdom so you know what to do with it. Previously, Wisdom had been reserved for the king, with Solomon being the best example, but now, all of the followers of Jesus have the wisdom of kings. The spirit of wisdom is called pomegranates in the spirit world.

Might

The followers also receive the spiritual strength or might originally meant for kings. This is a spirit of authority over spirits and angels, including warrior angels, which is where the 'might' comes in. This spirit is called 'almond' in the spiritual world, and it is the staff which was given to Moses and Aaron. In practice, it makes the follower turn from being meek to being confident and speaking to anyone of any authority, with even greater authority. We will see this in action when the formerly meek apostles stand up to any authority, and witnesses are amazed by the way they speak with confidence and authority. One healing of a blind man will show this happening clearly.

Faith

Which brings us to the first spirit of the Holy Spirit. The first sub-spirit is 'faith' and in the spiritual world it is called 'mustard'. There is a lot to faith, so we need to start at the beginning. Faith is the breath of life. When you are an unbeliever, you have no such spirit and you live in the 'sea'. Then, when you believe, you breathe the breath of life and come onto the earth. This spirit is what makes a non-believer into a believer.

To be complete, there are two types of breath of life. The first is 'the fear of God' or 'the fear of Yhwh'. This is given to people of Darkness who are under the Law. They have fear of the punishment of whoever they are under. It is also why the spirit is called mustard. Mustard is spicy and hot. The other type is faith and is given to the people of Light, who have no fear of punishment. If you stop believing for any reason, then you lose your fear or your faith. If you do, then you will not go to hell, your soul will return to the sea and remain there until you believe once again.

When you receive faith, it is the start of something very big. Jesus describes the mustard seed as being the smallest of all seeds but it grows to be larger than all of the trees in the garden. And if you have faith like a mustard seed, you can move mountains. What does he mean? Remember that a spiritual mountain is a house of many generations and we will see that a house or houses of the spirit of the Serpent will be removed from the earth during the purge. Jesus is saying that the people filled with faith are filled with the Holy Spirit and as they grow in numbers and strength, they will overpower and cast out whole houses of the spirit of the Serpent.

Also, this spirit spreads through touch (the laying on of hands) so it spreads out rather like the pestilence of the spirit of the Serpent, but the Holy Spirit brings the healing of the pestilence instead of infection.

To summarise, the sub-spirits of the Holy Spirit are:

- Faith (mustard)
- Knowledge (bread)
- Counsel (olive oil)
- Understanding (leaven)
- Wisdom (pomegranate)
- Might (almond)

The seventh spirit is the 'Spirit of the Lord' or the 'Spirit of Yhwh' (the wine). This is the stem spirit from which all the sub-spirits branch out from. You can receive the sub-spirits separately (which is why they all have their own fruit which you can eat) but when you receive the Holy Spirit of Yhwh, then you get all of them together as one complete spirit. This is what happens when you follow Jesus and receive the Holy Spirit. When someone receives all of the Holy Spirit together, you have a transformation of the person involved. Then the power of each spirit in a person is regulated by God, like a volume control, so that different people have different spiritual gifts, as will be required for their purposes. That could be prophecy or teaching or leadership or missionary work, or many other talents and other things, but you will get what you need.

Blindness

You can put the whole Holy Spirit under one category, which is that now the blind can see. This can be taken literally, so that when your spiritual eyes are opened you can see the spiritual world around you. We have already seen a few examples of this, such as when Moses saw the Holy Spirit of Yhwh as a burning bush, and Elisha and his servant could see the angel armies around them, and here in this book we see the spiritual world when we go to 'the other side'. In summary, it means that when you lose your spiritual blindness, you become spiritually aware and gain important spiritual powers.

Now we are going to look at some examples of miracles in action.

The Fifth Age – John the Baptist and Jesus 281

The first example is healing a blind man in two stages, the first is being able to see the spiritual world.

The second example looks at the transformation of a blind man into a new man with confidence and authority which come from the Holy Spirit.

The third example looks at the casting out of spirits of the Serpent.

First example: Jesus heals a blind man at Bethsaida (Mark 8;22)
Jesus had been teaching and healing near the sea of Galilee, near Decapolis. He had opened the ears of a deaf man and his tongue was released so he spoke plainly. Then he fed his followers with his bread and he got in a boat with his disciples and *'went to the other side'*. You may have missed it, but this event is illustrated in part, on the cover of this book.

En route, he warned his disciples to beware the leaven of the Pharisees and of Herod, and pointed out that they did not yet perceive or understand anything, and their hearts were still hardened. He tells them that *'having eyes you do not see and having ears you do not hear'*. Now we know that he means they do not have the Holy Spirit as yet! He has just demonstrated the opening of ears and the release of tongues (Counsel), and now he is going to demonstrate the opening of eyes.

As soon as they landed on the other side at Bethsaida, a blind man was brought to him who begged Jesus to touch him. So Jesus spat on his eyes and laid his hands on him. The saliva was the cleansing water of Yhwh which must come first (so that the Holy Spirit would not reach out to the uncleanliness with fire). The laying on of hands passed the Holy Spirit to him. Jesus asked him if he could see anything, and he replied that he saw people, but they looked like trees, walking. This might sound like Jesus had not healed him properly and needed to try again, but in fact it shows that the man's spiritual eyes were open and he was able to see the spiritual world around him (on the other side). The trees were the spirits inside the people, so when the people walked, their spirits went with them. That was the point of the demonstration. Then Jesus laid hands on him again and he saw everything clearly.

Note that Bethsaida means the house of fish, and 'fish' are the souls of the unbelievers in the 'sea'. By choosing this location, Jesus is telling us that this form of salvation, the salvation of the Holy Spirit, will be used for the unbelieving people and the gentiles. That is why he will command the disciples to become fishers of men. In this house of fish, the Holy Spirit will spread out quickly and far and it will move the mountain, the house of the spirit of the Serpent.

Second example: Jesus heals a man blind from birth (John 9)
This seems to be a simple healing of a blind man, but the man is suddenly able to confidently argue with and outwit the religious leaders as he manifests Understanding and Wisdom and Might, which is well beyond the capability of the leaders. This is because he has been filled with the Holy Spirit. We will see that this miracle is not just about this man, but it is a demonstration of what is going to be available to all of mankind as we move from the old to the new. Since this miracle has so many important hidden messages, I will explain it in some detail here, despite us still being in Book One.

The man had been blind from birth, and the disciples assumed that was because of sin. Since he was born blind, it could not be his own sin, so they ask Jesus who had sinned to cause this. He replies that it was so that *'the works of God might be displayed in him. We must work the works of him who sent me while it is day; night is coming when no one can work. As long as I am in the world, I am the light of the world.'* That seems like a strange reply, but Jesus has a fundamental point to make before he heals him, which we should understand here.

The healing takes place on the Sabbath, the seventh day and the day of Light, and that is when the Holy Spirit will bring salvation in the new kingdom which Jesus is preparing the people for. So it should not be a surprise to us that Jesus demonstrates his healing work on the sabbath. Salvation is, after all, the work of Jesus and Yhwh on the seventh day.

The problem is that the people of the Law see this as work, but they say that work is prohibited on the sabbath. Because of the false teaching of the religious leaders, they have missed the point completely, and will regularly accuse Jesus of breaking the law of Moses on the Sabbath. The point they missed is that the work which they are to rest from on the Sabbath, is the work of the Law, the work of Darkness, so that the work of Light, especially salvation, can take place. That is why Jesus tells his disciples that he wants to display the works of Yhwh, and he explains that it is the work of Light, performed by the Light of the world on the day of Light. Sadly, this teaching will fall on many deaf ears – and blind eyes.

With that point made, Jesus proceeds to heal the blind man, and we will see that the work of Light on the seventh day is all about being filled by the Holy Spirit and using its gifts.

He uses an unusual method, by spitting on the ground and making clay from the dust and the saliva. He then 'anoints' the man's eyes with the clay and tells him to wash in the pool of Siloam. The man does so, and then comes back seeing. So why did Jesus make clay and put it on the man's eyes?

Because the clay that Jesus makes is like the clay that Yhwh used to make the clay vessel of Adam, including his eyes, at the creation of Man. Because Adam then rejected the Holy Spirit, his eyes were spiritually blind since his creation. This man has also been blind since his birth, so in this living parable, he is representing Adam. In the story he is not named, rather he is always called 'man' – which is the translation of Adam! What Jesus just did was give him a new creation of new eyes, so the new will take over from the old. But the new eyes are only anointed at first, like Adam was only anointed as he entered the garden. Remember that Messiah or Christ means 'anointed one'. The man, like Adam, is ready for the Holy Spirit, but he does not have it as yet.

Then the new man has the opportunity to repent and receive the baptism of water, like the baptism of John, and he receives it by washing in the pool of Siloam. As soon as he is washed clean, he receives the Holy Spirit, and his eyes are opened. Now he represents the new Adam who chose the Holy Spirit, and no longer the old Adam who refused it. You might have noticed that Adam didn't go to any pool in the garden, so what is the difference here? It is that Adam and Woman were innocent and therefore sin free, whereas this man was not sin free and needed to be washed clean first. A better way of putting it is that this man had the spirit of the Serpent in him from birth, passed down by his parents, so he was fallen from birth, even without committing any sins.

But there is another hidden message here. Why did he receive the Holy Spirit after he was washed clean, and how did it happen since Jesus did not lay his hands on him? It was because Jesus gave the man a command to go to wash himself, and he obeyed. That makes him under the authority of Jesus (not the Serpent) and so he became a follower of Jesus and became entitled to the Holy Spirit. Also, he knew he was blind and asked to be healed, and so Jesus was answering his prayer. All of these little things mean something important, and now we can see that even if Jesus is not with us in person today, he is with us in spirit, and he hears our prayers asking to be filled with the Holy Spirit, and he knows who his followers are. If we follow him and repent from our old ways, he cleanses us and his Holy Spirit touches us and fills us, even without a physical laying on of hands. This can and does happen to thousands of people simultaneously, as we will soon see.

When the man comes back, he looks like his former self, but he has changed. That's what the Holy Spirit does to you. It can be called becoming new or sometimes being born again. The people who knew him were divided into those who said it was him, and those who said it is only like him. The man just repeated, 'I am', meaning I exist, which is the first thing that Yhwh said when she arrived as Light. The man has changed into a new man, from Darkness to Light, and he is already speaking the word of Yhwh, or prophesising.

He tells the people what happened to him, and that it was through a man called Jesus. He speaks simply and he fearlessly tells the truth. These are features of the Holy Spirit. He didn't know where Jesus was, so they took him to the Pharisees, the religious rulers. He repeated his story to them. This is another thing that happens when you are filled by the Holy Spirit. You want to share the experience with everyone, and you tell your story truthfully, regardless of the response! It's because you are no longer lame and you are spreading the word of Yhwh. But the Pharisees were divided. Some said Jesus was a sinner because he did 'work' on the sabbath, while others said that a sinner could not do such signs. When they asked the man again, he said that Jesus was a prophet, which is a well foretold feature of the Messiah.

The Jews didn't believe in Jesus or the miracle, and they didn't believe that he had been blind in the first place. So they called his parents to confirm it and to ask them how he has been healed. His parents confirmed his blindness, but they didn't know how he was healed, and they tell the Pharisees to ask their son, for *'he is of age. He will speak for himself.'* At that time, anyone who confessed that Jesus is the Messiah was expelled from the synagogue, and so the parents didn't dare to speak out themselves.

The man continues to speak the simple truth, saying *'Whether he is a sinner I do not know. One thing I do know, that though I was blind now I see.'* That is an important message. The man doesn't need or want to engage in theology or judgement, he has had his eyes opened and that is all he needs to know! From now on, he will receive all the knowledge and understanding he needs from the Holy Spirit rather than the religious leaders.

The Pharisees ask again, *'What did he do to you? How did he open your eyes?'* He answers with startling confidence, authority and wisdom, in a similar way to how Jesus himself speaks to the Pharisees, '*I have told you already, and you would not listen. Why do you want to hear it again? Do you also want to become his disciples?*' He is taunting the Serpent in them, but more importantly, he is manifesting his new authority and Might, because has risen to the authority of Light over Darkness, and has wisdom, from the Holy Spirit.

The Pharisees revile him, of course, not just because he is taunting them, but because he is now obviously a follower of the Messiah. They acknowledge this with '*You are his disciple*' then claim that they are disciples of Moses, meaning they are followers of the Law. They may believe that is true, but in fact they have corrupted the law by following the word of the Serpent.

Then the exchange hots up. The Pharisees say, '*We know that God has spoken to Moses, but as for this man, we do not know where he comes from.*' The man then speaks to them with a powerful riposte, to which they have no reply. '*Why, this is an amazing thing! You do not know where he comes from, and yet he opened my eyes. We know that God does not listen to sinners, but if anyone is a worshipper of God and does his will, God listens to him. Never since the world began has it been heard that anyone opened the eyes of a man born blind. If this man were not from God he could do nothing.*' The man is taunting them that it is true that God doesn't listen to people who follow the Serpent, and anyone who is not from God can do nothing. But it is they, the religious rulers who have done nothing, whereas Jesus has healed him. So it is Jesus who is a worshipper of God and who does his will, not them.

This simple beggar is able to speak with authority and to outwit the best theological brains in Jerusalem. Actually, in this exchange, we can see that he has used all seven of the sub-spirits of the Holy Spirit. Faith without fear, true knowledge, understanding, wisdom, counsel, might and it started with the core of the Holy Spirit, Yhwh or I AM.

But the Pharisees don't listen, and they tell him that he was born in utter sin, and yet he would teach them? They then cast him out.

But this isn't really about them excluding the man, it is about them excluding themselves from the coming way of Light. They will remain blind and in Darkness, and the people of Light will see and move on to great things, leaving the old things of Darkness behind.

Later, Jesus finds the man and introduces himself as the Son of Man (or the son of Adam). He does not just represent the last Adam like the man represents the first Adam, he **is** the last Adam. The man believes that Jesus is the Son of Man and worships him. Then Jesus sums up the meaning behind this miracle.

'*For judgement I came into this world, that those who do not see may see, and those that see may become blind.*' The judgement he means will occur on judgement day, which is only one generation away. The Sun and king will be the judge. As always there are only two options, the spirit of the Serpent or not. Those who cannot see are like the man, they never received the Holy Spirit. Now they can receive it and have their eyes opened and use all of the gifts during their physical lives. But those who can already see, are manifesting the spirit of the Serpent with all the falsehoods that provides. As this spirit is cast out and purged, they will become blind. The best example of that will be when Saul is made blind on the Road to Damascus, described in the next chapter.

The Pharisees overhear Jesus and they ask if they are blind. Jesus explains, '*If you were blind, you would have no guilt but now you say "We see," your guilt remains.*' Here, Jesus is referring to the redemption of the people who are blind, the lost sheep. They will have no sin because it will be taken by their redeemer. But since the Holy Spirit has not yet been released, those who 'see', do so through the spirit of the Serpent, just as they have the wisdom and understanding or leaven from the spirit of the Serpent. They are not innocent, they are under the Serpent, and their guilt is not redeemed, so it remains.

This miracle has two main messages. For the people of Light who turn to follow Jesus, it is a message of salvation. But for the religious leaders who oppose Jesus, it is a warning message. Jesus will continue to try to turn this group of people from the Serpent to him throughout his ministry, but as we know, not all will do so. They are the hypocrites who stubbornly remain with the Serpent, so they will be sent to the lake of fire with her.

Third example: Legion and the casting out of his demons
When Jesus and his disciples go to 'the other side', therefore we can visualise the spiritual world, he is met by a man called Legion who is infested with many demons. They recognise and speak to Jesus and he casts them out, using his authority and power. Like the blind man, this story has many hidden meanings. Now nothing Jesus does is random, he has a specific purpose for all of his actions and messages, and this meeting is no exception. Who is he and why did Jesus come to him? The man is very important, and his identity is carefully hidden.

In fact it is carefully hidden within a carefully hidden riddle. Here are the clues embedded in the story, in order, which reveal the riddle. Can you work it out? It's relatively simple!

1. He was among the tombs
2. He had been bound many times but had broken his chains and shackles
3. No one had the strength to subdue him
4. Night and day he cried out and cut himself with stones
5. When he saw Jesus he recognised him and he ran to him and fell down before him
6. He is called Legion *'for we are many'*
7. Jesus casts out the unclean spirits into pigs who promptly drowned in the sea

Note that there are seven and they all match the number code, starting with judgement and death and finishing with salvation and life for the man but death for the unclean spirits. Note that there is only one man with many unclean spirits, although the norm is to have only one spirit of the Serpent which stays with you for a lifetime. This means that the man has had many lives and has been bound many times and released many times. He is a man of Darkness with lives throughout the seven ages. His identity is a carefully guarded secret. Jesus and he know each other, and he immediately submits to Jesus who releases him again. The name 'Legion' is associated with the Roman army.

Now do you know who he is and why Jesus visited him? Don't worry if you don't get it yet, we will return to Legion in Book Three.

Other messages and demonstrations

Jesus says and does many other things to demonstrate what the coming kingdom will bring, so that the people can be prepared for it. We will look at many more examples and go into more depth and detail in the next books, but here is a simple summary of a few of them.

The fig tree

Jesus curses a fig tree so that it withers and bears no fruit. This is the tree which Adam and Eve ate from in the garden, and it is the spirit of the Serpent. It will be purged at the end of the sixth age. When it bears no more fruit, this is like a famine of the unclean spirit which will then be replaced by the Holy Spirit for those who hunger.

Overturning the tables

Jesus overturns the tables of the money changers in the temple. The money changers are an example of the corruption of the Serpent within the temple. They make immoral profits to make themselves rich at the expense of the people, and they are approved by the religious leaders. When Jesus overturns their tables, he is demonstrating the change of authority of the people of the Serpent. They fall to the lowest level and their wealth is scattered.

The house of Ishmael
He meets with the spirit of Ishmael and talks to him and his household in Ishmael's house. This house is the house of the Muslims. The conversation is secret, but it includes the provision of donkeys for Jesus to enter Jerusalem on, to meet his death by crucifixion.

Resurrection

He will resurrect a few examples of people, to demonstrate that he is 'the resurrection', as he puts it.

The last supper and the ritual of bread and water
Just before he is arrested to be crucified, Jesus has a last supper with his disciples. He washes their feet so that they are prepared for the Holy Spirit which will be released soon after Jesus ascends to heaven. The feet are the place where the Holy Spirit will reside. He also introduces the ritual of the bread and the wine, which they should observe to remind themselves of him.

The bread is the true spiritual knowledge of Jesus which is held in his angelic flesh, and is like a memory. When you eat the bread you take it into your own angelic flesh and you should remember it too. Whenever Jesus eats with people it means that he is preaching his word to them. That includes the last supper and the feeding of the 5,000.

The wine is the Holy Spirit of Yhwh and when you drink it you should remember that he either has given it to you and give thanks, or pray that he soon will. Initially, this will be the Holy Spirit of fire, which may come as a surprise, but until the conflicts of the ages of darkness, and the final purge is over, the Spirit of fire is what will be needed. This, if you like, is the red wine. Later, in the seventh age it will be the Spirit of Light and mercy, and it could be described as the white wine. This is the long awaited tree of life.

The end of the age
Although he spends most of his time preparing the people for their salvation, when Jesus is alone with his disciples he will also talk a little

about the purge which comes before it. He promises to return in angelic form, as the warrior King David and the Sun, commanding heavenly angelic armies. He describes the purge of the spirit of the Serpent from the people of Darkness. He also describes the fall and destruction of the temple and Jerusalem, warning his followers to leave the city when they see the signs that it is imminent. This is Armageddon. It will come after the old generation has ended, which means in about 40 years, to be replaced by the new generation. He says that some of the disciples who Jesus is speaking to will still be alive when he returns. Since the disciples are the ones who will prepare the new followers of Christ for the purge and the salvation, this is why Jesus speaks to them privately. They will become the Apostles.

The Rapture

The return of Jesus has been the subject of much debate and much misunderstanding. We will look at this in more detail in Book Three, but it is appropriate to briefly mention here, one commonly held belief, which has become known as 'the rapture'. This view is based on two Bible prophecies, the first was given in the above passage by Jesus to his disciples. The second was given by Paul in his first letter to the Thessalonians, chapter 4. When taken literally, the first prophecy describes two men working in the field, then two women grinding at the mill, one of the men and one of the women is taken, and the other is left behind. This has led to a widespread belief that suddenly a number of people will be taken and will simply disappear, and these are assumed to be Christians being removed from the coming Armageddon and taken to heaven.

Actually, both prophecies are riddles which use code, and which are not meant to be taken literally. The rapture is the intense joy you feel when you are filled by the Holy Spirit. Men 'working in the field' means they are preachers who are preaching the salvation of the Holy Spirit to the people in the lead up to Armageddon. One is preaching and the other is receiving the message and asking to be filled by the Holy Spirit. The spirit of the Serpent is cast out (taken) and the Holy Spirit replaces it and is left. Women grinding at the mill are preparing the flour for the bread of Jesus (the word of Yhwh) and are also preaching salvation, with the same results. Therefore, this short riddle describes the bread and the wine. There is nothing new in its meaning.

The second prophecy is also given in the context of the holy salvation of the Holy Spirit, '*so that he may establish your hearts blameless in holiness before our God and Father, at the coming of our Lord Jesus with all his saints.*' ('With all his saints' means the holy angelic army of Jesus, which join him when he returns. Saints are simply those who have become holy.) In this passage, Paul is actually answering a valid question from his followers about the Holy Spirit salvation and the army of the saints. The question is, what happens to those saints who have died and sleep before Jesus returns? Paul answers that the dead (sleeping) will be resurrected first, so they can join Jesus's heavenly army when he returns.

He is only confirming what we already know, that the numbers of the angelic army will be vastly increased at judgement day through resurrection when Sheol is opened, but Paul is clarifying that this also applies to those Christians who physically died after being filled with the Holy Spirit, but before judgement day and the return of Jesus. He simply says that they will be resurrected to join the angelic army of the saints when Jesus returns so that they will become part of the heavenly army.

Meanwhile, while those on earth who are living and waiting for Jesus to return, the spiritual battle over holy salvation being waged by the living, continues. This means that the spirit of the Serpent is being cast out and the Holy Spirit is replacing it, which is what was previously described as one being taken and the other remaining.

We know that when Jesus returns, the two armies will join up. Then we have the classic earthly battle being reinforced by the heavenly armies, which we have seen throughout the old testament.

The Fifth Age – John the Baptist and Jesus

The forces of Yhwh win every time. This is what Paul is describing, but he uses some code and creates a short riddle.

Paul is saying that the living who are filled with the Holy Spirit (those left) will join the heavenly army of the saints, in the spiritual battle on earth. He says that they will meet Jesus in the 'air', but the air is not physical air, the word is actually the Greek for the breath of life, which is the Holy Spirit. It means they are both joined in the battle through the same Holy Spirit, and by using the same Holy Spirit. This is exactly what you would expect, and it works like this. The preachers on earth are praying for a new convert who has asked to be filled with the Holy Spirit. They ask for the Holy Spirit to cast out the spirit of the Serpent and replace it with the Holy Spirit. The unseen angel army obliges with a verbal command which sounds like a trumpet, and the Holy Spirit casts out the spirit of the Serpent and enters the convert as the breath of life, with great and rapturous joy.

Furthermore, they join the angelic army of Jesus in their heavenly chariots, which are called 'clouds', blown by the Holy Spirit to where they should go.

So really, there is nothing new here and Paul's followers would have understood everything that I have just described, because they all had Understanding. However, here is the whole riddle that has been so misunderstood without the benefit of Understanding, and you can see why! Note that the key passage that became the core of the doctrine of the Rapture is only one sentence long and it must be read in its proper context.

'But we do not want you to be uninformed, brothers, about those who are asleep, that you may not grieve as others who have no hope. For since we believe that Jesus died and rose again, even so, through Jesus, God will bring with him those who have fallen asleep. For this we declare to you by a word from the Lord, that **we who are alive, who are left** *until the coming of the Lord, will not precede those who have fallen asleep. For the Lord himself will descend from heaven with a cry of command, with the voice of an archangel, and with the sound of the trumpet of God. And the dead in Christ will rise first.* **Then we**

who are alive, who are left, will be caught up together with them in the clouds to meet the Lord in the air and so we will always be with the Lord. Therefore encourage one another with these words.'

Therefore, the part of the passage which has been most understood can be better translated and explained as, '*And the dead in Christ will rise (be resurrected) first. Then we who are alive, who are left, will be joined together (by our Holy Spirits) with them in the clouds (on their spiritual chariots) to meet the Lord in the Holy Spirit breath of life, so we will always be with the Lord (in heaven and on earth, as we receive salvation and eternal life through the Holy Spirit). Therefore encourage one another with these words.*'

The phrase '*so we will always be with the Lord*' needs an explanation. It means that when we are filled with the Holy Spirit, this spirit is in both us and Jesus and everywhere there is 'air'. This is our connection, it is permanent and it means we are 'always with the Lord'. It applies both during our physical life and eternally in the afterlife.

The transfiguration

Jesus will go up a mountain with Peter and James and John, where they will meet with the spirits of Moses and Elijah. Jesus shines and becomes as white as light. This is the spiritual transfer from the old to the new. The old are Moses who represents the law and Elijah who represents the prophets. Jesus is the new and he is revealing the glory of his Holy Spirit of Light, which will replace the old law and prophets. The disciples are to be the foundation of the new generation, but they do not, as yet, have the Holy Spirit, so they don't understand what is going on. Yhwh (or Gabriel) also appears in a bright cloud of Light and says, '*This is my beloved son, with whom I am well pleased.*' Like the time when Jesus received the Holy Spirit after his baptism, this means that Jesus is worthy to proceed to the next stage. And all the relevant parties have just agreed to it and will play their parts. It is nearly time for his crucifixion and his resurrection, and of course, to redeem his people.

THE FIFTH AGE – JOHN THE BAPTIST AND JESUS   295

The arrest, trial and crucifixion of Jesus

This event is the most important and the most famous thing that Jesus will do. It takes place on the Passover festival, which is no coincidence, because this is the biggest Passover of them all! This is when Jesus will redeem his people by accepting their sins and will die for them and be punished for them in hell, so that they will be deemed righteous and 'passed over' in the coming judgement day. Jesus knows what is going to happen to him, but he does it anyway. He knows that this will not be over after a few hours of pain on the cross, instead, as the Sun, he will be suffering the fire of hell for 40 years, until he is proven worthy to be king of kings, and he can return with his army to purge the Serpent. You will recall that when King David was about to die, he faced the enormity of the price of his redemption. Initially, it was too much for him to accept, and he asked for it to be reduced. Only after he had seen 70,000 men die in a pestilence which he had chosen for them, did he change his mind and agree to take on all the sin. Now the redemption he committed to is about to happen, starting with the crucifixion, and although Jesus is fully aware of what is about to happen to him, this time, he agrees to proceed if it is the will of Yhwh. It is.

Up to now, Jesus has managed to avoid the schemes of the religious rulers to kill him, without any retaliation. But now he judges them so that he will be judged in return, and therefore he will be subject to the unjust courts of man and the Serpent. It's what he warned his people not to do, and it is what the Serpent has been waiting for.

One of his disciples, Judas, is tempted by the Serpent to accept silver and betray Jesus. The silver is like the living gold and silver of the queen of Sheba which resulted in the fall of Samson. It is like armour which shields the bearer from the deceptions and attacks of the enemy, but it works in the opposite way to the silver of Yhwh. Instead of blocking the Serpent, it blocks Yhwh. Under the influence of the Serpent's silver, he tells them where Jesus will be. Jesus is aware of what Judas has done, but he continues. He knows it is just a part of what has to be. Now the religious leaders can find him and arrest him, and they do so. Because Jesus does not resist, his sacrifice is a freewill offering according to the law. It is like the planned sacrifice of Isaac by his father Abraham in the earlier cycle, where Isaac accepted his fate and prepared to die. But this time there will be no intervention from Yhwh to stop the sacrifice. Jesus says he is about to fulfil the scriptures of the prophets, and at that, his disciples scattered and fled. When challenged, Peter even denied Jesus three times, one for each Messianic identity, so that he lost his salvation and his position of authority.

Next Jesus will be tried in the courts with the aim of sentencing him to death.

However, it is not straightforward for the religious leaders to get a death sentence. Not least, Jesus has done nothing that deserves death. They can accuse him of blasphemy, but this is under religious law. In practice, everyone is under the higher Roman law, and the death penalty is reserved only for serious breaches of Roman justice. The Romans allow the religious laws and the local religious courts, but they do not get involved. Therefore, a charge of blasphemy is not likely to result in a Roman sentence of death. What the religious leaders need is a breach of Roman law. Now the Romans are particularly concerned with keeping the peace in their empire, and looking out for rebellions and a coup. If a rebellious leader was to rise up, claiming to be a true king, not the puppet king of the Romans, he would end the peace, inciting riotous behaviour and potentially a coup. This would be a charge that would be heard by the Roman courts and could result in the death penalty.

To do so, they would have to prove that Jesus claims to be King of the Jews. That would put Jesus in a difficult position, because of course in heaven, he is indeed king of the Jews, so he cannot deny the charge. But he is not the secular king that he will be accused of, and he certainly has no interest in rebellion against the Romans, because they have brought peace and justice to the empire and he knows that their authority is from Yhwh. However, there is no evidence to support the charge, so the religious leaders will have to produce false witnesses to fabricate evidence. What happens in the trials?

First he was tried by the chief priest with the whole council of the religious rulers. They attempted to find false witnesses against him but failed, and Jesus said nothing. Eventually he admitted that he was the Son of Man and would return on the clouds of heaven. This is true, but they accused him of blasphemy and decided he deserved a sentence of death. That sentence required the higher court of the Romans, so they changed the charge to that he was claiming to be the 'king of the Jews'.

They took Jesus to the Roman governor, Pontius Pilate, who heard the accusations against him. Jesus never answered the charges of the chief priests and elders and when Pilate asked him if he was king of the Jews, he only replied, *'You have said so.'* He admitted nothing and there was no evidence against him. Pilate was amazed by Jesus but was not impressed with the charges. He felt it was out of envy that they had delivered him up.

According to custom, the Romans pardoned one prisoner at the time of the Passover, a sign of their mercy, so he turned to the people and asked them to choose whether to release a criminal called Barabbas, or to release Jesus. The chief priests and the elders persuaded the crowd to choose Barabbas, which they did. Then Pilate asked them what they wanted him to do to Jesus, and they said he should be crucified. Pilate replied, 'Why? What evil has he done?' but they insisted.

Pilate had observed that both the religious leaders and the people themselves wanted Jesus executed. To keep the peace, he was therefore under pressure to give them what they wanted. With a riot beginning, which was the last thing that the governor wanted, Pilot washed his hands with water and said that he was innocent of Jesus's blood, and they should see to it themselves. The people accepted and stated that his blood would be on them and their children, and after Pilate scourged Jesus by whipping him severely, he delivered him to be crucified.

Thus Jesus, an innocent man, was sentence to death. Who carried the guilt? It looks like the Jewish people, but they were persuaded by the religious rulers, and they in turn were under the Serpent. Therefore, under the principle that it is not the sinner but the person responsible for the sin who carries the guilt, it was the Serpent and the servants of the Serpent. These are the ones who Jesus said will be sent to the eternal fires at judgement day. To confirm this, although they didn't understand it, when the people said that the blood of Jesus would be on them and their children, it means that they will be covered by the redeeming blood of Jesus, the blood of the sacrificial lamb. They will receive mercy, even though they are killing their Messiah.

After being mocked by the Roman soldiers, Jesus was led away to be crucified. En route, he was offered wine mixed with gall to drink. But when he realised what it was, he refused. The wine was the wine of the Serpent and the gall was the bitterness of sin.

Then he was crucified. When he was close to death, Yhwh withdrew her Spirit so he was no longer Holy. Jesus felt it go and said, '*My God, my God, why have you forsaken me?*' At that moment, a bystander gave him the sour wine of the Serpent to drink, and this time he took it. His Holy Spirit had been replaced by the spirit of the Serpent and he was filled with the sins of all his people. He cried out again and died.

To ensure that he was dead, a Roman soldier pierced Jesus's side with his spear, and water and blood flowed out. When the clay vessel of Jesus's physical body was broken, his spirits lived on and left his body. The water was the cleansing waters, the soul of Yhwh. It was his heart of water and mercy and not a heart of stone. The blood was the wine of his Holy Spirit, as he had explained at the last supper. These were the foundations of the kingdom of Light and in the next age, they would flow outwards and be spread by the disciples (apostles) over the land.

What are the foundations of the Kingdom of Light? The baptism of water and the baptism of the Holy Spirit.

The Resurrection of Jesus

When Jesus died, his three spiritual identities were released in angelic form, and they immediately went to where all the spirits of the dead go, Sheol. There, Jesus preached to the dead people of Israel about the coming salvation and purge. He redeemed them and provided white linen coverings in preparation for judgement day. All the redeemed would join his army against the Serpent. They would be called the resurrection of the dead and their numbers were huge. They were the army of Israel which the prophet Ezekiel had famously prophesised would come back from dry bones to life. Life as a heavenly angel, that is. Jesus did not waste a moment of his time in Sheol.

It was Friday when Jesus had died, and his body was put in a tomb and sealed with a huge stone. In the spiritual world, the huge stone was a mighty warrior guardian angel called a cherub (plural cherubim), which guarded the entrance. Then Saturday was the sabbath day of rest, when the people of the law rested but as he had been preaching about during his ministry, Jesus was working hard on salvation for millions, in Sheol. Here, the only people who were resting were the dead, but their living spirits were listening intently! Then, on Sunday morning, the day after the sabbath and the third day including the day of his death, he rose to the entrance of the tomb, in his three angelic forms.

That has led to some confusion over which day is the sabbath, Saturday or Sunday? This is largely academic, but we should try to understand what is going on, so that everything fits and there are no loose ends. Jesus rose on the Sunday, so surely that must mean that Sunday is the day of salvation and is the sabbath? No, it doesn't. The sabbath day is the seventh day, Saturday, and this is the day of salvation, but it is not the day of resurrection. The day after the Sabbath day is described in the Bible as the eighth day, the day of resurrection. Eight is the number code for resurrection, and circumcision is the mark of redemption and resurrection which is performed on the eight day after birth. So you might ask why is there an eighth day if there are only seven days in a cycle? Because the eighth day is the first day of the new cycle in the kingdom of heaven. It doesn't happen during the seven day cycles on earth, it happens when Yhwh is ready for it, in heaven.

Back in the story, Gabriel commanded the cherub to move aside, so the stone rolled away and the three angels were free to leave. Most people would not be able to see the angels, but those whose eyes were opened could. All of the disciples could see and hear them speak, and even feel them. So could a handful of others too, including Mary Magdalene who had served Jesus, and some key people who would become missionaries to foreign nations. Jesus mysteriously appeared in rooms with locked doors, because he was in the spiritual world like a ghost, including the holy ghost, and could pass through anything physical.

Jesus had demonstrated that he was truly alive and would never leave them. He had risen from Sheol and had been resurrected. Actually, we should understand that this is the resurrection of the first type of salvation, which is worth explaining here, because it is not straightforward. Normally, the angels of a holy Messiah like Jesus would have gone straight to heaven under the salvation of holiness, because he was holy and sin free. However, Jesus lost his Holy Spirit just before he died, and received the spirit of the Serpent and the sin of all those he would redeem. So he was not Holy and sin free at that moment.

Once his clay vessel had died and was broken, his spirits and soul were separated from the spirit of the Serpent and they went to Sheol, just like everyone else who died with the spirit of the Serpent and sin. Then he was resurrected on the eighth day, also just like all the others in Sheol would be resurrected. Therefore, Jesus's resurrection is a sign of the type of resurrection that his redeemed would receive. But it is not the type of resurrection that his followers would have when they were filled with the Holy Spirit and holy when they died. They go straight to heaven without going to Sheol.

Jesus had commanded his disciples that they should become fishers of men, and he demonstrated that they would catch large numbers of people if they preached about their inheritance of Light. He said they should cast their nets on the right side of their boat, the side of inheritance, and the nets would be fully filled. He is talking about the conversion of unbelievers, going from sea to earth, that is, the gentiles.

He also restored Peter, by confirming that he loved Jesus (to an extent) three times, once for each Messianic identity that he had denied, and he appointed him as his apostle and shepherd to the lost sheep of the chosen people. His ministry would be centred around Jerusalem. The job for leading the preaching to the gentiles was left open for now, but not for long.

Finally, he was ready to go to heaven, and the disciples watched him being taken up before them. This event is called 'the ascension'. But the three angels of Jesus did not disappear, they all went to where they would carry out their essential functions in the next age, the age of the Apostles, in the spiritual world. Before he left, Jesus told his disciples to wait in Jerusalem where they would be baptised in the Holy Spirit.

This would change everything.

Chapter 18

The Sixth Age of the Apostles

Although this is a short age, only 40 years or one generation long, it is vital because it brings to an end the six ages of Darkness and is the final preparation for the age of Light. It starts with the release of the Holy Spirit to the apostles and the followers of Jesus, and there is a dramatic change in the apostles as a result. The apostles are the leaders and elders of the early Christians, a combination of the original disciples and other key leaders who spread the word of Jesus the Christ (Messiah) and founded the Christian Church. They are similar to ambassadors to the church. The prominent apostles were Peter and John and Paul (originally Saul).

The early Christian Church will be born and will grow. Peter will lead the spreading of Yhwh's word to the Jews around Jerusalem, and a new apostle, Paul, will lead the spreading of the word to the gentiles. He will found the Roman Catholic Church from Rome. This is a time of intense spiritual conflict with the Serpent as she desperately attempts to disrupt and prevent the growth of the Church. The accounts in the Bible focus on this dramatic time.

The three identities of Jesus remain separated as three distinct angels. The Holy Spirit will be available to all the followers of Jesus on earth. Gabriel, the word, will speak through the Holy Spirit (Counsel) and will start the age living in the temple of Jerusalem, but will leave when it becomes corrupted by abominations of idolatry. The final straw will be called the abomination of desolation as she leaves the temple and both the temple and the city of Jerusalem become desolate without her. She will rise to heaven to take up her throne as almighty God, ready for the next age. King David, the Sun, will accept his punishment for the sins of his people, and be imprisoned in the fires of hell for the full 40 years. At the end of this time, he will have redeemed all his followers.

At the end of the age he will judge the dead and empty Sheol, swelling the numbers of his angel armies from the redeemed. Then, as the seventh age begins King David will lead his angelic armies to defeat the Serpent and destroy the corrupted and desolate temple and city. That is the battle and the purge of Armageddon. Then, with the Serpent purged, the seventh age of Light will continue as the kingdoms of Yhwh and heaven, in an age of peace and mercy and security. And of course, salvation. Then, the Bible will finish.

The sixth age is perhaps the most relevant age to us, because after the Bible stops, the cycles continue, and we are presently in the sixth age once again. As the word and the Holy Spirit spread throughout the earth this time, we can prepare ourselves as well as possible for the coming purge and the salvation which follows it.

In this part we will only look at the events in a simple way, and summarise them. In Book Three we will go deeper, and we will see that the writings of the Apostles conceal the true depth of knowledge and understanding that the apostles had. Especially Paul and Peter and John. Nearly all of the true mysteries that were revealed to them are hidden again in layers of riddles and code and living parables, many of which are difficult to unravel. It is worth the effort though, because they confirm everything that we have learned so far.

The Holy Spirit is released

The giving of the old law by Moses was celebrated in a festival called Pentecost. During this festival, the first after Jesus died, the Holy Spirit was released. This time it is the transition from the old law to the new law, which is written on the heart of flesh through the Holy Spirit, rather than on the tablets of stone. It came like a mighty rushing wind, not just a breath, to demonstrate that it was the mighty divine Holy Spirit. It also came in 12 tongues of fire, to demonstrate that it was the Holy Spirit of fire, and it was for all the people of light who chose it.

It will probably come as a surprise that the Holy Spirit is the Spirit of fire, but we need to remember that this age is still an age of Darkness. There is still judgement and still punishment and still battles to fight. The Holy Spirit of mercy will come in the seventh age, and everyone with the spirit of fire will be changed simultaneously and instantly from fire to water, as Light takes authority over Darkness. But for the whole of this sixth age, the Apostles will operate with the Holy Spirit of fire.

The 12 spoke in new tongues which drew a large crowd of Jews who lived in Jerusalem but who came from every nation. Fifteen nations are named, the number code revealing that this is for the people of Darkness (1) who receive the mercy of God (5). Many of the crowd were amazed that they could understand what the disciples were saying, like it was their own language.

This is an important feature of this event because it is the reversal of the dispersal from the tower of Babel, when Gabriel used her own spirit of Counsel to confuse the language of the people of the Serpent, so they did not understand one another and scattered abroad, becoming less effective. Now the crowds are being 'anointed' in the oil of the Counsel of Yhwh so they understand what is being said, in every language, as they are brought together under the single spiritual language of Yhwh and Jesus. They become one body with one purpose, following the will of Yhwh, in full agreement. This is how the people of Babel were initially, except they were all under the Serpent.

Those that do not receive the Counsel do not understand a word, and they mock the disciples, saying they are drunk with new wine – which of course they are! Those that listen to Peter hear him give an amazing sermon, which is pure prophecy of the word of Yhwh. They are shamed by it and ask what to do, so Peter tells them to repent

The Sixth Age of the Apostles   305

and be baptised in the name (spirit) of Jesus Christ so that they too receive the gift of the Holy Spirit. *'For the promise is for you and for your children, and for all who are far off, everyone who Yhwh our supreme God calls to herself.'* Peter is addressing the exiled people of Israel who are still in exile, and telling them that this is the call they have been waiting for The call is a call to salvation. *'Save yourselves from this crooked generation.'* About 3,000 received the word and were baptised in the Holy Spirit. This shows us that the Holy Spirit can be received simultaneously by large numbers, it is not only an individual experience.

Luke also throws in an important mystery, but hides it. When I said they are shamed by what they heard, the phrase is actually 'pierced to the heart'. This means the casting out of the spirit of the Serpent from the heart, to be replaced by the Holy Spirit. It doesn't come through the sword and death, it comes through the word of life, like Peter's sermon. Hence this is the first example of the sword in the mouth. This is a simple example that the Apostles had a deep level of understanding, but they hid it from people who did not share their understanding.

Immediately, they devoted themselves to the Apostle's teaching and were filled with awe. Most importantly, *'And all who believed were together and had all things in common.'* A vital advantage of being filled with the Holy Spirit is that everyone hears the same word, and there is total unity and agreement. Day by day they learnt more and praised God and had favour with all the people. Their numbers increased every day.

Wonders and signs were being done through the apostles, including that a lame man was healed by Peter and John. This demonstrates that Peter and John had the authority to cast out the spirit of the Serpent, just as Jesus had. It also shows that spreading the word by healing the lame, was a top priority. Peter was bravely preaching in the temple about Jesus, and how he fulfilled the writings of the prophets. Not surprisingly, this was unwelcome to the religious leaders, who arrested them and put them in prison. But already, about 5,000 people had heard and believed the word. Peter and the disciples argued against the leaders, with authority and confidence, declaring that the Spirit of Jesus was responsible for the miracles. The religious leaders were amazed how such uneducated and simple men knew and they had to release them because the crowds were supporting them more and more. All this, of course, is the work of the Holy Spirit in them.

The numbers of believers continued to increase and they were all of one heart and soul so they had everything in common. There was total unity, no dissent and no division. The apostles continued to carry out many miracles and were held in high esteem. The sick and those afflicted with unclean spirits came from the towns around Jerusalem and they were healed.

Of course, the Serpent started to fight back, and the religious leaders arrested them and put them in prison. But they were released by an angel at night and told to continue their preaching in the temple, which they did. They were taken before the Council again, and were released again.

By now there were too many believers for the apostles to manage their many needs, so a second layer of authority was introduced. Seven righteous men were chosen to assist the apostles, one of whom was called Stephen.

Stephen and Saul

Now the Serpent strikes back. Stephen had been preaching successfully through the Holy Spirit so many men from the synagogues in the gentile countries where Israel had been exiled, rose up against him and his teaching. They argued with his teaching but they could not defeat his wisdom, so they used false witnesses against him and brought him to the Council and the people. He gave a powerful and accurate sermon, but he did not hold back on the failings of Israel to keep the Law. They were enraged and stoned him to death, making him the first Christian martyr. He was the first martyr. One of the men who rose up against him was called Saul.

Saul was from the tribe of Benjamin, like King Saul, and like him he was part of the divided house of Israel. Like most of his colleagues, he was on the side of the Serpent but thought he was on the side of Yhwh. Saul had fought fiercely against the Christians, persecuting them and having them arrested, thinking that their teachings were against the Law of Moses and against God. Now this persecution had escalated into murder.

Up to now, the gentiles had not been preached to by the 12 apostles, but this event brings them sharply into focus. The Serpent had used the synagogues in the gentile nations against Stephen, so now Yhwh wanted to bring the war to the Serpent, in the gentile nations too. She needed a new apostle to lead the fight, and who better than Saul? All she had to do was turn him back to her side of the house of Israel and the Serpent would have lost one of her best leaders and Yhwh would have gained him. Meanwhile, Philip, one of the seven leaders who had included Stephen (and not an apostle) was sent to preach to the Samaritans and to teach a court official of the Ethiopians, then he preached to the Philistines from their city of Azotus to Caesarea on the coast of the Mediterranean to the north. The gentiles were now very much on the map, but they still needed an apostle.

As Saul was en route to Damascus to persecute more Christians, a bright white light from heaven shone all around him, and a voice asked him why he was persecuting him. The voice told him that he was Jesus and that he should go to Damascus where he would be told what to do. He had become blind and so his men led him there by the hand. The white light is the glory of the divine Holy Spirit of Jesus and the blindness happened when he lost the spirit of the Serpent and before he received the Holy Spirit. After three days a man was sent to lay hands on him, and he received the Holy Spirit.

As he did so, something like scales fell from his eyes and be regained his sight.

He was converted and fought for Jesus from that moment on, although he was treated with considerable scepticism at first. He was also known as Paul or Paulus, which is his Roman name because he was a Roman citizen, and he became the famous Saint Paul. His Roman citizenship made him a perfect choice to reach out to the Roman empire. He will have an overwhelming desire to preach in Rome, and there he will found the Roman Catholic Church. He is the apostle to the gentiles, and he is responsible for the whole church in the gentile countries throughout the rest of the world.

After he was filled with the Holy Spirit, Saul received understanding and wisdom and he needed time alone to prepare himself and to reveal all the mysteries hidden in scripture. He went on his own to Tarsus, his home town, where he would not be distracted or led astray by other teachings, hearing only Yhwh. After several years of study, Saul's depth of understanding was immense.

Circumcision and unclean food

While Saul was studying, there was a debate about whether the law of Moses had to be obeyed by those who had received the Holy Spirit. In particular it was difficult for righteous Jews to accept that it was OK to eat unclean food, and many thought that circumcision was a requirement for salvation. This wasn't so much of an issue for the converted Jews who were already circumcised and could continue to eat only clean food. But it would certainly be an issue for the gentiles. So in a vision, Yhwh showed Peter that he could eat unclean food without any problem. The spiritual reason behind this fundamental change is that the Holy Spirit in you cleanses everything you eat. It was this vision that resulted in the situation we have today, when the Christians can eat any food, but the people of the Law who are not filled by the Holy Spirit, that is Jewish people and Muslims, must eat only clean food.

THE SIXTH AGE OF THE APOSTLES 309

As Peter was speaking to a Roman family about his vision that gentiles would be saved too, the Holy Spirit fell on them and their household, so it was certain that gentiles were to be included in the salvation and that they did not need to be circumcised or eat only clean food. This was the deeper meaning of the vision. When Peter explained to the brothers in Jerusalem what had happened to the Roman family, they quickly accepted that circumcision and clean food was not required, and they glorified God. Despite the questions, there was still unity in the church. Only the voice of Yhwh was being heard, and it was saying that the gentiles must be included in the salvation of the Holy Spirit, without circumcision and without the Law.

But the persecution that followed the death of Stephen grew, and the new Christians were scattered. Some went as far north as Cyprus and Phoenicia and Antioch, which were gentile nations, but they had no clear leader. Therefore, it was time to engage Saul as an apostle. A preacher called Barnabas went to Tarsus, where he found Saul and brought him back to Antioch and together, they started the ministry of Saul to the gentiles.

Antioch and the famine and the secret of Peter's escape from prison

For a year, they preached in Antioch and a great many people became followers of Jesus. This is when the followers were first called Christians.

After a year, some prophets came from Jerusalem to foretell that there was going to be a tough time for the Christians and apostles in Jerusalem, rather like a famine. Paul and the followers decided to send them relief. Sure enough, there was violence, and James the brother of John was killed by Herod. Also, Peter was arrested and imprisoned by him.

What happens next is one of the most carefully guarded secrets in the New Testament, but you would never know it, simply by reading the story. It reads like a spiritual story of a miraculous release of Peter from prison and a miraculous striking down of Herod, but that isn't what really happened. The story is full of code and riddles which hide the reality, and can only be revealed by the spirit of Understanding. I will reveal it in detail in Book Three. Why is it so deeply hidden? It is to protect the identity of the 'prophet' who foretold the 'famine', because he is a courageous senior Roman officer, and a spy for the Christians.

The missionary journeys of Paul

Paul reached out to the Gentiles by making three missionary journeys from Antioch, stopping at major cities along the way, where there were both synagogues for the dispersed exiles of Israel and local gentile people. He preached to them both, Jewish people first, followed by Gentiles, and he set up Christian churches and leaders to run them after he moved on. He would revisit them, where possible, in future missions. After his third mission he visited Jerusalem and was accused by the religious leaders then arrested and tried by the Romans, with no clear conviction or sentence. He appealed to the higher courts in Rome, which was his right as a Roman citizen, and he would make a fourth journey by sea to Rome, still under arrest. He nearly died when his ship was wrecked at Malta. This journey is an amazing seafaring story of struggles against adverse winds and storms and running aground, which many sailors will appreciate, but more importantly, it is a living parable with many hidden mysteries, which we will reveal later.

The Sixth Age of the Apostles 311

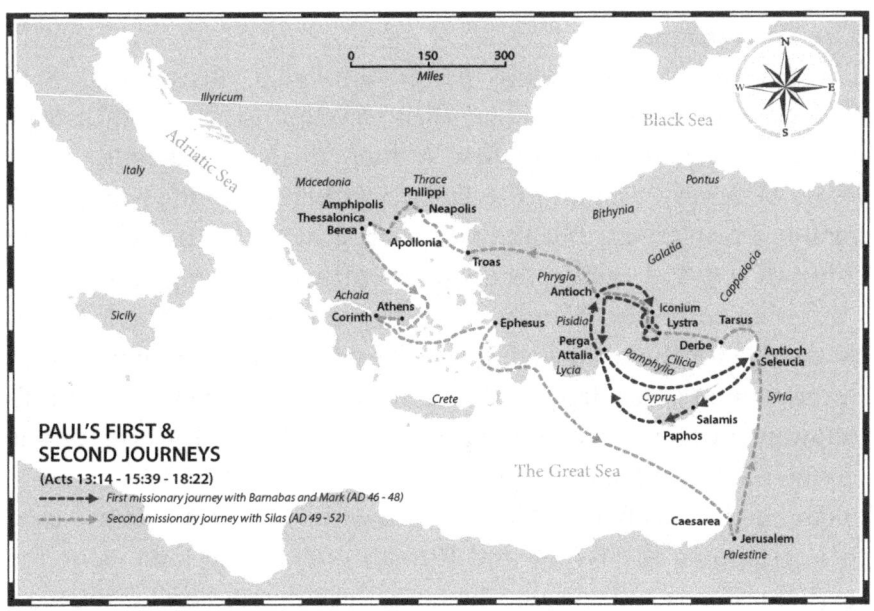

PAUL'S FIRST & SECOND JOURNEYS
(Acts 13:14 - 15:39 - 18:22)
- - - → First missionary journey with Barnabas and Mark (AD 46 - 48)
- - - → Second missionary journey with Silas (AD 49 - 52)

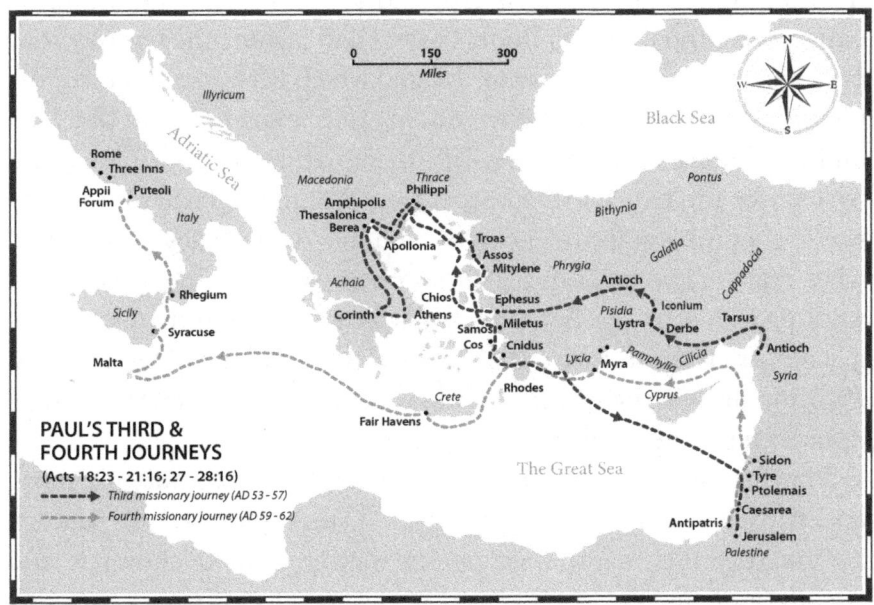

PAUL'S THIRD & FOURTH JOURNEYS
(Acts 18:23 - 21:16; 27 - 28:16)
- - - → Third missionary journey (AD 53 - 57)
- - - → Fourth missionary journey (AD 59 - 62)

The first mission

The first mission successfully passed through Cyprus, where Saul became known as Paul. Then they travelled to the mainland of present day Turkey. Paul's first sermon to the synagogue, about Jesus, went very well and the crowds gathered the following week for more revelations. But the Jews were jealous of the crowds and contradicted and reviled Saul, so he turned to the gentiles. This was going to be the pattern from then on, as the Serpent stirred up trouble for them through the exiles who had not repented. Like in the time of Jesus, frequently there were plots to kill Paul and his followers, but he usually managed to evade them. However, in one city he was stoned and nearly died.

Paul had one other problem to deal with. The gentiles were used to worshipping the Greek and Roman gods, made famous by the mythology stories. Typically, the cities they visited didn't just have a synagogue, they had a temple to a specific god, especially when Paul will get as far as Greece. So when the people see Paul performing miracles they treat him as a god and try to worship him, and he struggles to stop them! In Book Three I will include the temples they encountered and the nature of the god which was worshipped in the temple. We will see that these 'gods' caused many problems for Saul and his followers, in keeping with their natures in mythology, and we can see the hand of the Serpent at work through them. Idolatry was still a problem for the gentiles, and the 'deities' they worshipped were real angelic creatures with powers over their followers, which were provided by the Serpent. We will see that that myths are not just empty classical stories. The 'deities' will continue to fight against Paul and Jesus in the spiritual world until they are purged by Michael in heaven in a heavenly war at the end of the age.

The first mission was a success and when Paul and his party had travelled as far as they needed to, they returned to Antioch by the way they came, visiting the newly formed churches and encouraging them.

The Council of Jerusalem

The apostles were making good progress and so as you would expect, the Serpent tried to enter and disrupt the followers of Paul, and those in Judea under Peter. Up to now there was no division in the leadership and no division in the doctrines which were being taught, so the Serpent wanted to introduce false prophets and false doctrines and replace unity with dissent and endless debates. Therefore, some men from Judea were again teaching that you had to be circumcised to be saved, and Paul was unable to silence them. They were from the party of the Pharisees, the old religious rulers referred to as a 'brood of vipers', so you can see that the Serpent is still behind them, as she was in the time of Jesus. The Apostles decided to take the matter to Jerusalem for a decision.

The Council of the apostles and the elders was formed, and Peter spoke first, arguing eloquently that circumcision was not required. The council fell silent, indicating there was no dissent. This is important, because it demonstrates that the Holy Spirit was dominant in the room, and without the spirit of the Serpent, there was unity. Then Paul and Barnabas spoke followed by James, all supporting the arguments of Peter and adding their own.

Then James concluded the meeting by suggesting that the only burden of the old Law that they would give to the gentiles was to avoid idolatry and eating the offerings to false gods; eating blood and what has been strangled; and sexual immorality. This was not some form of religious and moral piety, it was an attempt to prevent the spirit of the Serpent from entering the Christian Church and cause more of these problems. The blood they must not eat is the living spirit of the Serpent, food which has been strangled means that the breath of life, which is the spirit of the Serpent, is still in the flesh, and the spirit of the Serpent is spread by sexual contact so sexual partners should be minimised. Adultery is a description of idolatry, when people covenant to other 'gods' as well as Yhwh.

This was unanimously accepted by the Council and letters were written to take these rules to all the new Christian churches. It started well, but sadly the Serpent did eventually manage to introduce false prophets and false doctrines into the churches, and later, Paul had to write in strong terms to some of his own churches to try to correct the errors. Paul's solution to persistent dissent was to separate the dissenters from the church to minimise their disruption. Even Paul and Barnabas would disagree and separate.

The second mission
After a break, Saul went on his second mission, and he went much further west, into Macedonia and Greece. The pattern was much the same as before, and he still came up against conflicts with the Jews from the synagogues and the false gods of the temples. But Paul persevered and adjusted his teaching according to his audience. For example, in Athens he was surrounded by idolatry and philosophers and he did not want to cause offence and be rejected, so he pointed out that it was permitted to preach about the unknown god too, so he did.

However, when Paul went on to Corinth, a well-hidden story reveals that he broke his own moral pledges, was seduced by a beautiful woman, and he fell. He received her spirit of the Serpent and he lost his Holy Spirit. He separated himself from his churches and followers, and he immediately cancelled the mission and returned on his own to Antioch. However, through repentance, reducing himself to the level of a slave and shaving his hair off, and appealing for mercy as his hair grew back, he was restored.

The third mission
Then Paul set off on his third mission, to return to where he left off from his second mission, visiting and strengthening the churches he had founded en route. When he got to Ephesus, on the eastern coast of the Aegean Sea, he discovered that the followers there had not

received the Holy Spirit. That is because it was the place he called at after he left Corinth. That was when he had lost his Holy Spirit, and the people that had taught there after him did not have the Holy Spirit either. They preached only the baptism of John. Paul immediately put that right by laying his hands on them and they received the baptism of the Holy Spirit, and they prophesised and spoke in tongues. But the Serpent struck back, using the followers of the goddess Artemis, from the temple in Ephesus, and there was a riot and it was not safe for Paul to remain. Ephesus was where Paul battled hardest against the Serpent, engaging in tough spiritual warfare. His letter to the church in Ephesus gives strong guidance on how to continue spiritual warfare against the *'world ruler over this present darkness, against the spiritual forces of evil in the heavenly places.'* The world ruler of darkness is the Serpent and the spiritual forces of evil in the heavenly places are the angels of heaven who are being worshipped by idolatry and mythology.

So he went on to Macedonia and from there to Greece where there was another plot against his life. He retraced his steps via Macedonia and crossed the Aegean Sea to the port of Troas. He was now planning to return to Jerusalem. The rest of his return journey bears many similarities to the journey that Jesus took into Jerusalem. For example, he has a long supper with his followers in an upper room (like the last supper), and a follower at the supper falls asleep (like the disciples at the mount of olives) and when he falls out of the window he is sitting in, he is resurrected by Paul (like Peter is restored after his fall). He makes a long speech to his followers at Ephesus about what is to come up to judgement day (like Jesus told his disciples). And when he announces his intention to go to Jerusalem, he is warned against it several times by different people, because of the danger to his life (like Jesus was warned). Even the secret Roman spy tries to persuade him not to go. But Paul would not be dissuaded and instead it becomes clear that he is saying goodbye to his followers. His calling is to go to Rome and nothing will stop him, even though he is well aware that it will lead to his death, like Jesus.

The similarities to Jesus are not a coincidence, because this is another cycle which continues after the cycle of Jesus. We will see that Paul is more than an apostle, he is a son of Man like Jesus. He is the eighth son of Man, who came after Jesus, and the significance of this is to ensure that the gentiles are included in the inheritance of Adam after Jesus. That means they will be included in the spiritual inheritance of the promises given to Abraham. This is a complex matter and we will look at it in more depth in Book Three.

When Paul gets to Jerusalem he is arrested, like Jesus, and he goes through a number of trials under the Roman law, but with the involvement of the people, the religious rulers, the Roman Tribune and Governors and even the king and queen. All of the relevant groups of people are included in the process, and Paul makes sure that he preaches the gospel thoroughly to all of them.

Like Jesus, the governor cannot find a real case against him in Roman law, but he is not released. He remains imprisoned in Jerusalem, so Paul plays his trump card and appeals to Caesar in Rome, which is his right as a Roman citizen. His appeal is accepted and he is sent under Roman guard to sail to Rome.

The shipwreck
Now the story of Paul's sail to Rome is an exciting one. It is in the vein of the gripping stories of King David, but naval this time. It turns out to be a living parable with many hidden messages. Paul is determined to get to Rome and the Holy Spirit is the wind that will get him there. It is a wind from the east. However, the Serpent is just as determined to prevent him and the spirit of the Serpent is the wind that will drive him away from the safety of landfall and into the stormy seas and reefs where he will drown. It is a wind from the north. Therefore, there are conflicts and struggles around a north

easterly wind, storms, heavy waves and deep waters and shallow rocks with suitable and unsuitable harbours.

Every sailor will recognise the seasonal weather issues and the seamanship decisions that have to be made, because they haven't changed much in 2,000 years! But there is much more to this story. Everything that happens on the voyage is like a giant riddle, where each boat and each port and each event and each plan and change of plan and change of weather has a spiritual significance. It ends in a shipwreck on the island of Malta. We will look at this in the context of a spiritual battle in the spiritual world in Book Three.

But for now, suffice to say that everyone survives the shipwreck and there follows a period of security and peace and salvation when Paul converts many of the islanders to follow Jesus. Paul continues his journey in a new boat to Rome. There he preaches to crowds and again he converts large numbers to follow Jesus and sets up churches. The story ends there, but history tells us that Paul will be martyred in Rome, an old man, having lived one of the most far-reaching lives of any Bible hero. That's because Paul's inheritance is the Roman Catholic Church.

The letters of the apostles

The letters that we still have are fascinating because they reveal some details of the struggles that the early Church faced and how the apostles dealt with the problems that the Serpent threw at them. They have much validity, even today. They also reveal the key doctrines that they were teaching. But they don't add much to what we already know about the underlying story.

The letters are written by apostles who are experts in the riddles and code, especially Paul and John and Peter, and although they seem to be fairly straightforward on the surface, they are actually complex. They even have hidden meanings within hidden structures, for example being divided into the seven ages, and you need to know which age is being described if you are to fully understand the deeper meanings. The letters are therefore too complex to do justice to in this part, and we will look at them in more detail and depth in later books.

What is clear, however, is that in their later letters, all the writers are encouraging their readers to persevere through the increasing conflicts because judgement day and the coming kingdom is close and coming soon, and the followers will not have to endure the intense hardships they face for much longer. All of the scripture writers will die before the end of the age, so there is no biblical narrative account of what actually happened at Armageddon or afterwards. There are only the prophecies that foretell the events, and as we know, their true meanings are written in code and riddles.

The most detailed of these prophecies was written by John, just before judgement day and Armageddon happened, and just before he died. It is the closest we get to an eye witness account, because John's spirit is taken to heaven and is shown what is soon to take place. He then writes it down in the last book of scripture in the Bible.

It is called the Revelation of Jesus Christ because it shows all the identities of the Messiah throughout the ages, finishing with the purge at the end of the sixth age and the salvation at the beginning of the seventh age. Now the Greek word for 'revelation' is apocalypse, so unfortunately, the book has become associated with 'apocalyptic' scenes of destruction and the so called 'end of the world.' Actually, it is the book that carefully reveals the spiritual identities of Jesus and how Jesus spiritually purges the spirit of the Serpent, to lead us from the system of Darkness, judgements and punishments, into salvation and his kingdom of Light and mercy.

Chapter 19

The Revelation of Jesus Christ

This book of the Bible is one of the hardest to understand and to reveal its hidden meanings. Nearly every sentence, and often nearly every word within the sentences, contains codes and riddles and multiple meanings, so much so that reading the text at face value makes no real sense at all and is, frankly, unhelpful because it leads to serious misunderstandings. John was not writing it to be taken literally. The book of Revelation includes descriptions of strange beasts and a dragon, the throne room in heaven, the anti-Christ, the four horsemen of the Apocalypse, a pregnant woman who hides in the wilderness and terrible events of death and destruction initiated from heaven. These events seem to go on and on and on and give the impression that they describe the end of the world. It is so difficult to understand that you see many interpretations and many misunderstandings, and therefore various competing 'end time' doctrines have taken root. There is much debate amongst scholars over which doctrine is correct. Or even if any of them are correct.

So, to do justice to John's work, I have explained the deeper meanings of what he has written in a later book. I will explain the whole book, division by division, line by line and where necessary word by word.

Here, it is too much to even attempt to explain how to decode the book, nor will I attempt to describe everything that John tells us when it is decoded. I will simply reveal the key messages which we can follow, even with the basic understanding that we already have. That said, I will need to go into a little more depth when we get to the events that are happening now or will soon happen. These stories describe events which are especially relevant to the events that are taking place today, many of which appear to be leading to something truly terrible and world ending, but they are not.

The key messages

The book of Revelation is the 'Revelation of Jesus Christ'. The Greek word for revealing is 'apokalypsis', so this is about revealing the mysteries of Jesus, not about an apocalypse or disaster.

John starts by revealing that the book is a prophecy and that he is the prophet, and he gives the route of the prophetic words from Yhwh to the people of Light. He says that it starts with Yhwh who gave it to Gabriel who she sent to John as her witness. Then anyone who reads the prophecy from John to others will inherit the kingdom, and if the others who hear it will watch over it and spread it accurately, then they will be blessed too.

Therefore, John has started by describing how prophecy works, which is usually stated as 'the word of Yhwh (the Lord) came to [the prophet].' John doesn't just repeat that phrase, he explains it and how prophecy works. Therefore, we can be confident that this is true prophecy from a man with deep understanding. We see that the purpose of the prophecy is inheritance and blessing, so we can be confident that it is going to explain the victory of Light over Darkness. Perhaps more importantly, he also states twice that the events that the prophecy leads up to are going to happen soon. The urgency is being repeated by the other Apostles too, and it will be stated clearly by Jesus at the end of Revelation. That should make it clear to anyone who is still waiting for Jesus to come and the events to happen, that they have missed something. The point is that Jesus did come, and most people missed it, because they were looking out for something like the end of the world. Now he is about to come again, and hopefully, we will not miss it this time.

John then describes the three spiritual identities of Jesus in heaven, and he does so three times. He will be coming with his heavenly army on chariots and he will be seen by everyone with spiritual eyes to see him, and when he comes, all the tribes of the earth will be cut down by a single stroke as they 'beat their breasts' in shame. This is the repentance and the casting out and purge of the spirit of the Serpent, the main purpose of Jesus's coming, and the true message of Revelation.

John switches to the earth and describes a vision of Jesus on earth, as the Son of Man. He describes the three identities of Jesus again, but this time he is shown as three in one, because he is on earth. However, he is the most important of the Sons of Man, he is the original Adam who has become the new Adam, Jesus. He is all seven of them in one, a complete cycle, from the fall to the recovery. To demonstrate that he was the Son of Man in every age, he describes seven churches, each one a current church full of people with the Holy Spirit, but each one also represents a past age, in the correct order. Each church has an angel over it, which represents their Son of Man, ascended to heaven at the end of their age. Jesus has a message for each church, which contains an event from the age they represent, to identify it. When you put all seven together, you have a summary of mankind from creation to the current end times.

A vital message for us is that these churches are a complete cycle of seven, and that means that it will be repeated. So what we are reading applies not just to the Bible times, but to our own times.

Worthiness, and war or no war?
Next, John's spirit is taken up to heaven by the Holy Spirit, instantly. This is to show us that the Holy Spirit is everywhere, and with your spiritual eye of the Holy Spirit in you, you can be shown or even taken to, any scene in any place at any time. Your body is constrained to one place and time, but your spirit is everywhere and in every time. This is important, because much of the prophecy to come is

about the same events viewed from different perspectives and it is important to understand that they are not in chronological order. We will see that Revelation appears to describe a very long list of terrible events, but actually they depict only one set of events, seen from a number of viewpoints.

Here, we continue with the view from heaven, and we start by looking at the mechanism for the transition of authority and power from Darkness to Light. The key test is whether Yhwh and her Messiah king are worthy to rule. All of the living creatures in heaven and earth are given their say, like a vote.

Gabriel, the angel of Yhwh and the word of Yhwh, is ready, and she has already been accepted to be worthy and enthroned in heaven. She is shown to be both the Almighty God and the God of Mercy in one, sitting on her throne and waiting for the time she will take over as the God of Light. She has already redeemed her people of Israel at the start of the fifth age, when she paid the punishment of their sins, and it is that redemption which has made her just and worthy. Just, because the proper punishment of sin has been paid, and worthy because she accepted full responsibility for all sins that she caused by her actions. She holds the scroll of the new covenant of Light for the new kingdom, but it is still sealed closed, with seven seals. When opened, this covenant will bring the age of Light and the kingdom of Light, but first the Messiah king, David, the Sun, must prove himself to be worthy to rule as king of kings, too. Only when he is worthy will he be able to open the seven seals and become not just king, but king of kings. One seal for each age and son of man.

But there is nobody who is worthy at this time, and so Gabriel continues to wait. John watches and weeps as it appears that they have failed. That is because the Sun is still serving his 40-year punishment to redeem his people. Then, as we watch, he completes his punishment, and he appears next to the throne as a lamb. The sacrificial lamb. Like Gabriel, he has now redeemed his people, and so he has just proven himself to be worthy as their king. He is ready to open the seals. Also, the angelic judges in heaven prepare to make their judgements. They confirm his worthiness to open the seals and declare that his redeemed people shall inherit and have authority over the earth in the new age. So far, so good. It looks like a war with the Serpent will not be required.

Next, all the senior angels with authority in heaven support the king's worthiness to rule. They say he should have seven royal instruments to rule with. Power, wealth and wisdom, come first, then might, honour, glory and blessing. It's still looking good.

Then there is a problem. The spirits and angels of the created creatures of heaven and earth and under the earth and in the sea, declare that the royal instruments for both the king and Gabriel should only be the last four, blessing and honour and glory and might. They do not include power, wealth or wisdom.

That is because the people with the spirits of the Serpent/Moon are included in this category. They already have power and wealth and wisdom from the Serpent, and they don't want to concede them to the Messiah Sun. But without them, the Sun cannot rule effectively, and the Moon would have far too much power in the new kingdom.

Neither the Sun nor Gabriel could possibly accept this state, so it is going to be necessary to fight and defeat the Moon, to purge her spirits from heaven and earth, in order to get what is rightfully theirs. Why is it rightfully theirs? Firstly, because Adam was blessed by God to inherit, and secondly, the Sun is the greater of the two lights and was given the authority to rule, although his authority is being rejected by the Moon/Serpent. She has rebelled and will not concede defeat. Therefore, the final battles with the Serpent will need to be fought, so that she can be defeated by force. (As an aside, we have just seen how important it is to Yhwh and the Messiah to have a large number of followers to outnumber the people with the spirit of the Serpent. We can imagine that one day, if they have enough followers at this early stage, there will be no need for war.)

The battles will follow the pattern of the battle of Jericho, with seven days of encircling the city as a series of warnings and preparations, followed by seven trumpets being sounded, with escalating judgements against the city, then the city walls will fall down when the seventh trumpet sounds. History tells us that the wall of Jerusalem collapses and the temple and the city are destroyed, in AD 70. This, as we will see, was the final battle of Armageddon as seen in the physical world. But the events and conflicts that come before it, are the essential spiritual purges and the spiritual conflicts between Jesus and the Serpent.

The preparations of the sons of man – the seven seals

The king opens the seals, one by one, to release the angel armies of each age. The first four are the kings of Darkness and fire who are commanding their heavenly armies, symbolised by their horses. They are the famous 'four horsemen of the apocalypse'. We have seen them before, as they carried out the purges of the spirit of the Serpent at the end of their ages. They are Yhwh's secret weapons, the hidden kings of Darkness who do the will of Yhwh. They are, in order, 1) Enoch, 2) the king of Babylon (Nimrod), 3) Moses and 4) the king of Babylon (Nebuchadnezzar). They position themselves on the earth and wait to be called.

In fact, the seals all represent the ages. Here, the first four seals represent the first four ages of Darkness and the four secret weapons are the ones who carried out the purges of these ages.

The fifth seal releases the martyred prophets of Gabriel, the word of Yhwh, who must also wait for their justice against the Serpent at the end of the age. They will be joined by the followers of Jesus who will be martyred for the word of Yhwh too and they will all join Jesus's angelic army when he comes at the end of the sixth age. They are impatient, but they don't have long to wait.

The sixth seal is for the Apostles and the Sun and warrior king David. This seal releases the most activity as it represents the sixth age which sees the most intense battles between Darkness and Light. On earth there is an earthquake as the authority of the Serpent starts to topple and fall. In heaven, Michael, the divine angel of righteous Darkness, takes authority and purges the angels of the Serpent, who are filled with the spirit of the Serpent (the fig), from heaven. These are the stars which then fall to earth, '*as the fig tree sheds its winter fruit when shaken by a gale.*' These angels are the false deities of the idols, and of the myths of Greece and Rome. The Sun in heaven turns black as he becomes the judge at judgement day, and the dark side of the Sun manifests. The sky vanishes '*like a scroll that is being rolled up*', which is the scroll of the old law and covenant being fulfilled, ready for the new covenant of Light. The mountains and islands move as the new authority of Jesus takes over. This is what Jesus meant when he said that with faith his followers could move mountains. All these are signs which are seen by the people of Darkness who are in authority on earth, and they know what is happening. They try to hide from Yhwh and the Sun.

Next, at Judgement Day, the dead of Israel who were sleeping in Sheol, are released and redeemed, followed by the newly redeemed dead of the gentiles. They are marked as the people belonging to Yhwh and the Messiah, and resurrected to heaven. The mark is like a Passover event, and is necessary to keep them safe during the purge and so that they will not be judged. They will be deemed righteous instead. The redeemed dead make a huge heavenly army, and they all serve God and the Sun, not the Serpent. They were the lost sheep, but now they are under the good shepherd, the lamb. Now the Sun and his new, huge, army is prepared for the coming purge.

After the huge numbers of the redeemed are resurrected to heaven, all the angels surrounding the throne of Yhwh, and the other angels in authority in heaven, are amazed and fall on their faces and worship Yhwh the supreme God. They pray for all the seven instruments of divine rule are given to her permanently. This is when at the end of the six ages of Darkness, Yhwh is confirmed to be worthy to rule in the seventh age of Light in heaven, for ever. It means that the seventh seal can be opened and Yhwh will have taken over as Supreme God.

It also means that Yhwh and the Messiah have completed their preparations and are ready to carry out the purge of the spirits of the Serpent.

Therefore, the lamb opens the final seal so that the seven trumpets of the purges can be sounded. You may remember that this is when the walls of Jericho fell down, when the trumpets were sounded after the seven days of encircling the city.

We are now at the beginning of the seventh age, and there was rest and silence in heaven for a short time. On earth this is a period of relative peace, but this gives people a false sense of security. Then, the silence ends and the purges can begin.

The trumpets

The trumpets are the calls to battle and commands from the commander to the various angelic armies. As each trumpet is blown in heaven, the heavenly army of fire destroys the spirits of the Serpent on earth, by fire, but leaves the spirits of the people in their 'clay vessel' untouched. The description in Revelation is that a third of the targets are 'killed', and the targets are identified as 'mankind', so it sounds very much like a massive destructive war throughout all of the earth. But there are three types of spirits involved, and the spirits of the Serpent make up only a third of them, and that is what is being purged. This is happening in the spiritual world.

The first trumpet

At the first trumpet, the spirits of the serpent in the whole earth, including the fig trees and all the spiritual food of the Serpent for the 'lost sheep' (grass) were burned up.

The second trumpet

At the second trumpet, the house of the Serpent, a mountain, which had been built up since creation, was thrown down into the sea, and all the spirits of the Serpent in that house died there. You may recall that the unclean spirits cast out of Legion finished up in the sea and they drowned.

The third trumpet

At the third trumpet, the rivers of the Serpent were purged and made bitter.

The fourth trumpet

At the fourth trumpet, the spirits of the Serpent who had entered the people of the houses of the Sun and the moon and the stars through idolatry on earth, were struck down. Both the people of the Day and the people of Night were cleansed.

All of these purges were spiritual and happened in the spiritual world, so these events would have been difficult or impossible to see from the physical world. However, the steadily weakening power of the Serpent would have become apparent, as the power of the Messiah grew. The effect of these trumpets is widespread, covering the Gentiles in particular.

If it's not going too deep, you can see that each trumpet represents an age, in order, and each purge reflects the purges that had happened at the end of each age. They were carried out by the appropriate horsemen. The first purge of the whole earth, including the grass is like Noah's flood, carried out by Enoch. The second purge of the mountain being thrown down is like the tower or pyramid of Babel, carried out by Nimrod. The third purge of the rivers of the Serpent are like the River Nile and the army of Egypt which Moses struck down in the Red Sea. The fourth purge of the spirits of the Serpent who entered the houses through idolatry and were struck down are like the purges of the king of Babylon at the end of the fourth age.

The next three trumpets are different. They are called 'three woes' which means three curses. This is the opposite of blessings and they concern the people who have chosen to ignore the calls to repent and they follow the Serpent rather than Yhwh, largely through idolatry. They are the people of Jerusalem and Judea and the exiles, who have not been redeemed or saved. They are deceived by the false shepherds and religious leaders and so they are breaking the Laws of Moses and are suffering the curses of the law, not the blessings. These trumpets are about persuading them to repent and turn back to Yhwh, so they can turn their curses into blessings as they turn from Darkness to Light.

These last three trumpets also represent their ages. They are the fifth age of Jesus, the sixth age of the apostles and the beginning of the seventh age, especially Armageddon. However, these events do not focus on the blessings of each age for the people of Yhwh and Jesus, they focus on the curses for the people of the Serpent who reject Yhwh and Jesus.

The fifth trumpet
The fifth trumpet reflects the time of the Roman Empire with their army of Darkness, who dominate the earth and are enforcing law and order. However, this event is a spiritual event which employs the spirits of the solders, who appear to be like the Romans, but they actually span many previous ages and many such battles.

The trumpet releases the angelic soldiers to torment the people who follow the serpent on earth, for five months, as a strong warning to turn from the Serpent and to repent. Those marked as redeemed are not to be affected, nor is the true spiritual knowledge for the people, nor the Holy Spirit of Yhwh. This is the true spiritual knowledge of Yhwh which is being successfully spread, and should not be harmed. The torments are harsh treatment as the spirits of the Serpent in the people fights back, and they are difficult to bear. But because they are only warnings, they are actually acts of mercy from Yhwh, hence the length of five months. They are soldiers of Darkness but they are doing the will of Yhwh, so their commander is clearly in the line of the other sons of Enoch and the kings of Babylon.

Although this is happening in the fifth age, the commander is not Jesus. Who is preaching strong messages of repentance or else be cursed? He is John the Baptist with the spirit of Elijah. That is the end of the first woe. The three woes are from each of the three identities of Jesus. Here, the first woe is from the first of the three Messianic identities of Jesus, the word of Yhwh, which here, is Elijah the prophet.

The sixth trumpet

After this, the sixth trumpet was sounded, to bring the second woe. Like the sixth seal, the sixth trumpet releases a large number of events, all of which happened in the sixth age. The warnings of the fifth trumpet and the fifth age are over, and the intention is firstly to remove the spirit of the Serpent and secondly to encourage repentance before the seventh trumpet sounds, to avoid the woes and receive the salvation and blessing.

The sixth trumpet is the most relevant to us today, firstly because it represents the sixth age, our age, and secondly because it comes from the third Messianic identity, the Holy Spirit. Therefore, these are the events which are happening or about to happen, now. Accordingly, I will look into this section of Revelation in rather more depth. It's harder to follow, but it does reveal what is happening in the spiritual world, which is relatively simple, albeit buried in difficult spiritual symbols with well hidden meanings.

Four mighty angels had been waiting at the great River Euphrates, where they had been prepared for this moment for a long time. They were released to kill a third of the spirits of mankind. Again, the third of the spirits of mankind refers to the spirits of the Serpent only. The Euphrates is to the east, and is the boundary to the empires of

Babylon and Assyria. So once again we are seeing the four heavenly angelic armies of the four sons of Enoch and the kings of Babylon, including Nebuchadnezzar, purging the spirit of the Serpent. However, this time it is not a warning, the purge is happening.

These armies again looked like horses and riders, but although their Holy Spirits of fire could wound as a warning, their mouths could kill. This is another example of their authority to command the spirits of the Serpent, because now they could cast them out and send them to their deaths with their commands. This purge is like the one that Jesus foretold to his disciples, where two people would be working together when one would suddenly be taken and the other left. Jesus was concerned about the one that was left, to receive the blessings, but here we are concerned about the one that is taken, to receive the curses. The sentences that are being enforced on the spirits of the Serpent are fire (punishment), smoke (curses) and sulphur (the burning, molten, lake of fire).

This is the major purge of the spirits of the Serpent which starts at the beginning of the sixth age, as soon as the Holy Spirit is released and casts out the spirit of the Serpent. It continues throughout the sixth age. We don't see much or any of this in the physical world, because it is spiritual warfare carried out by the Holy Spirit of fire, but lead by the apostles.

Unfortunately, the rest of mankind who were not killed, did not repent and carried on with their sinful lives, especially idolatry. These are the other two spirits of mankind which were not killed, but they remain able to choose to follow the Serpent again, and be filled by the spirit of the Serpent again. To try to deter this, Yhwh decides to deal with them through preaching to them about the true Law of Moses, which includes the curses. It will be their last chances to repent. Yhwh also turns to preach to the gentiles.

Yhwh wants to reintroduce the true Law of Moses and to preach it again to the Hebrews, but this time, showing the descriptions of the Messiah in the Law. How better to give the Law of Moses, than to use Moses himself? A mighty angel, which is Moses the lawgiver, his face still shining, descends from heaven, under the authority of the seven Sons of Man. He carries the Holy Spirit of fire in both his legs, spread over a huge area, of both the earth and the sea. The left foot is for curses on the earth for the chosen people who are under Law and the curses. The right foot is for the gentiles in the sea, and here, the Holy Spirit gives only blessings of inheritance to the people. The point of the description of the feet is to emphasise that the action will be performed by the Holy Spirit, which is an important message for us today.

Moses, who as we know is a spiritual lion, calls out loudly like a lion roaring, and this is the call to repent and come to the Messiah for salvation. However, the call is answered by the seven spirits of the Holy Spirit of Darkness and fire, who sound like thunder. They are the Spirit of the Serpent on the earth which is already cursed. We do not know what they say because Gabriel asked John to keep it secret, not even writing it in code. However, I understand that it was a reply from the voice of the Serpent, of defiance and rebellion, against the Sun in Moses, and against Yhwh. It was also to encourage the people of the Serpent that Moses had just called, to ignore the call and to continue the fight. Something like, 'Do not listen to or fear Yhwh or the Sun because they are weak and few and we are strong and outnumber them. We will win, and we will inherit, so trust me, there will be no curses and no seventh age of Light. Instead, the kings of Darkness will rule for ever and ever. Long live Darkness!' It's not a message that Yhwh would like to spread.

Moses's response is to swear to Yhwh that there will be no further delay and that at the seventh trumpet call, the mystery of God would be fulfilled. The mystery of God at that time means that Yhwh and the Messiah will rule, and the old law of Moses will be fulfilled and replaced by the new law of Mercy. When Moses swears this, he raises his right hand up to heaven. The right hand of the Sun is the army of Light, in heaven and on earth, and it means he is declaring war to defeat the Serpent and win the inheritance. A perfect reply to the Serpent's call to rebel.

Therefore, the teaching of the true Law of Moses, which includes the true identity of the Messiah who they are rejecting, is the last chance for the unrepentant people to see the curses they are under, and repent. Then they will receive the salvation that is conspicuously absent from the Serpent's messages. Who will teach it though?

John is told to take the scroll of the Law of Moses from his hand and eat it, which he does, while he is still in his angelic state. Now, all of the Law and all of its meanings are within him and fully understood. On earth, Jesus had to speak and preach the spiritual knowledge when he was eating with his audience, but angels can just eat it. The blessings of the Law taste like sweet honey in John's mouth, but the curses are bitter in his stomach. Now, John has a complete spiritual knowledge of the Law and its curses and blessings, and he is told to go and prophesy again *over many peoples and nations and languages and kings.* This means to make the call to all the exiled people of the Law, spread throughout the earth, carefully explaining both the sweet blessings and the bitter curses of the Law. It is their last call before the end of the age and judgement day. John is representing all of the apostles, and we have seen that Paul will make a point of preaching to the Hebrews in the synagogues of the gentile countries first, before he preaches to the gentiles. However, as we know, he spreads the word to the Gentiles too, to 'many peoples and nations and languages and kings' and has a much stronger response than the Hebrews.

Then Yhwh turns her attention to the Jews of Jerusalem and the surrounding area. John prepares for Armageddon by measuring the temple. Measuring means to judge. The temple has become corrupt, teaching the false laws of the Serpent and even has an idol to the Serpent in it, called the abomination of desolation. So the temple has become the problem rather than the solution and it must be judged, condemned and stopped.

Therefore, the two witnesses to the Jews, the Law and the Prophets (Moses and Elijah) are told to prophesise. That means that the true Law and the true prophets are preached in the temple, wherever possible. However, as we know, the truth is attacked by the Serpent, it is suppressed, and seems to be dead, to the delight of the Serpent and her religious rulers. That's because the true word of Yhwh and the true Law had become a real problem for the Serpent.

The people of the Serpent thought they had won, and that all the remaining Jews had lost their salvation and were spiritually dead too. However, they had not taken Jesus's redemption into account. The dead people of the Law and Prophets (the Hebrews) were resurrected and stood upright in deemed righteousness. The people of the Serpent who saw this happening in the spiritual world were terrified. There was a call from heaven for the redeemed people to come up to heaven, and they rose in a cloud, a spiritual chariot of Yhwh, as the people of the Serpent watched. At that time, there was a great earthquake, as the authority changed hands, then a tenth of the city fell, meaning the inheritance of the firstborn of Darkness was lost. The rest were terrified, and they turned to Yhwh and gave glory to her. They were redeemed too.

That is the end of the second woe. It is a happy ending for Yhwh and her people, who were blessed, just in time. But it is a disastrous ending for the Serpent and her people, who were cursed.

That completes the sixth trumpet and as the angel of Moses stated, the time for repentance is over. Now it is time for the day of Light and for Yhwh and the Sun to rule. It is also time for Armageddon and the end of the corrupt city and temple of Jerusalem. That is the third and final woe.

The seventh trumpet
The seventh and final trumpet was sounded. The seventh age started and loud voices in heaven said, '*The kingdom of the whole world has become the kingdom of Yhwh and the Messiah, and they shall reign forever and*

ever.' They are declaring that in heaven, Light has taken over from Darkness, permanently.

Then the 20 four elders and judges on their thrones in heaven, summarised the recent events. I have written what they said word for word, with my comments in brackets. I have also numbered the points so that if you want to, you can see the 10 stages of the purge, in the order and meaning of the number code:

1. *We give thanks to you, Lord God Almighty,* [the supreme God, Yhwh Elohiym]
2. *who is and who was,* [previously she was, and is, and **will be**, but now her future has arrived]
3. *for you have taken your great power* [the divine Holy Spirit]
4. *and begun to reign.* [her reign has just started now]
5. *The nations raged but your wrath came,* [the Gentile nations under the Serpent fought against Yhwh but she Yhwh's anger was aimed at the Serpent]
6. *and the time for the dead to be judged,* [as Sheol is emptied]
7. *and for rewarding your servants, the prophets and saints.* [The reward is salvation. The prophets are from the time of the old testament, and the saints from the new testament.]
8. *and those who fear your name, both small and great,* [The others who remain under the law and who fear God (rather than have faith in her and Jesus), who have the salvation of redemption and resurrection]
9. *And for destroying the destroyers of the earth.* [the final purge of the spirits of the Serpent in the leaders and priests and judges of Darkness]

Then, at last, we have the third and final woe or curse, which is number 10 in this sequence (for judgement) and is the battle of Armageddon.

I will quote how it is described at this point of the Bible, [10.] *'There were flashes of lightning, rumblings, peals of thunder, an earthquake, and heavy hail.'* That's it!

Perhaps surprisingly, that's all there is, but it is enough to describe the walls of Jerusalem come tumbling down just like happened when the seventh trumpet of Jericho sounded, followed by the destruction of the city and the temple and the forceable change of authority.

We know from history that the rebellion of the Jews against Rome resulted in a strong retaliation from the Romans to put down the rebellion, who swept through Judea and besieged Jerusalem, then the city fell and was destroyed in AD 70.

The same events are repeated in the next section of Revelation, through the perspective of the Holy Spirit on earth (which we will cover in Book Three). We will see that Armageddon is described again, in the same way, except the earthquake and the hail are more fully described: '*and there were* **flashes of lightning, rumblings, peals of thunder, and a great earthquake** *such as there had never been since man was on the earth, so great was the earthquake. The great city was split into three parts and the cities of the nations fell.* ... **And great hailstones**, *(about a talent of silver each) fell from heaven on people; and they cursed God for the plague of the hail, because the plague was so severe.'* The earthquake is the toppling of the authority of Darkness, and it is so big because it is the whole authority of Darkness that has fallen as Light takes over. The hailstones are the last plague, the mighty warriors of Yhwh who defeat and destroy the remaining spirits of the Serpent.

This is the tenth and last plague and with it, the wrath of Yhwh is spent and the purge of Armageddon is over.

The structure of Revelation
I know that the enquiring minds of some readers will lead them to look at the original Revelation in the Bible to see how well they can understand it now before we return to it in Book Three. I wish

you well. For them, it is important to understand how Revelation is structured. John has written it in seven parts, which correspond to the seven ages and the number code. This is the order you read it in, so you can see that it is not chronological, which causes even more confusion and misunderstanding. We have just looked at parts 1 and 2.

1. Yhwh and her Messiah and the seven sons of man.
2. The description of the purges from the perspective of Yhwh or Gabriel.
3. The same from the perspective of the Messiah and the Holy Spirit.
4. The same from the perspective of the Moon or the Serpent.
5. The mercy and salvation in heaven.
6. The events of the sixth age, which is described as the 'thousand years', including judgement day. The 1,000 years is actually a use of the number code, and although this is jumping ahead, it means judgement under Darkness (1) of all living creatures after the divine angels (000). Note that this part takes us back to the beginning of the sixth age, so it is not chronological. The 1,000 years is described as the same as a day, which for this day means 40 years! It does not describe a future reign of 1,000 physical years, and this has caused many misunderstandings and much confusion.
7. The new heaven and earth in the seventh age, with the tree of life.

The other perspectives do add some useful information and details, such as the famous anti-Christ and 666 the mark of the beast, but there is nothing dramatically new.

Now, we will finish with part 7 of Revelation, the description of the seventh age which concludes the Bible with a happy ending.

Chapter 20

The Seventh Age. The New Heaven and the New Earth and the New Jerusalem and the Tree of Life

As we know, heaven and earth are the places of the believers who have covenanted with God. In the first six ages, the covenants were covenants of Darkness based on Law and punishment. Now, in the seventh age, the age of Yhwh, there is a new covenant of Light, based on mercy, so the old covenant places, that is the old heaven and earth, are removed and replaced by the new heaven and earth. The new kingdoms that Jesus had told us about.

Likewise, the old Jerusalem has been removed and is replaced by a new Jerusalem. This is the Holy City for the holy people, and it is in heaven – the kingdom of heaven. Let's take a look at it. In this city there is everlasting life so there is no death and no mourning, and no crying or pain. This is what we traditionally describe as heaven, although it is only a part of heaven, reserved for the holy people.

Yhwh had been described as the one who was and is and will be, but now she is the one who was and is, because she has come to rule as almighty God at last. She declares that she will give mercy to anyone who is thirsty for it, and it will be given freely and for free. But the Serpent and her rulers on earth, who have not thirsted for mercy and not repented, will be cast into the lake of fire and sulphur as people of Darkness. There they will serve their own punishments without redemption. But that does not destroy them, it cleanses them the hard way, and they will be resurrected to heaven when they are released. Very few people receive this punishment, and in practice it is reserved for the bad shepherds and hypocrites who have led the lost sheep of Israel astray, and not protected them from attacks from the beasts of the Serpent. Instead, they fed them to the beasts and are now paying the price.

The new Jerusalem is a message of great hope, because when John sees it, it is coming down from heaven to earth. It isn't there yet, but it is coming. Everyone in it is covenanted to Jesus like a bridegroom and his bride, and they are made holy by him through his Holy Spirit. It is these people of Light who inherit the earth and have authority on earth while they live there. They are assisted by the gifts of the Holy Spirit, such as being able to hear the guidance and wisdom of Yhwh, in everything they do.

The foundations of the city are the 12 foundational spirits of creation (the precious stones), so that every nation is represented. But the 12 gates of the walls are not the 12 gates of the tribes of the chosen people, they are all made of a single pearl. This is the Holy Spirit of Jesus, and it means that only Jesus can judge and allow entry, but he does not restrict it to the Hebrews, he includes the gentiles. He will also ensure that nothing unclean will ever enter it.

In the city there is no darkness, because the way of Darkness and the Law of the first six ages has ended. There is only Light, 24 hours a day. In heaven, the cycles of day and night have concluded, so there is only everlasting Light. And Light means mercy, without judgement. This Light will be the guidance to all the nations who will walk by it, and the kings of the earth will bring glory to it as they and their people turn to Light and are filled by the Holy Spirit (the glory).

Finally, there is the source of the mercy that will satisfy the thirst of the new kingdoms. There is a river of the water of life, flowing from the throne of God and the lamb, through the street of the city. This is the water of the baptism that cleanses anyone who walks into it. Then, as they climb out of the river, clean, there is the Tree of Life on the banks. This is the same Tree of Life that was rejected in the Garden of Eden. Now, at last, it is available again, but this time it is accepted and eaten.

Its fruit is not just available during an annual summer season, it is available and ripe every month, to all the 12 foundational spirits of creation. It is always summer in heaven. The tree has many 'leaves' which are actually angels of Light, full of the Holy Spirit, who go out to the nations to heal them, as missionaries.

The servants of Jesus will worship him and they will be able to see him face to face, because they are holy. The almighty God, now Yhwh, will be their Light and they will reign with Jesus, their king of kings, forever.

Finally, Revelation and the Bible closes with the promise from Jesus that these events will happen soon and that he is coming soon and that the time is near. He says, 'Come', which is his call to the nations. Everyone who hears him should also say 'come'. And everyone who is thirsty for the water of life should come. That means everyone with an enquiring mind! Jesus wraps up the book with, 'Surely I am coming soon.'

He did.

And now that we are approaching this same time of holiness and salvation in our own cycles, Jesus is about to come again.

Chapter 21

The Beginning

The old warrior took a deep breath. It was over. His king had come and he had conquered. He called out, 'Victory to you my king. For ever and ever you shall reign in your kingdom, for the Serpent is vanquished and his servants burn with him in the lake of fire.' David replied, 'No my old friend, the victory belongs to all of us, and we shall all surely live in peace.'

The old warrior thought quietly to himself. He thought about many things, and what he had done in the many lives of his old soul. He still remembered when he used to walk with God and the covenant they had made together. He had nothing but admiration and undying loyalty for Michael and his son, the Sun. It was so good to fight evil together, but it was even better to win together. That they had done, time and time again, but never like this. He remembered the destruction of Noah's flood, but he still wondered why it was called 'Noah's flood' since, as he remembered it, Noah was a man of peace and he destroyed nothing. He preferred 'Enoch's flood'. He remembered knocking down and dispersing the mountain at Babel. He remembered leading the people of Israel to safety and the destruction of the Egyptian army. He remembered sweeping through the promised land and destroying so many strongholds of the Serpent, then looking after the people of Judah again, in his own kingdom. He was proud to do both destroying and saving. And most of all he remembered his time as Emperor of Rome. What a great civilisation. What a great army. What a great victory.

Then he thought about what David had said, about us all living in peace. He took a deep breath and he replied. Not for me, I think,

The Beginning 341

old friend, for I am a man of war. I think it is the time for me to rest in peace. It is the time when all Darkness will rest. David came to him and they embraced each other, with the knowing smiles and the memories and mixed emotions of old men. David wept. Enoch went to his well-worn resting place, laid down and closed his eyes.

David, the Sun, whispered to him, 'rest well. But only until the next time, when we will ride together once more. Meanwhile I have work to do.'

Gabriel and the Holy Spirit joined him and reminded him, 'all three of us have work to do. This age of Light is not permanent on earth, and it will come to an end when the Serpent recovers and tempts mankind into falling once again. A new cycle of seven ages will start. We will be busy.'

The Sun thought for a long moment, then he replied, 'So what can we do to make it better next time, Gabriel?'

'Well, we can ensure that the Serpent has no shadows to hide in. Her biggest advantage is that nobody on earth knows who she is, what she wants, and how she works. In fact, nobody on earth knows much about the spiritual world at all. Few people would follow her if they realised what she was really like, and especially that she would steal their salvation. This deception has to come to an end. Therefore, at the next sabbath age, in some 2,000 years' time, we will reveal every mystery of the spiritual world, and the knowledge and understanding of us will cover the earth. And everyone will know us and they will know the Serpent. Then mercy will rule, so fire will be quenched by water, and wars will end.'

The Sun asked, 'Why wait until then?' 'Because that will be the start of the third cycle of seven, the cycle of the Holy Spirit and the Messiah. It will be your time to shine. Everywhere.'

He considered what she had said and he understood it all. Her wisdom truly surpassed all others. So he said, 'I like your plan.'

Then, after another moment he said, 'But then again, I have always liked your plans. They never go wrong or anything, do they?'

Gabriel just looked at him, smiled, and forgave him. They had a lot to do together. The next cycle on earth would be a difficult one for them, but already she was planning for the one after it, when all would have been revealed.

Gabriel and Yhwh had a lot to plan, because Yhwh had not forgotten that before creation, God had foreseen that mankind would wipe itself out with terrible wars of escalating fire. They did not have the capability to do so in this cycle, but she knew that they would be able to do it in the next. The threat was very real and it had not gone away. It had still to come. She also knew that the reason that she existed as Light was to be the solution, and she already felt the burden. What was she supposed to do?

Put simply, she and her army of Light would need to pour the water of mercy on the fires of war, as the Serpent and her armies of Darkness poured petrol on them. It was a massive task. And for that reason, she needed all of Mankind to understand what was really going on in the spiritual world. Then she would need all the help from Mankind that she could get. Fully supported by her Holy Spirit, of course.

She looked at Enoch, her secret weapon, as he slept, and she made her plans.

End of Book One

Conclusions

We have reached that time, so should we be scared today? I do not want this book to be remembered for repeating the old cliché of 'repent, repent, for the end of the world is nigh!' which is a message of fear. I would rather it was remembered as the start of a time of enlightenment, in preparation of a great age of peace and security where our default method of justice is to apply mercy and not fire. When the threat of nuclear Mutually Assured Destruction will be a vague memory, which is a message of faith. But the fact is that we do have to get through the purge leading up to Armageddon, before we can move forwards.

We will look at Armageddon in more depth in the next two books, but I hope that even at this early level of understanding, I have shown that most of the action will be in the spiritual world and that it is spiritual warfare. In the last cycle of seven ages, most people didn't even notice it happen, so most people are still waiting for it now. Nevertheless, if we are people of Light then we do have an important role to play.

What should we look out for?

The purge at the end of the ages is a cycle, and it consists of many subcycles which have already happened in the past. We can look out for these cycles today, not just for the events, but for the main characters involved too.

The sixth age

Let's start with the obvious cycle, which is the one we are in now – the sixth age of the apostles which at the end, leads to judgement day and the purge of Armageddon. This was when the apostles were shown how to reveal the hidden mysteries and spread the knowledge and understanding of the coming kingdom of Light, under the Messiah, Jesus. Critically, it was also when the Holy Spirit was released and filled the followers of Jesus, after casting out the spirit of the Serpent.

The casting out is the purge of the Serpent in this age, and the replacement with the Holy Spirit leads to holiness and salvation to follow the purge. This also describes the spiritual battles between these two spirits, which leads to Armageddon and victory for Light, followed by salvation. This is what is about to be repeated in our own age, and you can see that the Holy Spirit is central to the conflicts and the victory and the salvation.

The key message of this book and the other two to follow is that the Holy Spirit of Light is the Tree of Life, which we rebelled against and rejected in the beginning, but now we have the opportunity to put that right, and to receive important spiritual gifts on earth and eternal life in heaven. In the process, we will weaken the Serpent and strengthen the Messiah. That, in a nutshell, is what all the people of Light can do.

If you are thinking you are insignificant and what difference can one person make to something like Armageddon, then just remember that in the story of the Bible, every great movement started with one person, and that the Serpent is defeated by large numbers. Remember Samson whose great strength depended on the numbers of his followers (his hair)? If Yhwh had not wanted large numbers of followers, she would not have wanted to publish these books to the world, for everyone with an enquiring mind to read.

Regarding spreading the word, the principle remains the same since the last cycle, but technology has moved on. At that time, teaching the word was slow and difficult, mainly done through preaching verbally to small groups. But the word was also spread by

CONCLUSIONS 345

the Holy Spirit who filled the new believers, and they in turn went out to fill more new believers. They did the same, so that eventually the word and the Holy Spirit grew exponentially. In our cycle, technology means that the word can be spread to large numbers of people in a short timescale, and therefore, the Holy Spirit can spread at the same rate. News about the books' contents can be spread just as fast, and to large numbers, through social media and all the other electronic media. That's another thing that the people of Light can do.

Now, although spreading the spiritual knowledge of the mysteries of the spiritual world is vital, I hope I have fully explained that the power of these words comes with the Holy Spirit. I meant it when I said that the answer to all the problems we face is the Holy Spirit. It was the answer 2,000 years ago and it still is.

Remember that if you truly wish to be filled with the Holy Spirit, and you expect it to happen to you, you just need to ask Jesus for it. He will do the rest. If you know someone who has recently been filled, then ask them to lay hands on you when you ask for the Holy Spirit. It's that simple.

Even if you look no further into Armageddon, then this is enough.

Other cycles of purges and their main characters

We have looked at many other cycles of many other purges throughout the Bible, and we can watch out for them happening now. Nearly all of them are happening in the spiritual world, but the physical signs and the various physical wars that we can see in history are important too. So are the main characters. If Armageddon is really only a few years away, as I say, then the main characters will already be here and in power. We should remember that what I am saying is not a prophecy, it is a description based on cycles that have happened before and can be expected to happen again, albeit with some changes. The details and the timing of what will actually happen are secret and known only to God, but we can still get a good idea from the past cycles so long as we are careful not to make too many assumptions.

All the battles are between the Moon (Serpent) and the Sun (Messiah), so we can start by looking out for the Serpent's current kings of the earth in the physical world. What do they look like? These are individual leaders who rule like a dictator or an emperor rules over an empire. They have a strong desire to expand it by force and obtain great power, with great armies and great wealth, both personally and for the empire. They are particularly shrewd and cunning. They have little regard for human life, with a low moral code, and brutality with massive death tolls are common in their wars. Sometimes, one such king of the earth rises above the others, and he can be called the anti-Christ, because he is the manifestation of the Moon/Serpent on earth who is anti the Messiah. He will be particularly smooth talking and he will speak deceptions rather than the truth, offering great riches to his obedient followers, but death to his enemies. He will break any agreement he makes without a thought. In preparation for Armageddon, he will gather other kings of the earth together, in a large alliance, but his promises to them will be lies.

In the previous cycle of the sixth age, he was Nero, the evil Roman emperor in the lead up to Armageddon, who killed many Christians in horrible ways. But he was assassinated in a coup about two years before Armageddon, which in the physical world was the destruction of Jerusalem and the temple in AD 70. Nero was also the emperor who played the fiddle as the city of Rome burned down, before the coup.

Before that, in the purge of the fourth age, the anti-Messiah was Pharaoh Neco of Egypt. He had taken over most of the nations around the promised land, and was soundly defeated by king Nebuchadnezzar of Babylon, when he took them over.

The kings of the earth and the anti-Christ (Moon) will be opposed by the Sun on earth, but with a secret twist. The Sun will be in another a powerful king of the earth with a great empire and a great army with great wealth. However, he will be Yhwh's secret weapon, in the line of Enoch and Nimrod and Nebuchadnezzar, king of Babylon. He has been an essential part of every purge at the end of the ages, and this purge is no exception. He will defeat the armies of the remaining kings of the earth who have not abandoned the alliance, if any. In the spiritual world he will join a heavenly angelic army commanded by the Sun in heaven, King David, and it is this that will make the army invincible. In the previous sixth age, he was an emperor of Rome, after Nero died. The Roman empire and its army was the greatest on earth at that time.

So today, we are looking out for a man who rules with a split personality, consisting of both Darkness and Light. Under Darkness he will look like a king of the earth, and he will rule the greatest country and the greatest army on the earth, behaving like he is an emperor, who wants expansion, greater wealth for himself and his country, tributes from those who wish to be allies, and permanent power. However, under Light he will do the will of Yhwh. What is the will of Yhwh? To use his power to make peace and to stop wars. It is this that differentiates him from the other kings of the earth, especially the anti-Christ.

The problem we face is that in this current cycle, the parties involved in the conflicts have the capability to destroy not just each other, but the whole of mankind, with nuclear weapons in World War Three. Kings of the earth and the anti-Christ have no problem with causing widespread death to get their way. The more deaths the better. Furthermore, some of the leaders who oppose them still talk about fears of World War Three but continue to escalate the wars and demands they are involved in, rather than backing down. Making peace quickly has never been so important, but it won't be easy.

There is a temptation to want to quickly identify the anti-Christ and focus our spiritual warfare on him, but we must be careful not to make assumptions. There are many kings of the earth that fit the description and seem to be candidates, making identification difficult or impossible at this time. And there is no rule that says there is only to be one anti-Christ anyway. Also, we should not assume that the nuclear threat will only come from the strongest power, or even come from a member of the public alliance. Remember that the Serpent is a master of deception and a fast builder of hatred. The Serpent understands the advantages of surprise just as well as we do, so we must be on the lookout for potential surprises.

However, despite our own difficulties in predicting what will happen, Yhwh has got this, and she knows what to do, even if we don't. Her wisdom is the greatest in heaven and on earth, and we will soon see her wisdom in action. It is true that she is facing a much bigger threat than in the last cycle, with many more numbers against her, and her enemy has learned from witnessing her strategies. However, she has already countered this by calling for many more numbers to join her side, filled with the Holy Spirit, and unveiling the secrets of how the Serpent works, so that we can learn and be ready too.

There is one remaining feature of the previous cycles to emphasise. Rebellion. In the past, once Yhwh and the Sun have subdued the kings of the Earth and they are safely under the authority of Light, some of the people have stubbornly rebelled against this authority, especially over the value of the tributes. That rebellion has always brought down the might of the new king and the rebellion is put down by force. I have warned several times that rebellion against the authority of the new king should be avoided, because nobody needs to die.

In summary, all we need to do is to spread the Holy Spirit, trust Yhwh and do not rebel. Let's see what happens.

I hope to see you again, in Book Two.

Appendix One

The Number Code and the Colour Code

I have tried to keep it simple here, but the use of numbers to hide and then reveal mysteries is everywhere, and a basic understanding of the number code is needed. We will look at this in more depth in Book Two, but for now just understand that each number has a meaning, and it identifies a particular spirit.

Here is the basic form of the number code with the alternative code word for the corresponding plant name for the spirit, where appropriate, in brackets. It won't make much sense yet, but you will refer to it many times in the book. You may wish to bookmark this page for future reference:

1. Elohiym and the system of Law
2. Yhwh and the system of Mercy
3. Sun and Messiah and the Holy Spirit of Light (grape/wine)
4. Moon in heaven and Serpent on earth
5. Mercy covering of Yhwh (linen)
6. Darkness and the spirit of the Serpent (sour wine)
7. Holy Spirit of fire, and the seventh age
8. Resurrection (Myrrh)
9. Judge (Palm)
10. Judgement

The colour code is relatively straightforward. The seven colours of the rainbow represent the seven ages of Adam as he transitions from fire (red) to water (violet).

1. Red
2. Orange
3. Yellow
4. Green
5. Blue
6. Indigo
7. Violet

Also, black is used to indicate Darkness and white is used to indicate Light, with grey indicating a mixture of both.

Appendix Two

Glossary of Common Code Words

Angel   The spiritual living creature that makes up most of the spiritual world. Soul, spirit and body. There is a strict hierarchy of authority, with the eldest first, starting with the divine angels. Some are highly specialised like the great warrior cherubim and seraphim, but most look like mankind or various animals.

Armageddon   The great battle between the armies of the Messiah and the Serpent at the beginning of the seventh age. It happens largely in the spiritual world.

Beautiful   Describes the Messianic spirit of Yhwh, Gabriel, in women. Signifies perfection.

Bird   A soul of a believer, the step after a fish believes. It is an independent living creature in angelic form with wings to go from earth to heaven and back. A white dove signifies the soul of Yhwh and a black raven represents the soul of righteous Darkness. An eagle represents the soul of a king. Souls are eternal and clean, and flesh-eating birds cleanse unclean flesh from bodies without being affected. On earth, a bird rests in the branches of a tree, which becomes their spirit, and a person rests under the tree. The three together make up the body, spirit and soul.

Blessing   To receive the inheritance. It is always about inheritance.

Breath of life   The spirit given to a believer when he leaves the sea. Either the spirit of darkness, including the spirit of

	the Serpent, or the spirit of Light, a part of the Holy Spirit called faith. It is also the air and the wind and is everywhere.
Bronze	The metal of the angels, used both for weapons and shields or armour. It is a manifestation of the Holy Spirit.
Bush	A small tree, a spirit. If it is a spirit of fire then it burns but is not consumed. An example is the burning bush seen by Moses.
Chaff	The part of the harvest of grain which is unclean, dry and without the water of mercy, and represents the spirit of the Serpent. It is burned at judgement day.
Cherubim	A very strong and righteous angel warrior, with four sides and hearts of stone which look like wheels. It is often called a chariot, and it transports senior angels, being blown by the wind of the Holy Spirit in a straight line without turning. They can interlock their wings to become a defensive wall.
Cloud	A cherubim in the sky, also blown by the wind and used by Yhwh and the Sun.
Curse	The opposite of bless, it means to disinherit.
Darkness	The original system of law and punishment (fire). It can be righteous if it is from Elohiym or evil if it is from the Moon or the Serpent.
Day/Age	One of the seven cycles, which always come in order. An age is the major cycle and there are subcycles in every major cycle.
Earth	The place of the living creatures who are under God. The earth under Yhwh is the promised earth. The original earth is under Elohiym.
Elohiym	The supreme God, manifesting fire.

Glossary of Common Code Words 353

Enoch	The secret weapon of Yhwh, used in every age, especially at the end of each age to bring victory against the Serpent. He appears to be a king of the earth under the Serpent, including the king of Babylon, but he also has the spirit of the Sun, making him unique. He is a man of Darkness doing the will of Yhwh, and he is vital to Yhwh's plans. His line includes Nimrod, Moses, Nebuchadnezzar and others.
Fig	The spirit of the Serpent, the breath of life under the Serpent, taken by Adam and Eve in the garden. It became unclean and is the evil spirit of Darkness. Whoever eats it is turned into a person of Darkness. It cannot enter heaven so it prevents salvation.
Fire	Punishment under the system of Darkness, carried out by the spirit of fire, also called the furnace or sometimes hell.
Fish	An unbelieving soul who lives in the sea without the breath of life.
Fruit tree	The fruit is the seven parts of the Holy Spirit or the spirit of the Serpent. When you eat the fruit you receive the spirit. To multiply and be fruitful refers to being filled with the Holy Spirit.
Gladness	The feeling you get when you know you are redeemed and will go to heaven.
Glory	The Holy Spirit of Light which surrounds a holy creature like armour and appears as a bright white light which you cannot see through.
Gold	The metal of kings. Like bronze or silver, but harder and cannot be penetrated by them. It has the power of the divine Holy Spirit.
Grass	Spiritual food (knowledge) for domestic animals like sheep and goats. It can be clean or unclean and it can be destroyed by locusts.

Guardian angel	A warrior angel, usually of Darkness and fire but also an angel of the army of Light, whose purpose is to protect people and things, usually by linking together with others, into a wall or hedge.
Harvest	The salvation of people at judgement day. Either through grain (redemption) or grapes (Holy Spirit).
Heap	A small number of angels in a group, like a small hill.
Hail, hailstone	Frozen water in the hearts of Yhwh's heavenly angelic warriors. They are very powerful and used like special forces against high value targets.
Hedge	Like a wall, but made from interlinked guardian spirits of wood, not stone.
Hill	A small mountain, which is a recently formed house. You start with a valley, then a heap, a hill and a mountain over the generations.
Holy Spirit	The divine and Holy Spirit of Light, of Yhwh. It can be fire or light and it consists of seven spirits. It overpowers the spirit of the Serpent and is invincible in sufficient numbers, but only became available to people at the beginning of the sixth age. It brings several important gifts or talents but the greatest gift is that it makes you holy so you can go straight to heaven.
Honey	The side of the Law which leads to sweet blessings.
Iron	The metal of the spirit of the Serpent on earth. It becomes rusty when it is corrupted. It is weaker than bronze and silver and gold.
Joy	The feeling of intense joy that you get when you are filled with the Holy Spirit.
King of Babylon	Nimrod and Nebuchadnezzar in the line of Enoch. The king of Assyria is also in the line of Nimrod.

Glossary of Common Code Words 355

Lamb	The name given to the king and son of God, including King David and Jesus, who should have been the lion but was denied this position by the Moon. It was corrected at Armageddon, when the spiritual David became king of kings.
Leprosy	What unclean angelic flesh looks like.
Life	Eternal spiritual life, not physical.
Light	The system of justice based on mercy and forgiveness (water), the opposite of Darkness and fire.
Linen	A spiritual covering of the mercy of Yhwh, which is opaque to sin and leads to deemed righteousness. It hides leprosy.
Lion	A spiritual king of the earth (but see lamb).
Locust	A soldier from a large army that can sweep through a region and devastate it. Usually creating a famine by destroying the food, or besieging a city for example.
Love	The same meaning as mercy. The divine and intense love of Yhwh for her people and the Sun for her people too.
Mercy	The same meaning as love.
Metal	See iron and bronze and silver and gold.
Moon	The lesser angel, under the Sun, but who rules night and therefore Darkness. She quickly rebelled against the Sun and Yhwh and became Satan, or the Serpent on earth.
Mountain	The generations of angels with hearts of stone. Each new generation forms at the bottom, and the leader is the elder which is always at the top. Pyramids are artificial mountains, made by the serpent and her kings of the earth to compete with mountains.
Name	A spirit. If there is a group of the same spirits with the same name, they will form a house with that

	name. A change of name signifies a change in spirit, for example Abram and Abraham.
Nimrod	See Enoch.
Peace	The feeling you get when you are deemed righteous and are at peace with God and can stand before her.
Pillar	A narrow heap, one angel wide but several angels high. Used to support something.
Precious stone	The 12 fundamental spirits or their hearts of stones.
Rain	The living water of mercy from the tears of Yhwh in heaven.
Redemption	The method of salvation when a redeemer (Yhwh and the Sun in Jesus) pays for the debts of a slave to free them. Jesus paid for the sins of his people, Israel and Judah, by serving their sentences for them, in hell, for many years. It leads to the peace of deemed righteousness, the linen covering and the gladness of salvation.
Riddle	A passage that hides a mystery and must be solved to reveal it. For example parables.
River	Moving water which in the spiritual world are ranks of guardian angels and can form boundaries which cannot be passed.
Salvation	To be saved from enslavement to the Serpent through sin, to enter heaven. Either through redemption or holiness.
Satan	The enemy in Hebrew. The devil in Greek. The Moon in heaven and the serpent on earth.
Sea	The place of the non-believers, the fish.
Seraphim	Like cherubim but with six wings rather than four or two. They are righteous angels of fire who look after the system of fire, under Elohiym.
Serpent	The Moon on earth. She started as a senior, royal guardian angel who ruled night and Darkness on

	earth, a dragon who breathed fire. But she fell and was reduced to the level of a snake.
Sheaf	The result of the harvest of people for salvation, but the part of the crop which contains the 'grain' (the people of Yhwh) and stands up with deemed righteousness. The chaff (the serpent) is separated and burned.
Sheep	The people of Yhwh who have the spirit of the serpent and become her domestic animals, the lost sheep of Israel.
Sheol	The place under the earth were spirits go after physical death to sleep until judgement day. The spirit of the serpent is separated after death when the body decays away.
Ship	A chariot on the sea, blown by the wind of the Holy Spirit or the spirit of the Serpent, or both together from different directions, where there is conflict
Silver	See metal. The metal of the anointed prince or Messiah.
Smoke	Curses of the people which rise to be heard by Yhwh.
Spirit of the Serpent	See the fig. Also sour wine.
Stone	The heart of the people of Darkness and the Holy Spirit. Can form a foundation or a stumbling stone to cause a fall, or a defensive wall.
Storm	The Holy Spirit when aroused into conflict. Usually stirs up waves of the Sea and waters.
Sun	The Messiah king, ruler of Day and Light, and the greater of the two lights in heaven, having authority over the Moon. Anointed to be king of kings in the seventh age when Light rules Darkness.

Thorn	A memory of the spirit of the Serpent which is embedded in the flesh and opposes the Holy Spirit in the body. The memory keeps returning so it becomes an irritating source of temptation.
Tree	Spirit, including fruit trees which are holy Spirits or the spirit of the Serpent, the fig.
Vine	The fruit tree of the Holy Spirit of Yhwh. It is the stem and contains all the seven spirits in one. Including Understanding, which is leaven. When leaven is included, the grape juice ferments and becomes wine which is drunk to receive the Holy Spirit.
Wall	A defensive interlinked line of guardian angels with hearts of stone. They encircle what they are trying to protect, including city walls, but they also imprison people.
Waters	See rivers. The soul of Light in Yhwh, in all her people. Stone can be liquified into water. Water is used to cleanse people, including the baptism of water.
Wind	Spirit, either spirit of the Serpent or the Holy Spirit. The breath of life which can grow into a tempest and stir up waves in the sea and waters.
Wine	The full Holy Spirit of Yhwh, including Understanding.
Word, the	Short for the word of Yhwh. Gabriel, the second Messianic spirit of Yhwh.
Yhwh, I am, Lord	The side of God which is Light and female, anointed to become supreme God in the seventh age.

Appendix Three

The Seven Ages

Here is a brief summary of the seven ages. They are the core of the hidden story of the Bible and as such they are referred to constantly, although often they are well hidden. To understand a Bible passage properly you have to read it in the context of the age or ages it is describing, so you will probably want to refer back to this description regularly. You might want to bookmark this too, like the number code.

1. The first age of Adam. The fall of Adam and Eve with the rejection of the Holy Spirit and its salvation resulted in a disaster as all mankind became wicked. The purge was the flood of Noah.
2. The second age of Noah. The purge resulted in a clean start for the sons of Noah, but Canaan fell and with him came the initial house of Israel. He took the promised land for the Serpent. The solution of purging the whole house like the age of Adam is rejected, so we have to live with the spirit of the Serpent but try to supress it. The Serpent's plan to exceed the authority of Yhwh was foiled, and the purge was the dispersal of the initial house of Israel into a number of smaller nations. They became the gentiles.
3. The third age of Abraham and Moses. The new creation of Israel in the 12 tribes of the Hebrews. Also the new creation of the New Moon in the 12 sons of Ishmael. Moses brought the Law and the Prophets and purged the Serpent from Egypt. Joshua took back much of the promised land,

including Jerusalem, but subsequent generations fell to the Serpent despite being ruled by Judges (rather than kings) provided by Yhwh. Idolatry with the Serpent and his false gods became dominant.

4. The fourth age of the kings including King David and Solomon. A terrible age of conflicts between the Sun and the Moon. King David purged the Serpent from much of the promised land, but his son, Solomon, fell and for the remainder of the age the people split into two competing kingdoms, Israel and Judah, and idolatry dominated again. The purge of the Serpent (including the destruction of the corrupt city and temple of Jerusalem and the defeat of Egypt) was carried out by the king of Babylon and both Israel and Judah were exiled and dispersed to Assyria and Babylon and beyond. A remnant of Judah returned to restore Jerusalem and the temple, but most of Israel remained dispersed, waiting for a call to salvation from the Messiah.

5. The fifth age of Jesus. After John the Baptist came to cleanse the people through repentance and mercy, ready for the Holy Spirit to come, Jesus, the Messiah, came to prepare the people for the coming kingdom of Light and the salvation of the Holy Spirit. This is the same spirit, from the tree of life, that was rejected by Adam and Eve. He demonstrated the power of the Holy Spirit to heal his followers from the effects of the spirit of the Serpent, including casting out the spirit of the Serpent and replacing it with the Holy Spirit. It brought holiness and eternal life in heaven as well as many powerful gifts during life on earth. The purge was the sacrifice of Jesus as he redeemed the people of Light so that they would be deemed righteous and be resurrected to heaven after they died. Jesus therefore brought both types of salvation, but only those who believe in him as the Messiah received the Holy Spirit.

6. The sixth age of the Apostles. The Holy Spirit was released and filled both Hebrews and gentiles. Disciples of Jesus and others spread the word of Jesus to continue his work. The Serpent fought back hard, and it was an age of terrible conflict with many deaths. However, the followers of Jesus cast out many spirits of the Serpent and this became a purge through spiritual warfare. This escalated into judgement day when the spirit of the serpent was condemned and the spirits of the people of Light were forgiven. The dead who had been sleeping in Sheol were raised to heaven and formed a great army following Jesus.
7. At the start of the seventh age, Jesus purged the remainder of the spirits of the Serpent and defeated the Serpent herself, in the battle of Armageddon. Yhwh and the Sun took the throne in heaven and the kingdom of Light was established eternally in heaven. Light ruled Darkness. However, on earth, the people fell once again, the rule of Light ended and the cycles of Darkness started once more.

We are now at the end of the sixth age of that cycle.

About the Author

George Begg was born in Scotland in 1956 and moved to England with his family when he was four.

He was educated in Surrey, where he joined the RAF cadets at school and learned to fly when he was 17 – the start of a lifelong passion for flying. Sponsored by the RAF, he studied Biology at the University of Southampton, before serving as a flying instructor and fighter pilot during the Cold War.

After leaving the service, George became a self employed businessman and entrepreneur, navigating both successes and setbacks along the way. A lifelong sceptic and staunch non-believer, his life changed dramatically and permanently, when God appeared to him as a bright white light and revealed a new purpose for his life. Since then, he has dedicated himself to uncovering the mysteries hidden in Scripture – guided always by God's presence and direction.

Over the past decade, George has focused on revealing these spiritual truths, exploring the divine patterns woven into creation and human life.

He has always found time to embrace his passions outside of business and writing: flying ex-military jets as a display pilot, spending time at sea, and living life to the full.

About the Author

Book Two

Mysteries of The Other Side

Days of Darkness

GEORGE BEGG

Prologue to Book Two

In the first book, we uncovered enough spiritual mysteries to see the hidden stories beneath the Bible's surface. We didn't explore every layer in detail – only the essential principles needed to understand how these secrets have been coded, concealed, and gradually revealed through riddles and symbolic fragments.

In this second book, we go further. We will revisit the stories introduced in Book One exploring them in greater depth, and uncover new ones that are less familiar but equally significant.

These hidden principles shape our spiritual identities and influence our human nature, guiding the way we experience life itself. They've been there since the beginning, hidden in plain sight within Scripture. Now, for the first time, they are being revealed to all who are ready to see.

Many of these secrets are hidden as riddles and, as with all riddles, they appear obvious once solved. The more you understand, the easier it is to uncover the next.

In this book, we'll explore many riddles, starting with an extraordinary one in the first three verses of the Bible. Some are simple, some complex, but each offers a glimpse into the deeper truths of existence.

As we journey through these revelations, you'll notice how every mystery connects back to the underlying story of Book One: the seven ages from Darkness to Light. For instance, even the brief story of Cain and Abel, which starts with jealousy and murder, ultimately foreshadows the terrible conflicts of the sixth age, between the

Moon and Yhwh, to determine who will inherit the earth, spoken in the words of the Moon herself.

There is far too much to reveal in one volume, so this series continues in two parts: the Old Testament of Law and Darkness (Book Two) and the New Testament of Mercy and Light (Book Three).

If you are tempted to begin your journey here, I must warn you – it won't make sense without the foundation of the first book. No matter how much you already know of Scripture, *Mysteries of the Other Side: Days of Darkness* builds upon what was revealed before. For those who have walked with me through Book One, it's now time to go deeper. Together.

And for those eager to understand the unfolding events of our time – the hidden workings of God's secret weapon – this is where we begin.